The Doctrine of the
Incarnation Opened

The Doctrine of the Incarnation Opened

An Abridgement with Introduction and Response

EDWARD IRVING

Edited by Alexander J. D. Irving
Introduction by Graham McFarlane
Response by Daniel Jordan Cameron

PICKWICK *Publications* · Eugene, Oregon

THE DOCTRINE OF THE INCARNATION OPENED
An Abridgement with Introduction and Response

Pickwick Publications
An Imprint of Wipf and Stock Publishers
199 W. 8th Ave., Suite 3
Eugene, OR 97401

www.wipfandstock.com

PAPERBACK ISBN: 978-1-7252-9183-6
HARDCOVER ISBN: 978-1-7252-9182-9
EBOOK ISBN: 978-1-7252-9184-3

Cataloguing-in-Publication data:

Names: Irving, Edward, 1792–1834, author. | Irving, Alexander, J. D., editor | McFarlane, Graham, 1949–, introduction writer | Cameron, Daniel Jordan, contributor

Title: The doctrine of the incarnation opened : an abridgment with introduction and response / Edward Irving, edited by Alexander J. D. Irving, with an introduction by Graham McFarlane.

Description: Eugene, OR: Pickwick Publications, 2021| Includes bibliographical references.

Identifiers: ISBN 978-1-7252-9183-6 (paperback) | ISBN 978-1-7252-9182-9 (hardcover) | ISBN 978-1-7252-9184-3 (ebook)

Subjects: LCSH: Irving, Edward, 1792–1834 | Jesus Christ—Humanity | Incarnation | Theologians—Scotland

Classification: BT220 I78 2021 (paperback) | BT220 (ebook)

08/26/21

Contents

Contributors

Editor   A. J. D. Irving

Introduction   G. McFarlane

Sermon Specific Introductions   A. J. D. Irving and Christopher G. Woznicki

Critical Response   D. J. Cameron

Transcribers   Jacob Hussain

Calvin Edwards

Neulsaem "Sam" Ha

Craig Devereaux

Bryce Dunn

Ben Evans

D. J. Cameron

Ben Hammond

Editor's Preface

A number of people have been instrumental in the production of this volume. A team of transcribers have generously devoted their time to the laborious task of reproducing the text. Some of this team were already known to me, and others have become new friends. I am very grateful to each of them for their hard work and cheerful efficiency.

Alongside this transcription work, a team has also made a variety of creative contributions. Christopher Woznicki has made the valuable creative contribution of introducing specific sermons and providing a summary of the abridged content. Daniel Cameron, author of *Flesh and Blood: A Dogmatic Sketch Concerning the Fallen Nature View of Christ's Human Nature*, has written a critical reception of Irving's Christology. Graham McFarlane, author of *Christ and the Spirit: The Doctrine of the Incarnation According to Edward Irving*, introduces the volume with an essay that presents the cultural and theological context of Irving's Christological sermons.

Irving's original publication covered some 450 pages and is inaccessible to a modern reader for a variety of reasons. In an effort to manage the cost of this volume and to make Irving's distinctive Christological and trinitarian ideas more accessible, sections of the original text have been omitted. These omissions are indicated in the text and summaries of abridged content can be found in the sermon specific introductions. Moreover, a note of where to find the full text in the original volumes is indicated in the footnotes.

Irving's text has, for the most part, been left unaltered. However, to aid the reader, some minor editorial decisions have been taken. First, the text has been divided into sections. To limit the imposition of alien categories of thought and expression, so far as is possible, the headings of these sections take their wording from Irving's text itself. Second, the occasions where Irving quotes long sections of Scripture are formatted according to the contemporary conventions. In addition to this, the lengthy way in which Irving introduces these texts ("in the seventh verse of the second chapter of Paul's second letter to the Corinthians") has been replaced by placing the reference in brackets at the end of the quotation (2 Corinthians 2:7). Third, paragraph breaks have, on occasion, been added. Finally, while Irving's spelling and punctuation have been retained, his use of capitalization has been modified to more closely conform to contemporary norms.

The sermons, which is how the following chapters were first delivered, follow a clear logical progression: the origin of the incarnation; the goal of the incarnation; the method of the incarnation; the events of the incarnate life and death of Christ and the effects of the incarnation. The aspect of Irving's thought that has garnered most attention is the method of the incarnation, which is to say, God the Son's assumption of a fallen human nature. It is in this doctrine that the trinitarian character of Irving's soteriology is cast in greatest relief, as it is in the power of the Spirit that the incarnate Son overcomes the distorted and alienated will of human nature and offers it in obedience to the Father as a sacrifice of praise. It is this aspect that this abridgment focuses on most directly. Given the contentious nature of Irving's Christology, some suggestions for further reading, both critical and in favour of Irving's view, are provided at the end of this volume to supplement Graham's introduction and Daniel's response so to provide further perspective.

Whether he was right or wrong regarding his conviction that the Son, by the will of the Father, assumed fallen human nature, twisting distorted human will back into accordance with the will of the Father by the power of the same Spirit, Edward Irving's singular focus was to direct our attention off ourselves and onto the purpose of God manifested and accomplished in Jesus Christ by the power of the Spirit. For Irving, an understanding of the redemptive death of Christ that was *exclusively* framed within extrinsic, forensic, and penal categories is grossly unsatisfactory. In this connection, Irving's description of the Christian doctrine of salvation suggests the influence of Athanasius. The saving act is one that digs deep into the human condition, overturning it from its fallen core and liberating it from the power of sin. The Saviour, who has life in himself, enters creation (that, as made from nothing, always has nothingness on the borders of its existence), which has turned in will from the ground of its existence, and is disintegrating into non-existence so to actualize a will and a life orientated to the Father. The one who is eternally begotten from the Father shares life with that which is created from nothing so to include us—who are contingent and temporal—in his relation to the Father, which is one of necessary mutuality and eternal delight.

The distinctive way in which Irving understood the divine purpose to be actualized in the person and work of Christ—specifically, the status of the human nature Christ assumed, the role of the Spirit in relation to sanctifying the human nature of the incarnate Son, and the implications for Christian discipleship—are and will remain contentious areas of his doctrine. However, the publication of this volume is intended to facilitate an estimation of Irving in which his more controversial doctrines are held in correlation with his broader theological vision.

The reproduction of this collection of sermons has been undertaken with Irving's singular focus in mind: to point believers beyond ourselves with our vacillating mood and devotion to the certainty of the divine will to be *for us*. This is in the prayer that our assurance of salvation might be anchored not on our interior states, our moral attainment or sacramental activity, but on the eternal purpose of the Father, covenanted with the Son, to draw all things together under Christ in the power of the Spirit. This is the Gospel of which Edward Irving was a servant: there is no depravity so deep, no suffering so dreadful, no death so complete that it is beyond the reach of God in Christ, who penetrated into the depths of human sin, suffering and death and lived the life of the faithful Son by the power of the Spirit. The crucified Jesus has been resurrected, inaugurating a new humanity to which we are joined, and he has returned to the Father's right hand, pouring out his Spirit on us that we too might (even today!) know freedom from the power of sin and the rule of death.

A. J. D. IRVING
The Feast of the Cross, 2020

Introduction

Graham McFarlane

> "Life's but a walking shadow, a poor player,
> That struts and frets his hour upon the stage,
> And then is heard no more. It is a tale
> Told by an idiot, full of sound and fury,
> Signifying nothing."[1]

IRVING AND HIS CONTEXT

It is hard to imagine a more protean time, with all the benefits as well as the challenges and excesses that ensue, than that experienced in the half-century or so that spans the end of the eighteenth century into the first quarter of the nineteenth century. Such is the 'scene' in which Edward Irving was to strut his own hour upon his Caledonian and London stages. In every aspect of Irving's life, whether in his Scottish borders' upbringing in Annan, family seat of Robert the Bruce, with contemporaries the likes of Thomas Carlyle and Robert Murray M'Shane, or in his later London Caledonian Chapel charge, where he would become, for a short season, London's go-to preacher, there was change.

Internationally, the scene was mercurial, due mainly to two significant events. First, there was the Revolution that birthed the newly declared (United) States of America, having emerged, July 4th, 1776. Second, the French Revolution had ended by 1799, reshaping forever the political scene on the continent and sending shock waves throughout the western world.

---

1. William Shakespeare, *Macbeth*, Act V, scene 5, http://shakespeare.mit.edu/macbeth/full.html, accessed, 09/07/2020.

The historic significance of these revolutions cannot be ignored when considering Edward Irving since, culturally and nationally, Scotland had had its own cornucopia of revolutions which resulted eventually in a significant number of Scots, around 50,000, living in the Thirteen Colonies by the time of the American Revolution.[2] In addition, whilst not all the ills of late eighteenth-century and early nineteenth-century British society can be levelled at the foot of the Gallic guillotine it would be naïve not to take into account the resultant underlying social and cultural insecurity of the time in the light of these French upheavals and their repercussions. No doubt, a form of "revolutionary horror"[3] permeated the zeitgeist that, in turn, overshadowed social intercourse on every level and brought with it the kind of social and existential angst that precipitates and even legitimates great change.[4] Without doubt, Edward Irving's world was mercurial. It was also exciting: the world as it was then known was undergoing significant change that brought with it new opportunities and horizons.[5] One can imagine the frisson of interest and discussion that would have enveloped the young Edward Irving, aged sixteen, now in the third year of his MA at the University of Edinburgh, on the news that Napoleon had invaded Spain in 1808.[6] There is little doubt that the *Edinburgh Review*, founded in 1802 and one of the most influential intellectual magazines of nineteenth-century Britain, would have fed the minds and imaginations of Edinburgh's students, especially given the compact nature of the city.

Nationally, and nearer to home, his own kirk, the Church of Scotland, was undergoing significant challenges. Following on from the previous century's Marrow Men,[7] Irving's time saw the rise of what can be described as

2. https://allthingsliberty.com/2013/10/scotland-american-revolution/

3. Henry Cockburn describes it in terms of, "Everything rung, and was connected with the Revolution in France; which, for above 20 years, was, or was made, the all in all. Everything, not this or that thing, but literally everything, was soaked in this one event." Henry Cockburn, *Memorials of his Time*, 2 vols (Edinburgh: A&C Black, 1856), 1:79.

4. It is of interest to note that Thomas Carlyle published a two-volume history of the French Revolution, in 1837, https://www.gutenberg.org/files/1301/1301-h/1301-h.htm, accessed 10 July 2020.

5. Something of this excitement runs through Irving's life like a golden thread: that the son of an Annan Tanner who was educated at the University of Edinburgh would consider missionary work in France, let alone turn down a Presbyterian charge in Jamaica, would make his name amongst the most gifted of London intellectuals.

6. An interesting note is that both men, Irving and Napoleon, shared a common love of the Scottish cycle of poems reputed to originate from the narrator and author Ossian but more likely an assembled collection of ancient Gaelic literature by James MacPherson and published around 1760–65.

7. See D. Lachman, *The Marrow Controversy, 1718–1723: An Historical and*

the 'Evangelical' party within the Church of Scotland with its devotion to the Bible along with the traditions and historical documents of the Church as distinct from the 'Moderate' party which was known more for its intellectual approach in theology. Economically, by the 1820s the dust from the previous half century had finally settled and a middle class with growing social power began to emerge in Scotland. The fear of a revolution was replaced by the fervour for reform. Indeed, it was Irving's first great mentor, Thomas Chalmers, Scotland's greatest 19th century churchman,[8] who after the Ten Years Conflict and the subsequent General Disruption, 1843, would go on to establish the Free Church of Scotland, taking with him a third of the clergy of the Church of Scotland, mainly from the North of Scotland and the Highlands.

Theologically, it is helpful to be reminded that a fissure of instability has always run through the Church of Scotland and can be accredited to its theological DNA. To affirm, *ecclesia reformata, semper reformanda secundum verbum Dei*: the church is always being reformed according to the Word of God, is to disavow any notion of ecclesial or theological stasis and thus protection from change. Admittedly, this disposition has always brought with it an awkward tension with the theological status quo and so it is not surprising that it sets a significant backdrop to Irving's own context and theological method. Thus, it is right to note that, in Irving's case, his ministry as well as his theology bore the hallmark of his Reformed tradition. In the former he pursued a personal piety in his own life and practice that corresponded to Scripture. In the latter Irving was equally driven by his understanding of both Scripture as well as the Incarnation of the Word of God that were expressed not in terms of dry intellectualism but in their transformative and hope-bearing impact in the lives of those in his charge as well as in his own personal piety. It was his duty to speak out against, if not reform, anything that he or others deemed to be in the way. It is not surprising, then, that Irving does not stand a solitary theological figure at this time. Rather, he stands within a striking theological coterie of like-minded countrymen and friends—clergyman John McLeod Campbell as well as countryman, lawyer and independently minded layman Thomas Erskine of Linlathen—in seeking to free the Gospel, in various ways, from the restrictions of the Calvinism of their day. Each sought to reconstruct and re-appropriate key aspects of the Gospel in relation to their ecclesial cultures. For McLeod Campbell, it concerned the Gospel's universal offer

---

Theological Analysis (Edinburgh: Rutherford House, 1988).

8. Donald McKim, *Encyclopedia of the Reformed Faith* (Louisville: Westminster John Knox, 1992), 61.

of salvation to a congregation disempowered by the egregious effects of a federal Calvinist understanding of election that eviscerated any notion of certainty regarding one's saving faith. Salvation, here, lay not in the finished work of Christ on the cross but in the pre-creation electing will of God about which no one has any knowledge. In this theology there is little if any confidence in the finished work of Christ and its personal application as the grounds for assurance of salvation. How does one ever know if one is elect, and if not elect, what assurance of salvation? What results are congregations devoid of any dynamic spiritual life based on personal assurance of salvation. All they can to is to persevere in the face of an eternal damnation that may or may not be their elected end. McLeod Campbell's answer was simple and clear albeit costly for him:[9] it is that assurance is the essence of faith and necessary to salvation.[10] Thomas Erskine, on the other hand, was not so bound by his native Kirk and was free to seek clarification on the nature of faith. He argued against the consequence of double predestination wherein faith is understood as a work, that is, where one's subjective response to the Gospel operates like a work rather than as the receiving of the objective and completed work of Christ that has merit to all who receive it.[11] Like McLeod Campbell, Erskine's theology prioritized divine love over divine wrath and, unlike McLeod Campbell, Erskine's theology ultimately led him to a universalist position regarding salvation.

Personally, it should not come as a surprise, then, to note that Irving's 'hour' upon this particular historic and theological stage was impacted by these various and shifting international, national, social, theological, ecclesial and personal tectonic plates. The French Revolution unleashed a national missionary zeal in Irving's generation, albeit it one purposed in 'saving' the despoiled French. It is not surprising, then, that prior to being called to be Thomas Chalmers' assistant, Irving was very much set in his pursuit of being a missionary, rather than filling the pulpit. His giftedness in languages would clearly benefit him here: by thirteen he was fluent in Greek and Latin, by twenty French and Italian, with Gaelic coming later being an essential condition for taking charge of the Caledonian Chapel, Hatton Garden, London in 1821.[12]

9. John McLeod Campbell would also lose his licence to minister in the Church of Scotland and went on to be minister of an independent church from which he was to publish his original *The of Atonement*.

10. John McLeod Campbell, *The Nature of Atonement* (Reprint, Grand Rapids: Eerdmans, 1996).

11. Thomas Erskine, *The Unconditional Freeness of the Gospel in Three Essays* (Edinburgh: Waugh and Innes, 1828). *The Brazen Serpent; or Life Coming through Death* (Edinburgh: Waugh & Innes, 1831).

12. It is unclear as to how much Gaelic Irving mastered. What is of note is that in

Closer to home, Irving's brief 'career' exposed him to a wide range of social expressions. On the one hand, as a schoolmaster in Haddington, Edinburgh and then first master in Kirkcaldy, east coast Scotland,[13] he will have mixed in more genteel circles where he would meet his future wife, Isabella Martin as well as teach Thomas Carlyle's future wife, Jane Welsh. On the other hand, the Glasgow of Irving's day exposed him to the very worst of social poverty. Glasgow was a city of extremes. It was economically depressed in the early nineteenth century. The city saw an outbreak of typhus in 1817 with devastating impact on the poor. It is to the credit of Thomas Chalmers and his legacy that he stood out amidst the silence of the Kirk in relation to the various social ills experienced by Glasgow's poor. However, on the other hand, industrialization created an emerging middle class in Glasgow who were able not only to support an assistant for the renowned Thomas Chalmers, but also to raise staggering funds to build churches and schools, as well as provide for the poor, in Chalmers' newly established parish: it was to the Kirk that the poor were dependent, in Scotland, until the Poor Relief Act, 1845 passed this responsibility to local authorities. In many ways, Irving is a synthesis of these two realities. If there is one identifying hallmark to Irving throughout his adult life as a clergyman, it is the testimony of all who knew him regarding his devotion to the poor in his care as well as their respect and love for him.

Theologically, Irving's passion for the Word of God and its application in the life of the believer as well as in parish ministry received oxygen from the rising 'Evangelical' wing within the Church of Scotland. It is likely, however, that the seeds for this churchmanship were sown much earlier in his own upbringing and shed light on the independent nature of the young Irving. Instead of attending his local kirk, the Church of Scotland, in his hometown of Annan, Irving attended a Secessionist Church in the neighbouring town of Ecclefechan, six miles inland, which was home also to Thomas Carlyle. Thus, it would be there that Irving would be exposed to an Evangelical and missionary spirit, as well as the aggressive attitude that Secessionists took towards the Established church.[14]

Socially, it was this serendipitous ecclesial alliance from his youth that the later Irving would continue to enjoy the company, opinion and criticism

---

order that he might take up the charge at Hatton Garden a special act of Parliament had to be passed to allow an incumbent to preach in English, as well as Gaelic. No one less than heir to the throne, Prince Frederick, Duke of York, gave his support to this successful legislature.

13. It was in Kirkcaldy that Adam Smith wrote *The Wealth of Nations*, 1766.

14. *Scottish Christianity in the Modern World: In Honour of A. C. Cheyne*, edited by Stewart J. Brown, George Newlands (Edinburgh: T.&T. Clark, 2000), 20.

of Thomas Carlyle, and his wife, once Irving was located in London. For once established in London, Irving engaged with the leading thinkers of his day, a camaraderie that was not unfamiliar to him given the fact that his secessionist friend would become one of London's most sought after figures with regards his religious views as well as his thoughts on theology's relations with literature and science. Indeed, it says something about Irving that both Carlyle and Samuel Taylor Coleridge, both of whom introduced German Romanticism to Britain, wanted Irving to support their own causes. We capture a sense of their own opinions on Irving in their own words. Thus, Coleridge writes of Irving that he "possesses more of the spirit and purpose of the first Reformers, that he has more of the Head and the Heart, the life, the Unction, and the general power of Martin Luther"[15] and Carlyle that, "He was never heard to speak an unkind word of any of his numerous opponents, far less of any of his friends. [. . .] One who knew him well, and may with good cause love him, has said, 'But for Irving I had never known what the communion of man with man means. His was the freest, brotherliest, bravest human soul mine ever came in contact with. I call him, on the whole, the best man I have ever (after trial enough) found in this world, or now hope to find.'"[16]

In addition to his lifelong friendship with Carlyle, Irving's Hatton Garden ministry exposed him to a wider trench of London society. Having been referred to by Sir James Mackintosh in Parliament, Irving's reputation grew such that the Caledonian Chapel, more accustomed to the dourness of its original congregants, now drew the very highest of society through its doors, whether royalty, government or high arts. For someone who self-declared that his "notions of pulpit eloquence differ from many of my worthy brethren. In truth I am an adventurer on the ground untried, and therefore am full of anxieties"[17] there is a sense of unpreparedness for this sudden audience. In this, essayist Charles Lamb was somewhat perspicacious in

---

15. S.T. Coleridge, *The Collected Works of S.T. Coleridge, Vol. 10: On the Constitution of the Church and State*, edited by J. Colmer (Princeton: Princeton University Press, 1976), 143.

16. T. Chalmers, "Life of Rev. E. Irving," *The Christian's Penny Magazine. A Weekly Miscellany conducted upon The Principle of the Protestant Reformation and suited to Every Denomination of Christians. Vol. I., New Series, for 1837*, No. 53, December 30, 1837, 426, 427. That said, Carlyle was to reminisce of Irving seven years later that, "He is one of the greatest Blockheads, with all his other qualities, that God ever made."

17. Cited in David Malcolm Bennett, *Edward Irving Reconsidered: The Man, His Controversies, and the Pentecostal Movement* (Eugene, OR: Wipf & Stock, 2014), 52. This may explain Dorothy Wordsworth's comment regarding Irving's preaching that "he wholly wants taste and good judgement" most likely due to Irving's Scottish tendency to give full range to his feelings, a quality deemed somewhat uncouth in more genteel English society, ibid., 55.

describing Irving as an "archangel slightly damaged."[18] Whilst Scottish diaspora history demonstrates the largesse and capacity of the Caledonian mind, spirit and temperament in wilder and more remote climes, this same character is less disposed to being uprooted and replanted in more refined Anglo-Saxon soil. To some extent, Irving's brief albeit explosive entry onto the London stage bears witness to the unsuitability of one so temperamentally Romantic in style, though not in orthodoxy, and Reformed in disposition, though not in its federalist extremes.

IRVING AND HIS THEOLOGY

Irving, like all other theologians, was a product of his context. The various factors above set the general backdrop to Irving's theology. More particularly, his Christology reflects a rich tapestry of influences coupled with an equally thoughtful and expressive mind. Without doubt he is a systematic thinker albeit not in the conventional sense of the method. His systematic approach is evidenced in the consistency and rigour evidenced in the interconnectedness of his thought.[19] In Irving we meet a thinker whose overall theological framework is robust in its trinitarianism, all the more of interest given his predominantly deist, if not unitarian, context. This trinitarianism, in turn, is exactingly perichoretic: there is no hint at all of any social trinitarian turn in Irving's thought. Nor is it in any sense 'intellectual.' It is birthed from the revelation of God in the incarnation of the Word, the eternal Son, of God. In his own words, Irving articulates his trinitarian methodology:

> It was not until the Son came into manifestation as a man, until the Word was made flesh and dwelt among us, became our

18. Charles Lamb, cited in Alma Clej, "Coleridge, Samuel Taylor" in *Encyclopedia of Literature and Politics: Censorship, Revolution, and Writing*, edited by M. Keith Booker, 3 vols (Westport, CT: Greenwood, 2005), 1:62.

19. Something similar to how Kevin Vanhoozer puts it: "The Bible is much more than a collection of truths to be organized into a comprehensive system. That way leads to what we might call *hard* systematic theology. I recommend a 'soft' systematics that acknowledges a unity to truth, though not like the truth of geometric axioms, which are not suitable for expressing redemptive history. There are things that theologians must make known, but they primarily concern what God has said and done in history. What unifies Scripture is the story of God's determination to see through his purpose for creation to the end, a story in which Israel and the Church loom large, with Jesus Christ as its hinge and center. If you aspire to 'systematic' theology in the sense of articulating the general coherence of what the Church proclaims on the basis of Scripture, you do well." Kevin J. Vanhoozer, "Letter to an Aspiring Theologian. How to Speak of God Truly," *First Things August 2018*, https://www.firstthings.com/article/2018/08/letter-to-an-aspiring-theologian, accessed 11 July 2020.

> Saviour, the long-expected Messiah on earth, the long-looked for
> Christ and Lord in heaven, for whom all things were created, that
> the truth of the glorious Trinity became a grand and manifest
> truth for ever. Because so soon as the Son became manifest He
> made known the Father, to whom He always inferred back as the
> eternal Father of the Son, and in Him the great originator of all
> things, and principal party to the eternal purpose which the Son
> came forth to reveal. "No one has ever seen God: the only Son,
> who is in the bosom of the Father, he has made him known." By
> the same act also did the Spirit become manifest; for . . . Christ's
> becoming outward and visible was the act of the Spirit.[20]

The radical nature of Irving's trinitarianism is not to be undervalued. In his day, Unitarianism, rather than the trinitarianism of orthodoxy, continued its eighteenth-century stranglehold. It should be remembered, too, that with Friedrich Schleiermacher deism was on the ascendency with the first edition of *Der Christliche Glaube* (*The Christian Faith*) published in 1820/21 with a revised edition in 1830. Whilst there could not be two more opposite theological thinkers on the Trinity they were equally united in their understanding of its centrality in Christian thought. For Schleiermacher, it was the coping-stone of all Christian doctrine (der Schlubstein der Christlichen Lehre),[21] albeit one relegated to an appendix due to the fact that any understanding of God as Trinity cannot be extrapolated from the Christian's feeling of absolute dependence upon God. For Irving, the doctrine of the Trinity was "the foundation of all orthodox doctrine"[22] and it was this that would mould his every theological and pastoral thought. However, what distinguishes the two is their *leitmotif.* For Schleiermacher it is a thoroughgoing anthropological agenda—theology works itself out from the human *sensus divinitatis* and any subsequent feeling of absolute dependence from which the existence of God might be affirmed. However, for Irving, his *leitmotif* was thoroughgoingly *theological* in which this foundational doctrine of the Trinity takes on a much more central position in both his methodology and theology:

> Ye may be able to state out the redemption, without a Trinity
> of persons in the Godhead: I lay claim to no such ability. Your
> Trinity is an idle letter in your creed; but it is the soul, the life of
> mine. Your Christ is a suffering God; I know it well: my Christ

---

20. Edward Irving, *The Collected Works of Edward Irving in Five Volumes,* edited by Rev. G. Carlyle (London: Alexander Strahan), 5:87–88.

21. Friedrich D.E. Schleiermacher, *The Christian Faith* (Edinburgh: T.&T. Clark, 1928), 739.

22. Edward Irving, *The Collected Works of Edward Irving in Five Volumes,* edited by Rev. G. Carlyle (London: Alexander Strahan), 5:350.

is a gracious condescending God, but a suffering man. In your Christ, you see but one person in a body: in my Christ I see the fulness of the Godhead in a body. My Christ is the Trinity manifested not merely the Trinity told of, but the Trinity manifested. I have the Father manifested in everything which He doth; for he did not His own will, but the will of His Father. I have the Son manifested, in uniting His Divinity to a humanity prepared for Him by the Father; and in making the two most contrary things to meet and kiss each other, in all the actings of his widest, most comprehensive being. I have the Holy Ghost manifested in subduing, restraining, conquering, the evil propensities of the fallen manhood, and making it an apt organ for expressing the will of the Father, a fit and holy substance to enter into personal union with the untempted and untemptable Godhead. And who is he that dares stand up and impugn these eternal truths? Be he whom he may, the devil himself, with all his legions, I will uphold them against him for ever; and I will say moreover, that in upholding these, I am upholding the atonement, the redemption, the reconciliation, the regeneration, the kingdom, and the glory of God.[23]

At the heart of Irving's theology is an understanding that our knowledge of God is derived from a very particular theatre, namely, the mess and obfuscation of the human condition and then the manner by which it is rescued from its current state of impotence in relation to become a mature expression of its original creation. Thus, building upon his Reformed origins Irving holds to the belief that knowledge of God comes out of knowledge of the human condition.[24] With Irving, then, we are confronted by a theological method that is radically premised on three principles:

1. Our knowledge of God is derived from what can be extrapolated from the historical and personal way by which our human brokenness is resolved in and through the life, death, resurrection, ascension and glorification of Jesus Christ. In this, human knowledge of God is subjective, primarily passive, and initially helpless;

23. Edward Irving, *Sermons, Lectures, and Occasional Discourses, in Three Volumes, Vol .I. The Doctrine of the Incarnation Opened in Six Sermons* (London: R.B. Seeley and W. Burnside, 1828), 76–77.

24. Calvin begins his *Institutes of the Christian Religion* with two complementary assertions: 1.1. *Without knowledge of self there is no knowledge of God and* 1.2. *Without knowledge of God there is no knowledge of self.* https://reformed.org/books/institutes/ books/book1/bk1ch01.html, accessed, 19 July 2020.

2. The messy business of divinity, of theological understanding, centres on the dynamics, on the how, this human problematic is overcome in the person and work of Jesus Christ. In this, Irving follows the fourth-century Cappadocian father Gregory of Nazianzus' theological method, namely, that: *to akatalepton atherepeuton, the unassumed is the unhealed*;[25]

3. How this overcoming occurs offers us understanding into the identity of the God who overcomes for us in Jesus Christ. From the standpoint of another ancient patristic maxim, *opera trinitatis ad extra indivisa sunt, the external operations of the Trinity are indivisible.*

In each of these three criteria Irving's theological method and theology follow an *orthodox* as distinct to *heterodox* theological line. He affirms the ancient paths: that knowledge of God is gifted to us through divine action towards us; that for the incarnation of the Son of God to involve the human condition at its point of failure then the salvation offered serves no purpose and has no potency; that what we see of divine action within the economies of creation and re-creation reflects who God is in Godself.

What drives Irving's Christology throughout the ensuing sermons is a theological method centred on a very particular understanding of the Incarnation that has two foci. The first can be located in his 1825 sermons on God the Father given in his early years at the Caledonian Chapel in London that were later published. These sermons have a measured tone that differ from Irving's "bursts of bold and splendid oratory" that made Irving's name.[26] It is these sermons, however, that provide Irving with the theological depth necessary for him to develop his later Christology, a feat made all the more remarkable given the strong Unitarian presence in both his own parish and the surrounding area in North London. These sermons appear to be the means by which Irving worked through to an articulation of the doctrine of the Trinity that is as perichoretic as any that might be read in contemporary Orthodox trinitarianism. In addition, there are clear resonances of sixteenth-century Richard Hooker, Irving's preferred 'go-to' theologian, and as well as echoes of seventeenth-century Puritan divine, John Owen, as well as Augustinian resonances best articulated by Richard

---

25. Alasdair Heron comments that Irving's use of this theological method is "in its way . . . a reprise of the Irenaean conception of *anakephalaiosis* or *recapitulation*." Alasdair Heron, "A turning-point in British Christology in the nineteenth century: Erskine, Irving and Campbell" in *Jesus Christ Today. Studies in Christology in Various Contexts,* edited by Stuart Georg Hall (Berlin: de Gruyter, 2009), 164.

26. MOW Oliphant, *Edward Irving.* 5th ed. London: Hurst and Blackett, no date, 220.

of St. Victor.[27] Without doubt, for Irving, divine agency *has to be* trinitarian solely on the grounds that this is what we see when we look at the way in which God, in Christ the incarnate Son of God, reconciles himself to the world and overcomes sin in the flesh, through the empowering agency of the Holy Spirit.

The second of these foci is given by Irving himself in his introduction to the sermons and is indicative of his own self-understanding as a pastor-theologian. These sermons are to be dogmatic, not controversial, in their method. In this, Irving is correct: there is little sense in Irving's manner towards his reader of him wanting to be sensationalist. To the modern mind, admittedly, his approach has a certain pomposity about it, and it is not difficult to imagine Irving delivering his sermons with the theatrics alluded to by so many of his contemporaries. Yet, in content, Irving is considered in how he reasons, whilst being pre-critical in method, all the same, there is a sense that his argument is weighty with the personal and theological reflection expected of his day. There is almost a sense, were he in more critical methodological climes, that Irving would have provided his sources and support for his thoughts in robust footnoting. However, this was not the case. What should not be forgotten is that Irving read not so much the publications of great thinkers but enjoyed their actual conversations and they of him. To some extent, this theological method was more conducive to Irving's theological nous and imagination.

The sermons, in turn, have a wholly pastoral and didactic intention: their intention is to instruct his church, those under his ministerial and pastoral care. They are, for Irving, a form of spiritual warfare in which he demonstrably contends for the gospel "as it was once delivered to the saints." As such, these sermons are fed not only by his dogmatic concerns but also by the pastoral issues of his day. The evidence of Irving being 'Evangelical' and not 'Moderate' in disposition, is the ultimate intention of engaging the scratch where those in his pastoral care itch rather than presenting a more intellectual and abstract series of thoughts on the matter.

When the dogmatic and the pastoral are combined, we note, third, how Irving's method seeks to connect what he says with other elements of Christian thought, especially the doctrine of the Trinity. In this, Irving reflects the holistic nature of his theological method akin more to a computer software engineer aware of how one aspect of the software interconnects and impacts others. We see this demonstrated best in the way Irving draws out the perichoretic relations between the Father, Son, and Holy Spirit, the

27. See, Richard of St. Victor, *The Book of the Patriarchs, The Mystical Ark, Book Three of the Trinity*. Classics of Western Spirituality Series (Mahwah, NJ: Paulist Press, 1979).

way in which he unites creation with redemption and the practical application Irving brings to his theology: it is there to serve the people of God,
not to tickle intellectual ears. Perhaps here we are privy to the influence of
Hooker on Irving's method rather than the more rigid manner of his Scottish contemporaries.

Lastly, and as a direct consequence of his desire to show the interconnectedness of Christian thought, Irving seeks to show the perichoretic
nature of the Trinity in this the fullest act of the Godhead towards human
beings, namely to show the works of each of the divine persons in making the Word flesh. Only after outlining these methodological criteria does
Irving state his theological content, namely, the doctrine of Jesus Christ's
human nature. Again, the clarity in Irving's intention is clear. The humanity
assumed by the eternal Son of God is a humanity fallen, that is, mortal and
corruptible, in line with the Scot's Confession.[28] This humanity, in turn, is
not self-sanctifying but, rather, is pneumatically sanctified; that is, whatever
freedom from sin or eternal existence it has is the work of the Holy Spirit.[29]

Of course, it is with his particular, some might argue 'peculiar,' understanding of the humanity assumed in the incarnation that Irving's notoriety
began, and his social standing declined. For it was in these sermons that
Irving expounds an understanding of the incarnation that caused offence

28. "So that we confess, and undoubtedly believe, that the faithful, in the right use
of the Lord's Table, so do eat the body, and drink the blood of the Lord Jesus, that He
remaineth in them and they in Him: yea, that they are so made flesh of his flesh, and
bone of his bones, that as the Eternal Godhead hath given to the flesh of Christ Jesus
(which of its own condition and nature was *mortal and corruptible*) life and immortality, so doth Christ Jesus his flesh and blood eaten and drunken by us, give to us the
same prerogatives." See, Chapter 21—Of the Sacraments, https://www.fpchurch.org.uk/
about-us/important-documents/the-scots-confession-1560/#c6, italics added.

29. https://trinityinyou.com/edward-irving-sermons-on-the-incarnation/. See David Lee, *A Charismatic Model of the Church: Edward Irving's Teaching in a 21st-century
Chinese Context* (Newcastle upon Tyne, UK: Cambridge Scholars, 2018), esp. Chapter
3, "Irving's Theological Method: The Humanity of Christ, Church and Divine Purpose."
Regarding Irving's theological method, Lee identifies five characteristics by which Irving reveals his own understanding of the dynamic and broad-sweeping movement of
God's redemptive-kingdom' perspective (ibid., 76–82). They are: *biblical* in that Irving's
Christological statements are supported by his interpretation of various biblical texts,
albeit in a pre-critical nineteenth-century manner; *respectful* to his doctrinal heritage;
systematic and unitary in that Irving works out his thought from his theological centre,
namely, the humanity of Christ. In this we see Irving the critical and constructive theologian; *synthetic* in fusing church ethics with Christian doctrines, the practical with
the spiritual, the theoretical and the intellectual; actively *contextual*, in that he engages
his ecclesiology with the political, social and historical context of nineteenth-century
Britain, For example, in 1830 in good Secessionist tradition, Irving took a petition to
the Houses of Parliament and met the Prime Minister, Lord Melbourne, for a national
fasting on behalf of the suffering of the poor.

and scandal. In essence, in positing that the Son of God assumed the very humanity in need of redemption, namely, a fallen and 'sinful' humanity, Irving opposed both the Presbyterianism of his day that read this as saying that the Son of God actually sinned, and the Roman Catholicism of his day that would eventually become the dogma in Pope Pius IX's bull, *Ineffabilis Deus*, concerning the Immaculate Conception, 1854 of the Virgin Mary's immaculate conception as the means the result of which ensured the sinlessness of Jesus Christ, being one without original sin.[30]

It may be helpful at this point to add three clarifications to Irving's use of 'sinful' regarding the humanity assumed in the incarnation. First, Irving provides us with his own *methodological* reason for using this term in relation to the incarnation. As Irving puts it:

> To make flesh was the great end, work, and accomplishment of the Incarnate God, and was brought about by the consenting and harmonious operation of Father, Son and Holy Ghost, according to their eternal and necessary relations and operations; the Father sending the Son; . . . the Son assuming flesh; [. . .] The Holy Ghost proceeding from the Father and the Son, to be its life and strength, and holiness, its resurrection and glory. To this flesh we have applied the word 'sinful,' or 'of sin' in order to express the state *out of which God took it*; the words 'sinless and holy,' to express the state into which God brought it.[31]

Second, there is the *pragmatic*, something deeply ingrained in Scottish common sense and its theology:

> That Christ took our fallen nature is most manifest, because there was no other in existence to take. The fine dust of Adam's being was changed, and the divine goodness of his will was oppressed by the mastery of sin; so that, unless God had created the Virgin in Adam's first estate . . . it was impossible to find in existence any human nature but human nature fallen whereof Christ might partake with the brethren. I believe, therefore, in opposition to all . . . who say the contrary, that Christ took unto

---

30. Coleridge was to comment, "Irving's expressions are highly inconvenient and in bad taste, but his meaning such as it is, is orthodox—as is plain enough to common reason. The body of Christ—as body only—was not capable of sin or righteousness, any more than my body or yours; that his *humanity* had a *capacity* of sin follows from its own essence. He was of like passions as we are—and was tempted. How *could* he be tempted, if there was no formal capacity of falling?" Samuel Taylor Coleridge, 14 Aug. 1833, *The Collected Works of Samuel Taylor Coleridge, Volume 14: Table Talk, Part 1*, edited by Carl Woodring (Princeton: Princeton University Press, 1990), 422–23.

31. Irving, *Sermons, Lectures, and Occasional Discourses*, i-ii.

Himself a true body and a reasonable soul; and that the flesh of Christ, like my flesh, was in its proper nature mortal and corruptible; that He was of the seed of David; that He was of the seed of Abraham, as well as of the seed of the woman; yea, that He was of the seed of the woman after she fell, and not before she fell. Even the time for making known the truth that Christ in human nature was to come did not arrive till after the fall, because it was determined in the counsel of God that He who was to come should come in the fallen state of the creature, and therein be cut off—yet not for himself—to the end tit might be proved that the creature substance which He took, and for ever united to the Godhead, was not of the Godhead a part, though by the Godhead sustained.[32]

Third, there is the *pastoral* concern Irving had for those in his charge. Of what use is a Saviour untouched by the most basic vicissitudes of human experience, a humanity incapable of overcoming its basic condition and unable to experience the life for which it was created? What use is a preacher who cannot explain the dynamics of spiritual life so that they can be embraced and enjoyed? There is a sense of the 'how-does-this-work' perspective in Irving's mind that was first seen in his disposition and ability in mathematics as a young scholar. Add to this the practical bent in his theological tradition and it is altogether expected that Irving would enquire into the nuts and bolts of the gospel he preached. If the freedom of the Gospel is to have any meaning, it must first be proven in the life of Christ through whom Christian liberation comes. The imputation of Christ's own righteousness, for Irving, is nothing other than what was actually achieved in the humanity assumed by the eternal Son of God and sustained through the indwelling Holy Spirit in the man Christ Jesus.

Given subsequent responses to Irving's Christology, he was denounced by Henry Cole in October 1828, called a heretic in James Haldane's 1829 tract, called before the London Presbytery in 1820 and deposed from the ministry of the Church of Scotland by the Annan Presbytery, March 1833, subsequently for his health to decline and ultimately to die, most likely from the subsequent exhaustion both mental and physical, five years from Cole's denunciation, on 7th December 1934. Carlyle was to write, "This mad City [. . .] killed him; he might have lived prosperous and long in Scotland, but here was in him a quality which the influences here took fatal hold of;—and now—Alas! alas!"[33] As in life, so in death, there is an irony in Irving's final

32. Edward Irving, *The Collected Works of Edward Irving in Five Volumes,* ed. Rev. G. Carlyle (London: Alexander Strahan), 5:87–88.

33. Thomas Carlyle to David Hope, https://carlyleletters.dukeupress.edu/volume

resting place being alongside St Mungo, the crypt of Glasgow cathedral, a site set apart for only the Kirk's finest and best.

CONCLUSION

There will always be those for whom Irving is held only in derision: an idiot full of sound and fury and who for them, in the end, signifies nothing. It was the case in his own day, and it remains today. It is no surprise, then, that Irving continues to divide opinion whether this be within his own Church of Scotland, its wider Reformed constituency or further afield to what might be identified as more Evangelical. However, for others Irving's theological dénouement is more positive, in no small part due to the fact that Irving has become a contemporary conversation partner through the energy of the late Colin Gunton who was first alerted to Irving's trinitarian currency through his colleague Andrew Walker. It can equally be said that Irving offered Gunton the stimulus he needed in order to advance his own trinitarian thinking.[34] Since then, in the past four decades, there has been a resurgence in Irving's thought, whether regarding his views on the Incarnation, his dispensational views concerning the second coming of the Lord Jesus Christ, his ecclesiology, his place as one of the founders of contemporary Pentecostalism or his contributions to contemporary trinitarianism. To date several noteworthy and scholarly contributions continue to keep Irving's legacy alive, for good or for ill. Tim Grass offers a comprehensive part-biography of Irving with special interest given to aspects of Irving's parish ministry and brings the man, Edward Irving, to life.[35] More theologically, Oliver Crisp leads the vanguard in critical and scholarly engagement in decrying Irving's notion of Christ 'sinful' flesh with his 2007 volume.[36] Those of a critical stance often lump Irving with T. F. Torrance—and even Barth—as representing a particular school of thought.[37] Graham McFarlane

/07/lt-18341219-TC-DH-01, accessed 13 July 2020.

34. Colin E. Gunton, "Two Dogmas Revisited: Edward Irving's Christology," *Scottish Journal of Theology* 41.3 (1988) 359–76. C. E. Gunton, *Theology through the Theologians: Selected Essays 1972–1995* (Edinburgh: T.&T. Clark, 1996).

35. Tim Grass, *The Lord's Watchman: A Life of Edward Irving (1792–1834).* (Eugene, OR: Pickwick, 2012).

36. Oliver Crisp, *Divinity and Humanity: The Incarnation Reconsidered* (Cambridge: Cambridge University Press, 2007).

37. Donald MacLeod, *The Person of Christ* (Downers Grove, IL: IVP Academic, 1998). Daniel J. Cameron, *Flesh and Blood: A Dogmatic Sketch concerning the Fallen Nature View of Christ's Human Nature* (Eugene, OR: Wipf & Stock, 2016). Cameron addresses the wider Scottish debate from Irving through to Torrance and so is less

offers the first of several engagements in Irving's Christology[38] and within the last decade, of note, several scholarly pieces of Irving research that engage his Christology have emerged.[39] Each in its own way shows the incredulity in relegating to Irving any notion that he is a 'poor player' but, rather, that his theology has proven to be a rich vein of thought for further dialogue during the trinitarian renaissance of the past three to four decades in western theology. The 'stage' on which Edward Irving's Christology first made its appearance, it would appear, is still very much inhabited. The Christological sermons which follow offer an accessible window through which contemporary readers may avail themselves of Irving's theology with the hope that rather than signifying nothing will, rather, prove not only Irving's own credibility as a theologian but also of his relevance to his readers today.

---

engaging Irving and more so T. F. Torrance.

38. Graham W. P. McFarlane, *Christ and the Spirit, The Doctrine of the Incarnation according to Edward Irving*. (Carlisle, UK: Paternoster, 1996).

39. Byung Sun Lee '*Christ Sinful Flesh': Edward Irving's Christological Theology within the Context of His Life and Times* (Newcastle upon Tyne, UK: Cambridge Scholars, 2013); P. Elliott, *Edward Irving: Romantic Theology in Crisis* (Carlisle, UK: Paternoster, 2014); David Lee, *A Charismatic Model of the Church* (Newcastle upon Tyne, UK: Cambridge Scholars, 2018); E. Jerome Van Kuiken, *Christ's Humanity in Current and Ancient Controversy: Fallen or Not?* (London: Bloomsbury T.&T. Clark, 2017).

Author's Preface

These sermons on the incarnation were intended to open that mystery after dogmatical, and not a controversial, method; as being designed for the instruction of the church committed to my ministerial and pastoral care, of whom I knew not that anyone entertained doubt upon that great head of Christian faith. To open the subject in all its bearings, and connected with the other great heads of divine doctrine, especially with the doctrine of the Trinity, and to show the several offices of the divine persons, in the great work of making the word flesh; this truly was the good purpose with which I undertook and completed the four sermons upon the Origin, the End, the Act, and the Fruit of the incarnation. When I had completed this office of my ministry, and, by the request of my flock, had consented to the publication of these discourses; and when the printing of them had all but, or altogether, concluded; There arose, I say not by what influence of Satan, great outcry against the doctrine which, with all Orthodox churches, I hold and maintain concerning the person of Christ: the doctrine, I mean, of his Human nature, that it was manhood fallen, which he took up into his divine person, in order to prove the grace and the might of godhead in redeeming it; Or, to use the words of our Scottish Confession, that his flesh was, in its proper nature, mortal incorruptible, but received immortality and incorruption from the Holy Ghost.

The stir which was made in diverse quarters, both of this and my native land, about this matter, as if it were neither the Orthodox doctrine of the church, nor a doctrine according to godliness, showed me, who am convinced of both, then it was necessary to take controversial weapons in my hand, and contend earnestly for the faith as it was once delivered to the saints. I perceive now, the dogmatical method which I had adopted for the behalf of my own believing flock, would not be sufficient when publishing to a wavering, gainsaying, or unbelieving people; and therefore it seemed to me most profitable to delay the publication until I should have composed something fitted to re-establish men's minds upon this great fundamental doctrine of the church; which having done, I resolved to insert the same as two other sermons—the one upon the method of the incarnation, and the other upon the relations of the Creator and the creature, as these are shown out in the light of the incarnation. And, for this timeous interruption by evil tongues, I desire to give thanks to God, in as much as I have been enabled thereby not only to expound but to defend the faith, that the son of God came in the flesh.

I would not add another word upon this subject, were it not that I know how ready the ear of this generation is to take up an evil report, and how much it does prejudice a man to be even suspected of a great vital error in his faith. Therefore, to set myself straight with honest hearted men, who may have been poisoned by malicious slanders, I will state in a few words, what is the exact matter in dispute between us and these gainsayers of the truth.

The point at issue is simply this: whether Christ's flesh had the grace of sinlessness and incorruption from its proper nature, or from the indwelling of the Holy Ghost. I say the latter. I assert that in its proper nature it was as the flesh of his mother, but, by virtue of the Holy Ghost quickening and inhabiting of it, it was preserved sinless and incorruptible. This work of the Holy Ghost, I further assert, was done in consequence of the Son's humbling himself to be made flesh. The Son said, "I come:" the Father said, "I prepare Thee a body to come in:" and the Holy Ghost prepared that body out of the Virgin's substance. And so, by the threefold acting of the Trinity, was the Christ constituted a divine and human nature, joined in personal union forever. This I hold to have been the Orthodox faith of the Christian Church in all ages: it is the doctrine of the Scottish church, expressed in these words of the twenty-first article: "as the eternal Godhead hath given to the flesh of Christ Jesus which of its own nature was mortal and corruptible life and immortality," &c. And, moreover, I assert, that the opposite of this doctrine, which affirmeth Christ's flesh to have been in itself immortal and incorruptible, or in any way diverse from this flesh of mine, without respect had to the Holy Ghost, is a pestilent heresy, which coming in will root out atonement, redemption, regeneration, the work of the Spirit, and the human nature of Christ altogether.

Now, I glory that God hath accounted me worthy to appear in the field of this ancient controversy, which I hold to be the foundation stone of the edifice of Orthodox truth. With all this I hold the human will of Christ have been perfectly holy, and to have acted, spoken, or wished nothing but in perfect harmony with the will of the Godhead; which to distinguish it from the creature will, He called it the will of the Father: For that there were two wills in Christ, the one the absolute will of the Godhead, the other the limited will of the manhood, the Church hath ever maintained as resolutely as that there were two natures. These two wills, I maintain, were always concentric or harmonious with each other, and the work achieved by the Godhead through the incarnation of Christ was neither less nor more than this, to bring the will of the creature, which had erred from the divine will, back again to be harmonious with the divine will, and there to fix it forever. This is the redemption, this is the at-one-ment, which was wrought in Christ, to redeem the will of a creature from the oppression of sin, and bring it to be at one with the will of the Creator. All Divinity, all Divine operation, all God's purpose, from beginning to the ending of time, and throughout eternal ages, rest upon this one truth, that every acting of the human nature of Christ was responsive to, and harmonious with, the actings of the divine will of the Godhead. What a calamity it is then, what a hideous lie, to represent us as making Christ unholy and sinful because we maintain that He took His humanity completely and wholly from the substance, from the sinful substance, of the fallen human creatures which he came to redeem! He was passive to every sinful suggestion which the world through the flesh can hand up onto the will; he was liable to every sinful suggestion which Satan through the mind can hand up to the will; and with all such suggestions and temptations, I believe him beyond all others to have been assailed, but further went they not. He gave them no inlet, He went not to seek them, He gave them no quarter, but with power divine rejected and repulsed them all; and so, from his conception until his resurrection, His whole life was a series of active triumphings over seen in the flesh, Satan in the world , and spiritual wickedness in high places. If now, after this honest and true statement of the issue, anyone will advance to the perusal of this treatise on the incarnation with a prejudice against the orthodox truth, or against me its expounder, be the guilt of the breach of charity on his own head; and may God deal with him better than he deserves!

I commend my book unto Thy patronage, O Thou enlightener of every man who cometh into the world! I submit my work and the review and censure of that righteous judgement which will yet beholden up on all the works of all men; and meanwhile unto thee, oh Holy Spirit, whose minister I am, I offer these various thoughts and counsels, that Thou may use them for the sake of the faithful in Christ Jesus, whom I love in my heart, and for whom I desire patiently to bear all pains and travails of this mortal estate. And, O Father of my spirit, I fervently pray unto thee, that thou wouldst in Thy great mercy forgive whatever, in these and all my writings, may be inharmonious with Thy only holy mind, or derogatory from the honour and glory of thine only-begotten son, or vexatious and hindersome to the work of the Holy Spirit, remembering not the sins of Thy servant neither suffering them to make the least of Thy little ones to offend. Amen and Amen.

EDWARD IRVING

Dedicatory Epistle

To My Flock and Congregation

Dearly beloved in the Lord,

*These Sermons on the Incarnation, and the most Orthodox and whole-
some doctrine therein set forth, you received with all acceptance; and the el-
ders whom God had set over you made choice of them to stand first in these
volumes, which I now publish for the edification of the body of Christ. To you,
therefore, over whom the Lord hath made us overseers, I do offer these fruits
of my meditation and ministry on your behalf; and entreat you, in the name
of Jesus Christ, whose act of surpassing love they are intended to unfold, that
you would receive them with favour and affection from the hand of your Pastor and Teacher, who loveth you much. I cannot refrain, dearly beloved, from
expressing to you all the growing attachment which I feel towards you, because
of your patient hearing of the whole testimony of God, and your observance
of his holy ordinances and reverence for the persons of us who administer the
same; and I entreat you, in the several stations appointed to you of God, to be
faithful witnesses for Christ until his coming; standing fast together in faith
and love and Good conscience, with your loins girt and your lamps burning,
as those who wait for his appearing.*

*May the great Bishop and Shepherd of your souls feed you with the bread
of life all the days of your earthly pilgrimage and receive you at length unto his
kingdom and glory.*

> *Your affectionate and dutiful Pastor,*
> *Edward Irving*
> *November 10th, 1828*

Introduction

to "The Origin of the Incarnation"

Irving identifies the ultimate ground of the incarnation of God the Son as the will of the Father to be God *for us*. This divine will to redeem has its primordial expression before the foundation of the world in the covenant between the Father and the Son. The will to create, redeem, and welcome into communion with himself is singular and consistent throughout God's actions toward creation, culminating in the incarnate life of God the Son.

Correspondingly, Irving identifies the *human* will as the origin of sin. This is a significant element of Irving's hamartiology. Sin is an internal—a spiritual—disorientation, which manifests itself through extrinsic action, but it cannot be reduced to the latter. Salvation, therefore, must involve the alienated will being overcome. As such, atonement cannot be reduced to penal terms alone. Instead, in accordance with the pre-temporal divine will, God the Son became human, assuming the fallen human will, and triumphed over it in the power of the Spirit.

The doctrine of the Trinity, then, is foundational to Irving's theological vision. The Father enacts his will to save through the Son by the Spirit as the Son assumes human nature into union with himself and surrenders human will to the Father by the power of the Spirit. This has a couple of immediate implications. First, the inward reclamation of humanity, Irving believes, far exceeds a theory of the atonement that is exhausted by Christ's suffering the penalty of sin. Therefore, Irving presses us to consider the atoning work of Christ in ontological rather than forensic categories. Second, the saving work of God is revelatory: the life of Christ reveals the triune God at work to save. In this, Irving places before us the necessary connection between revelation and salvation, reminding us that the

2

knowledge of God is never static, as it were, but has the actuality of God's act to save as its foundation and context.

A portion of this sermon—some twenty pages in the original volume—has been omitted. In these pages, Irving describes the vicarious sufferings of Christ as the substitution of the innocent for the guilty. Irving is alert to the objections that his listeners might have to the proposition that the innocent might suffer for the guilty. Characteristically, Irving elucidates this doctrine in trinitarian terms: the incarnate Son is not an unwilling and fearful vessel, but rather the eternal Son, who delights to do the will of the Father. This saving substitution is not best understood as a cold legalistic exchange, but in the personal categories of will as it is the Father's will to permit and surrender his Son, the Son's willingness to obey, and the Spirit's willingness to bring about. As such, Irving provides a filial framework for the forensic exchange whereby sin is imputed to Christ and his righteousness gifted to us. This being established, Irving moves to an extended exegetical section in which, from 1 Peter 3.18 and Colossians 1.19–23, he demonstrates the close relationship between the incarnation, the vicarious suffering of Christ, and reconciliation. His discussion includes recognizably Reformed theological categories such as Christ's active and passive obedience, the justification of believing sinners, the propitiation of the wrath of God and the cleansing of sin.

The final sections of the sermon, which are included in this abridgement, are taken up with pastoral comments regarding assurance of salvation. Irving encourages his listeners to establish their assurance of salvation on the unchangeable will of God to be for them. He warns against establishing trust on either the institutional church or on their own personal spiritual growth. The former he sees as formalistic and the latter he sees as an effect rather than a foundation of salvation. Against these, Irving encourages us to focus our minds on the Father's purpose before the foundation of the world to send the Son in the power of the Spirit.

AJDI

1

The Origin of the Incarnation

Sacrifice and offering thou didst not desire; mine ears hast thou opened: burnt offering and sin-offering hast thou not required. Then said I, Lo, I come: in the volume of the book it is written of me, I delight to do thy will, oh my God: yea, thy law is within my heart.

PSALM 40.6–8

Dearly beloved brethren, on this day which we have set apart for showing forth the Lord's death by the sacrament of the supper, I consider it to be due unto his honour, and a right acknowledgement of our faith, that we should begin to meditate, and to set forth in order the great work of his incarnation, and the benefits which flow thence into our souls; to the end that, when God beholdeth us to be one of mind and spirit to honour and glorify his Son, he may be well pleased in us and make himself known to us in the breaking of bread. And may the Holy Spirit, who receiveth of the things of Christ to show them unto us, at this time so anoint us all with his holy unction of truth, that we may be able to search into the deep things of God, and to present them for the edification of the church, which is his body, the fullness of him who filleth all in all.

THE FALL OF HUMANITY AS THE IMMEDIATE, BUT NOT EXCLUSIVE, ORIGIN OF THE INCARNATION

The immediate cause of the incarnation, was the fall of man and the consequent invasion of sin, and the subjection of all earthly things to the prince of darkness. I say that this was the immediate cause, or, as we may say, the occasion of it: for, if man had not fallen, there would never have been upon this earth any such event as the incarnation, whereof the first fruit is to recover that which Adam lost, and, at the least to reinstate mankind and their habitation in that condition wherein they were created. This fall of man was also the formal cause of the incarnation; that is to say, what gave to the purpose of God its outward form and character, requiring his Son to take upon him the nature of man, and not of angels, to be under the law and to bear the curse of death, as it is written:

> for as much then as the children are partakers of flesh and blood, he also himself likewise took part of the same; that through death he might destroy him that had the power of death, that is the devil; and deliver them who through fear of death were all their lifetime subject to bondage. (Hebrews 2.14–15)

But, if we would ascend to the first cause of this great act of the Godhead, we must seek it in God himself, who worketh all things after the pleasure of his own will, and to the praise of his own glory. The fall of man was not an accident which fell out against the disposition into the hindrance of God's universal and all-including scheme of creation, and providence, and grace: but though the will of man was free,—that is, under his own single control, and not in bondage of a stronger as now it is,—yet was the act of his disobedience both known and foreseen and permitted of God, though not in such a way as to overrule, or constrain, or in anyway to bias his mind to evil, but all the contrary.

And as it was foreseen, so was it provided for; and as it was permitted, so was it overruled for the greater glory and honour of the most holy and righteous God, and for the total and eternal extinction and abolition of the active power of sin. Therefore is it most necessary to reach to a higher and more remote source than the full, or even the creation of our first parents, in order to attain into the great and first cause of the mystery of the Lamb slain from the foundation of the world. And the rule is general, that we must wholly disentangle every spiritual subject from the conditions of space and time, which are only the forms of its manifestation, ere we can arrive at his proper bearings or handle it in a way profitable to the spiritual life.

THE ORIGIN OF THE INCARNATION BEFORE
THE FOUNDATION OF THE WORLD

Accordingly, it is written concerning this mystery of the incarnation, in various parts of Scripture, that it came not within the coasts of time, but had its origin before the foundation of the world. In the beginning of his gospel, the testimony of John is given to this effect, "Behold the Lamb of God, which taketh away the sin of the world" (John 1.29): concerning which Lamb he testifies, that he was "slain in the foundation of the world [. . .] whose names are not written the book of life of the Lamb slain from the foundation of the world" (Revelation 13.8). But lest anyone should say this doth carry the offering of Christ only to, and not beyond the foundation of the world, I have Christ's testimony concerning himself: "Father, I will they also, whom thou hast given me be with me where I am; that they may behold my glory which thou hast given me: for thou lovedst me before the foundation of the world. Sanctify them through thy truth: thy word is truth" (John 17.21).

And lest this should be interpreted of the Father's love to him anterior to an independent of his *mediatorial* office (although it is, to my mind, nothing less than an absurdity in contradiction to imagine that the Father can contemplate his Son otherwise than in the fullness of all his offices, there being no application of time to the Godhead), I have to shew you a passage which places the sacrifice of the lamb, yea, and the foot and the foreordination and appointment of it, before the foundation of the world:

> forasmuch as ye know that ye were not redeemed with corruptible things, a silver and gold, from your vain conversation received by tradition from your fathers; but with the precious blood of Christ, as of a lamb without blemish and without spot; who verily was foreordained before the foundation of the world, but was manifest in these last times for you. (1 Peter 1.18–20)

In which idea that the apostles were rooted and grounded, you cannot read one of their epistles without perceiving; where you shall find that it is not in the fall of man they date the origin of our redemption, but in the eternal council of God, which he purposed in himself before the world began, as it is written:

> who had saved us, and called us with an holy calling, not according to our works, but according to his own purpose and grace, which was given us in Christ Jesus before the world began; but is now made manifest by the appearing of our saviour Jesus Christ, who has abolished death, and have brought life and immortality to light through the gospel. (2 Timothy 1.9)

In which passage, that which is seen and temporal with respect to the Messiah, is regarded merely as the manifestation of that purpose which the Godhead had purposed in himself before the world was, before any world was; all good purposes being ever present with him, and the execution of them all ever seen in the fullness of the Word, contemplated in him as their great architect, and fabricator, and upholder. But the full development of this doctrine is to be found written in the epistle to the Ephesians; of which Paul himself doth witness the great depth, saying, that when we read it, we may understand his knowledge in the mystery of Christ. If you read it with me, at the third verse of the first chapter, you will find that the apostle carries us out of *place*; At verse 4, out of *time*; at verse 5, out of the *present age*; and at verse 6, out of all *external cause*; at verse 7, he rehearseth the act of its *revelation in time*; and in verses 8–10, consummates the *act*; in verse 11 he takes in the *personal interest*, and in verse 12 he shows the *end of the purpose*.[1]

THE DIVINE WILL IS THE ULTIMATE ORIGIN OF THE INCARNATION

The doctrine, therefore, concerning the incarnation, upon which the primitive church was founded by the apostles, and to which the Reformers brought us back, and from which are fast swerving again is this: That it is a great purpose of the divine will which God was minded from all eternity to make known unto his creatures, for their greater information, delight and blessedness; to make known, I say, to all his intelligent creatures, the grace and mercy, the forgiveness and love which he beareth towards those who love the honour of his Son, and believe in the word of his testimony. In order that thereby his children, comprehending more fully the beauty and loveliness of the divine majesty, might desire him the more, and cleave unto him with an entire fidelity. Which aspect, if I may so speak, of the divine character, could never be beheld by a creature unfallen; forasmuch as grace and mercy, and forgiveness, do necessarily presuppose and require guilt, and offence, and hatefulness, for the objects upon which to put themselves forth, as necessarily as the power, and wisdom, and order, and harmony of creation require a chaos, and confusion, and darkness which they may adorn, and order, and bless. And as God did not at once command the created world to come forth as we now behold it, but first permitted a chaos which was without form and void, in order that by successive acts of wisdom and goodness, he might order it into beauty and light; so also did he permit that in the moral part of his works there should be a rebellion, and

1. Italics added.

darkness, and disobedience, in order that by successive acts of compelling grace, he might lead out the harmony and unity of all his chosen, "against the dispensation of the fulness of the times when he shall gather together in all things in Christ, both which are in the heavens and which are on the earth" (Ephesians 1.10).

And in thus proceeding, he doth manifest the grace or favour which he beareth even to sinners who honour his Son, giving his Son thereby a very great exaltation before the heavenly host, which they perceive that for his sake the Father of all can forgive sin. This, then, you will bear in mind, that the incarnation of his Son is the way by which God revealeth the more tender aspect of his being called *grace*—that part of the divine substance which could not otherwise have been made known. And therefore the gospel is called a mystery, because it was long hid to all, and yet in a measure hid unto all, being still only in the act and progress of unfolding itself. Abraham had a distant prospect of it, and Moses had a material model of it, the psalmist a royal foretaste of it, and the prophets a national manifestation of it, which yet themselves understood not, though they believed; and our Lord verified Abraham's distant view, substantiated Moses' shadow, answered part of the predictions of the psalms and the prophets, prepared the way of the Spirit to open the mystery more perfectly to the apostles, and promised that he would come again to manifest, clear up, and accomplish what still lay shrouded in the mystery: and this we look for him to accomplish against the dispensation of the fulness of the times. And to this agree the words of the apostle, when speaking of the insight which had been given unto him,

> Whereby, when ye read, ye may understand my knowledge in the mystery of Christ; which in other ages was not made known unto the sons of men, as it is now revealed unto his holy apostles and prophets by the Spirit; that the Gentiles should be fellow-heirs, and of the same body, and partakers of his promise in Christ by the gospel. (Ephesians 3.4–6)

And further:

> Unto me, who am less than the least of all saints, is this grace given, that I should preach among the Gentiles the unsearchable riches of Christ; and to make all men see what is the fellowship of the mystery, which from the beginning of the world hath been hid in God, who created all things by Jesus Christ: to the intent that now unto the principalities and powers in heavenly places might be known by the church the manifold wisdom of God according to the eternal purpose which he purposed in Christ Jesus our Lord. (Ephesians 3.8–11)

Upon which word "now," I remark, that we, that the principalities and powers in heavenly places, that all created beings, shall have no other revelation than we now possess in the church concerning the manifold wisdom of God; though, as it opens more and more, and is by the Lion of the tribe of Judah unsealed more and more, it shall be more and more discovered what treasures of wisdom and knowledge are hid in Jesus Christ, in whom it hath pleased the Father that all fulness should dwell: "That in the ages to come he might show us the exceeding riches of his grace, in his kindness towards us through Christ Jesus." (Ephesians 2.7)

Take this, therefore, my beloved brethren, for the true principle of the work of the incarnation, that it was a purpose which God purposed in himself, to make known by Jesus Christ, and by all who shall honour and cleave to him, the riches of his grace and mercy to the chief of sinners. And taking this for the true account of the matter, be comforted and strengthened and edified, in knowing that there is nothing accidental nor circumstantial in the work of your redemption, but that it is complete in him in whom ye believe and trust;—that as the men are carried safe who cleave unto the lifeboat, while the men that rashly commit themselves to the billows are dashed to pieces, or, to keep to the sacred emblem, as the souls who believed Noah and took refuge in the ark were saved, while all the rest perished, so you have nothing to fear if ye cleave to Christ, and resign yourselves to the shelter of his brooding wings. Oh, our fathers knew the comfort of this doctrine of the unconditional, uncircumstantial, unaccidental, the substantial, eternal, and unchangeable election in Christ Jesus; and, receiving it, they grew into his similitude, and were strengthened to do works of his holiness. But we have confounded the security of the divine purpose which includeth the church, and embraceth every spirit which believeth in Jesus, and which is the argument for believing in him, that we may be so kept in safety for ever; this we have confounded by looking continually at the varieties of the moods and frames of the natural man, and changing conditions of the visible church, which have no more to do with the constancy of that purpose in which we are wrapped up with Jesus, than this changing atmosphere and cloudy canopy over our heads hath to do with the fixed stars of heaven, and the constant light and heat of the glorious sun.

THE ORIGIN OF SIN IN THE CREATURE'S WILL AND THE CHARACTER OF SALVATION

So much have I to say in the general way which one topic of a discourse can contain, concerning the first and great cause of the incarnation of our Lord and Saviour Jesus Christ; and now I pray you to observe these two things, which naturally flow from what hath been said:—

First, in order that God might not be the cause of sin, and so all ideas of good and evil become confounded, it was proper, as from his own essential goodness it was necessary, that every creature which his finger framed should be made perfect in its kind, fit to shadow forth some portion of the Creator's worthiness, and to execute some part of his all-consistent and all-gracious will. Wherefore every creature being framed obedient to a good law and blessed in the obedience of the same, it must follow that if any creature fall from its primitive condition and frame of righteousness, it must do so by positive transgression of that ordinance under which it was placed by its Creator, and therein held by strong obligations and inducements, yet by no means so strong as to preclude a fall, which were infallibility itself and unchangeableness,—a state of being which pertaineth, as I conceive, at present to God only, but unto which all the redeemed are working their way, with all those heavenly and earthly things which, in the dispensation of the fulness of times, are in Christ Jesus to be gathered together into one.

I mean to say, that we have no tidings, nor records, nor, as I think, ideas of any unchangeable but the one unchangeable, the I AM, and therefore we ought not to wonder that angels and mankind should fall, or impute their fall unto God the Creator, because he had foreseen the occurrence thereof, and taken measures that there should thence redound glory to himself in the highest, peace on earth, and good-will to the children of men, new faithfulness and delight to the morning stars and the angels of God. The fall of the creatures therefore involveth guilt, and that of the deepest dye, if indeed there be deeper and deeper dyes of guilt; which, though it be a true idea to a creature already in a fallen state, is not so, as I take it, to a creature who hath not fallen, in whom any insurrection of the will, or disobedience of the act, doth constitute the very essence and substance of sin, which may afterwards be varied by particular accidents, but cannot, as I take it, be changed in its essence.

Now brethren, when guilt had been incurred, as it appeareth that it must occur in the fall of any creature, how is that creature to be delivered from under the state of guilt? How is the Almighty in shewing forth his love and mercy to the unfallen, and revealing that other aspect of himself, to approach this guilty creature who hath flown off to wander in the evil and erroneous maze of an independent will. This is the question which ignorance and presumption and wickedness findeth no question, but resolveth into God's indiscriminate mercy; but which wisdom, and righteousness, and modesty, findeth the mystery of mysteries, the perplexities of perplexities;—insomuch, that the very wisest of the heathen did say, he believed

God would, in the time he judged best, send forth some one from himself to teach mankind that mystery of mysteries, how a holy God could pardon sin. If it can be done, it can be declared; but the difficulty lieth all in the accomplishment of it. For it would ill answer either the end of the Creator or the wellbeing of his creatures, that he should make known that new and tenderer aspect of his character, which is grace, at the expense and obliteration of that other, which is righteousness. This would make the Father of lights to be a changing and revolving light; whereas he is the Father of lights, in whom there is no variableness nor shadow of turning. Besides, it is in virtue of his holiness that sin is sin; for if you take away the holiness of God, all distinctive is for ever confounded; and seeing the sinning creature is the evidence and token of his holiness, if that sinning creature were to be pardoned by a single act of love, love would have strangled holiness; or there would be a reign now of holiness, then of love, and no one could say when there might be another shift from love to holiness: and therefore, such an arbitrary redemption, even if possible, would be no redemption to depend on.

Wherefore, in the love, the holiness must shine forth, as the light of the sun shineth forth in company with its heat. The new manifestation of Jehovah's being must illustrate the old, not cast it into the shade. The new knowledge must be the old waxed more clear and manifest; no extinction nor obliteration thereof. And therefore I observe:—

Secondly, that seeing, not to drive all order within the universe into confusion, and all integrity into distraction and put all righteousness to shame, there must be with the divine power a faculty of preserving holiness, and of forgiving sin, I am at my wit's end to know how: here I stand non-plussed, my faculty of reason serving me not a jot. If I could conceive of sin as an accidental thing, which an accidental punishment could remove out of the way. I were in no strait or dilemma; for in that case, after we have suffered a while God may remain satisfied. But what a base notion of God is this; as if there were any proportion between the guilt of sin, and as much pain and punishment, in the mind of the most Holy! That notion of the universalists would dethrone my God at once from all my reverence, and set him lower than myself; forasmuch as I would despise myself for wreaking out so much punishment upon him who had offended me, and, without more ado, taking him by the hand as if he were cleansed.

Not but that pain and penalty will and must ever attend on sin, but that an age and an age of ages of pain and punishment will never, never wipe away sin. Sin is an alienation of the will; it is a spiritual act against a Spirit, against the good and gracious Father of spirits; and the root of the punishment is in the will; the strength of its bondage, the yoke of its thraldom, is upon the will; and it is only the recovery and restoration of the will, in its own act, which can put us again even on good terms with ourselves, much more with the gracious God whom we had offended. But what is to bring back the will of a spirit which of its own accord hath swerved away, which did not choose to stand when all was in its favour? What, I say, is to bring it back again when its whole bent is gone the other way, with all the malicious powers of darkness overloading and overbearing it? Tell me how this is to come to pass, and you shall be my prophet, priest and king. For verily to do this pertaineth only to him who is my Prophet, Priest and King.

Conceiving thus of sin as an eternal and unchangeable, an *original* condition of the will, which no punishment can alter, which all the accidents within the coasts of time cannot alter, I stand at that pass over which nothing can carry me but Almighty power; and I may say, with reverence, that not even power Almighty of itself can deliver me. Almighty power cannot reconcile this contradiction, that holiness should be preserved, and the creatures who have offended holinesss be, by a bare act of will, reinstated. We stand here upon the brink of a chasm, over which, with reverence be it spoken, even Almighty power cannot convey us without some further revelation than that of his omnipotence. The unity of the Godhead availeth us not here, where our reason refuseth to move forward without the revelation of more persons than one in the Godhead; from which the revelation of the mystery cometh.

Therefore the divine evangelist beginneth by declaring the eternal divinity of the Word, saying, "In the beginning was the Word and the Word was with God, and the Word was God" (John 1.1); and, after dilating upon his uncreated essence, upon his divine works in the times of old, when the heavens and the earth were created by him, and life and light were bestowed by him and of him, he addeth:

> And the Word was made flesh, and dwelt among us, full of grace and truth. And of his fulness have all we received, and grace for grace. For the law was given by Moses, but grace and truth came by Jesus Christ. No man hath seen God at any time; the only-begotten Son which is in the bosom of the Father, he hath revealed him. (John 1.14, 17–18)

John comprehended the mystery at which I declared, a little ago, that human reason must stand for ever nonplussed, and which no knowledge of God's unity can ever resolve. Therefore, after declaring the eternal Godhead of the Word, and at the same time intimating the mystery of his personal distinctness, by saying, not merely that he was God, but also that he was with God, he proceeds to declare his incarnation,—"he became flesh;" and the end of it,—for the purpose of revealing to us that grace of God to the sinful, and truth to those with whom he had entered into covenant, which could never have been known if we had not fallen, and would never have been known had the Son not been willing and free to take upon himself the remedy of our condition. Oh, what volumes are contained in these words, "Grace and truth came by Jesus Christ!"

Grace; that is, the knowledge of the love and mercy which is in God, of the whole mystery of good-will and peace which is in the gospel; the condescension of the holiest to the most unholy, his holiness unsullied by the condescension, yea, made infinitely more bright; the condescension of the Almighty to the weakest; all that is included in the word Father, Redeemer, Saviour; a mystery into which the angels desire to look, and which the apostle who had profited the largest therein, could only admire with silent admiration, saying, "Oh the height and the depth and the length and the breadth of the love of God in Christ Jesus; it passeth knowledge" (Ephesians 3.18).

Truth; that is, the fulfilment of all promise, the keeping of all covenant, the answer of all expectation, which had been given since the world began, and the assurance of all faith, which might be rested thereon until the world should end. This grace and truth came, not by the *word*, but by the *Word Incarnate*, by *Jesus Christ*; that is *Jah the Saviour* and *Anointed One*. For it was in the act of becoming flesh that all grace and all truth was embodied, his name, Jesus Christ, importeth it. His name, the Word, importeth only his divine essence and separate personality from all eternity.

TRINITARIAN BASIS OF GOD AS JUST AND JUSTIFIER OF SINNER

Now, brethren, from this separate personality of the Word is derived the resolution of the great mystery, "how God can be just and justifier of the ungodly;"[2] and from this point we must begin to speak in the language of the Trinity; for no one can speak of the redemption but in that language, as may be seen in the eighteenth verse, which, after having spoken of the grace and truth that is in Jesus Christ, the Evangelist thus begins, "No one hath seen God at any time" (John 1.18); but he cannot conclude it in the language of unity, and is forced to add, "the only-begotten Son, which is in the bosom of the Father, he hath revealed him" (John 1.18). The Father's holiness of will remaineth unaltered; he remaineth the unchangeable enemy and implacable destroyer of sin. His holiness continueth, like a fire, to consume the transgressor now as when sin first entered the world. But man's

2. Irving appears to be referring to Romans 4.4.

transgression did not reach to, or in any way affect, the relation between the Father and the Son, between whom no creature intermeddleth, or can any wise intermeddle.

This is secret, deep, and unsearchable; and the joys of it are not to be apprehended by created minds, nor discoursed of by human tongues; therefore was it possible, within the depths of the divine nature, for the Father to forgo the delight which he had with his Son in his own bosom, and to permit him to come forth on the ministry of redemption, in order that, after suffering for a while, he might return again with the honour of redemption added to the honour of creation and providence. In this, I say, there is no impeachment of the holiness of God, while there is a great manifestation of his love, in not sparing his only-begotten Son, but giving him up to the death for us all. Nay, but there is a great manifestation and illustration of his holiness likewise, if when his dear Son, his beloved before all ages, took upon himself our nature, his holiness should pursue him as man, as flesh, with that awful severity it pursueth sinful flesh; if, when he was found within the accursed realm and blighted barren region of sin, the most direful scourges thereof should seize him, and smite him, and cleave to him even as unto others; if, against him, the law should stand up in all its offended majesty, and measure him without abatement at every point; and if Satan also and the powers of darkness, and if death also and the grave and if hell also and its legions should combine against him, even as against any other of the children. Which being truly fulfilled in the manifestation, the holiness of God was, in a most marvellous way, illustrated in the midst of his love; yea and over his love. Yes, I will say *over* his love; for holiness is the column of the divine majesty and power, the root and trunk of that tree, of which goodness and wisdom, mercy and love, are the various branches, flowers and fruits. Which holiness, I say, is more illustrated and honoured in the incarnation of Jesus Christ than it would have been in the destruction of a thousand worlds fallen, forsaken, and abandoned because of sin. So that, on the part of the Father, unchangeableness is preserved, hatred of sin is preserved, the stability of righteousness is preserved, while love, and grace, and mercy find their proper manifestation toward sinful men.

THE NATURE OF THE INCARNATION AND THE REDEMPTIVE OBEDIENCE OF CHRIST

Let us now turn and consider how this great act affects the condition of the Son; for ignorant men take upon them to scoff at this great work of the incarnation, as if it were a substitution of the innocent instead of the guilty, against all reason and justice, and to the subversion of all reason and justice in the breasts of men. Thus they speak in ignorance not understanding what they say, nor whereof they affirm. But first, I pray you to observe, that there was no necessity, to speak after the manner of men, obliging God to find an atonement for sin;—which is manifest from the condition of the angels who kept not their first estate, and are reserved in chains of darkness unto the judgement of the great day. Their case was passed by, while ours was chosen for the manifestation of grace and truth: which is, therefore, devoutly to be contemplated as an act of sovereignty in the midst of mercy; for there must be sovereignty in all God's acts, else he were no longer gracious; and it is to be ascribed to no other cause than his own electing love, which is an ultimate fact and principle that cannot be passed beyond. It needed to be shewn that God could punish sin unchangeably; or, in other words, that the proper nature of sin is to propagate and increase itself for ever. There must be a monument of all the divine attributes, and this of the fallen angels is the monument of his unextinguishable hatred of sin. The earth shall be redeemed, and the spirits of just men shall be made perfect, who shall thenceforward be the monument to all the universe of grace. And where is the monument of God's justice and severity against sin for the universal host to contemplate? Hell with her prince of darkness, her rebel angels, and all reprobate men, shall be that monument for ever and ever. "They shall go forth and look upon the carcases of the men who have transgressed against me; for the worm dieth not, neither shall their fire be quenched" (Isaiah 66.24). It is thus that every attribute of God shall have its proper manifestation, or be realised in some object which his creatures may behold and admire.

Bearing this in mind, that the great object of the incarnation, whereof we discourse, is to bring into visible manifestation and real being the monument of God's grace and mercy, and that the Father worketh nothing but by the Son, it is clear that it properly became him, who created angels and men, and all things, and thereby gave the demonstration of God's creative attributes of power, wisdom, goodness, &c.,—him, who is at last to judge all things; and by constituting hell, to give the demonstration of God's attributes of justice and holiness, abhorrence of sin, &c.; that same one it did become to give the intermediate demonstration of God's mercy, and grace, and forgiveness in recovering, redeeming, and regenerating the earth, and in constituting its blessedness forever. And besides these three great demonstrations of the Godhead, creation, redemption, and judgement, no others are known unto me.

Now, with respect to the part which the Son bore in this great covenant, made and sealed before the foundation of the world, I pray you to remember what I observed above, that the essence of sin is spiritual, in the will; and that the inward darkness and trouble, the outward suffering and sorrow, are only the consequences, and I may say the accidents, which cleave unto a will or spirit which hath cast off the authority of God, and become a law unto itself: therefore, the work which the Son had to perform was to redeem the will of man from its bondage to sin and Satan; or rather, I should say, from the curse of God, declared in paradise against transgression. Which deliverance to accomplish, he must come into the very condition of that which he would redeem; become flesh, and take up into himself the very conditions of a human will, or human spirit; that is, become *very* man, and himself wrestle therein against flesh and blood—against principalities—against powers—against the rulers and darkness of this world—against spiritual wickedness in high places. If it pleased him to undertake this, no one will say that he was hindered from undertaking it. If he had love strong enough to make the sacrifice, there was no unrighteousness, there was no dishonour—unless mercy, and love, and grace be a dishonour.

For the suffering which it caused him—first, the hiding of the light of the Divinity; secondly, the being subject unto a law, being himself both the Lawgiver and the law; thirdly, the encountering his own creatures, and being under their continual malice and persecution; fourthly, the presence and very close communion in which he dwelt with all manner of sin, touching, tasting, hearing, seeing, feeling it, and being in all points tempted like as we are, yet without sin; lastly, the undergoing of death and burial;—these things which I cannot now handle particularly, are but the outward accidents and apparent attendants of that humiliation into human nature which he underwent. The merit of the act lay not in these outward visible things, nor is it by them to be appreciated: even as the heinousness of sin is not thus to be measured, but standeth in the reprobate will; so the righteousness of Christ is to be appreciated by the willingness with which he undertook humanity, and underwent the fiery proof; and if you would have *apparent* proofs of that willingness, they are to be found in the meekness, gentleness, patience, long-suffering, and forgiveness with which he endured it.

And that this is the highest view of the Lord's work, the reasoning of St Paul upon the saying of the psalmist "Sacrifice and offering thou didst not desire; mine ears hast thou opened: burnt-offering and sin-offering hast thou not required" (Psalm 40.6). He rejects the Jewish, or rather the ceremonial form of the work, even as I have endeavoured to raise your views above it, to the higher view of it which is contained in the following verses: "Then said I, Lo, I come: in the volume of the book is written of me; I delight to do thy will, O my God: yea, thy law is within my heart" (Psalm 40.7–8)—in which the true end of his advent or incarnation is declared to be to do the will of God, and to have his law written on his heart; or to give the example of a man, who, as a man, should overcome all the enemies of a man, and reobtain the possession of that dominion of man which had been lost in the fall.

Now let us observe St Paul's reasoning upon this text: "Above, when he said, Sacrifice and offerings, and burnt-offerings, and offering for sin thou wouldest not, either hadst pleasure therein; which are offered by the law; then said he, Lo, I come to do thy will, O God. He taketh away the first, that he may establish the second" (Hebrews 10.8–9). It is the active obedience of Christ, in the perfect submission and obedience which he yielded, in the doing without any failure all the will of God, that he became the author of salvation for all them that believe. The suffering which he came under was, as it were, but the putting of that will to proof; and the well-pleasing in the sight of God was the enduring of the fiery proof, and the continual declaration of it, "Yet not my will, but thine be done" (Luke 22.42). Hence it is, that, in the Gospel of John, the Lord's discourse is but as it were one acknowledgement of his Father's will, and obedience to his Father's commandment; or, as it is written in that same psalm (Psalm 40.9–10): "I have preached righteousness in the great congregation: I have not refrained my lips, O Lord, thou knowest. I have not hid thy righteousness within my heart; I have declared thy faithfulness and thy salvation: I have not concealed thy loving-kindness and thy truth from the great congregation." And, brethren, it is by the will of God that we are sanctified still, as St Paul reasoneth, and as St John confirmeth: "He came unto his own, and his own received him not. But as many as received him, to them gave he power to become the sons of God, even to them that believe on his name: which were born, not of blood, nor of the will of the flesh, nor of the will of man, but of God" (John 1.11–13).

I consider it, therefore, to be rather a low view of the Redeemer's work, to contemplate it so much in the sense of acute bodily suffering, or to enlarge upon it under the idea of a price or a bargain, which is a carnal similitude, suitable and proper to the former carnal dispensation, and which should, as much as possible, be taken away for the more spiritual idea of our sanctification by the full and perfect obedience which Christ rendered unto the will of God; thereby purchasing back, and procuring for as many as believe in him their justification and sanctification by the Holy Spirit, which is their conformity to the will of God, and reliance on his eternal purpose. For whosoever is brought into conformity with the will of God is thereby included in his purpose. It was a great act of power in the Son—a demonstration of his almighty power to take up flesh and strengthen it against all the powers of hell—to take up flesh and purify it against all the powers of sin and corruption. But no one will say it was impossible, for it hath been accomplished; and no will say that there was any violation of the principles of eternal holiness and justice, for the Son to do what was within his power, or for the Father to suffer him to do it.

With respect to the communication of the gift to others, we do not now entreat: at present we are considering only of the purchase of the gift; and this, as hath been said, was by his obedience and perfect fulfilment of God's most holy law, which had been offended by our first parents and by all their posterity. And it was the offended law, or, in other words, God's unalterable, immitigable[3] holiness, which perpetuated the punishment. If one of Adam's children could have stood up and kept the law, he would, in virtue of his own innocency, have lived in it, and known neither suffering nor death. The man, Christ Jesus, did this, and in virtue of his work, now liveth, it being impossible that he should be holden of death. By which life of obedience the law stood honoured: it was proved to be *holy*, it was proved to be *just*, it was proved to be *good*, and it was *satisfied*.

I may say the *holiness* of God's law was never manifested upon the earth till now, because it was never kept. In the idea it was holy; but never in the reality, till Christ said "Father, I have glorified thee on the earth; I have justified the work which thou gavest me to do" (John 17.4).

The *justice* of the law might well be doubted, and its cruelty believed, at least its disproportion to human conditions: forasmuch as every man had smarted and suffered under it, and no one has been able to attain unto the keeping of it. It might have been supposed the law of a tyrannical, or arbitrary, or even a malicious being, inasmuch as it had punished all and acquitted none. This was a great, a very great apparent stigma, which the perfect obedience of Christ in human flesh removed, proving unequivocally that it was made for flesh, and would have blessed humanity had its gracious intention and adaptation not been crossed and prevented by the fall or our first parents, and the consequent apostasy of the will of man, and its alienation from every thing which is holy, and just, and good; for the goodness of the law,—that is its kindness and bountifulness, and fruits of blessedness,—were all contradicted by the fact of such long and universal misery as had been upon the earth. The divine purpose in creating human nature, and putting it under his holy, just and good law, seemed to be wholly frustrated; the very end of creation seemed defeated; there was no glory of God redounding from it, but glory to the enemy of God. The world had gone into chaos, and the great achievement was, out of the chaos to bring something more perfect than before. To justify the ancient constitution of law and government under which the world was established at first; to retrieve, to do more than retrieve, the honour of the

---

3. Archaic term meaning 'unable to be made less severe'.

Creator,—to make it more glorious. This was the first end for which Christ gave himself to become man from the foundation of the world. To this agreeth the reasoning of the apostle Paul in his Epistle to the Romans:

> "Do we then make void the law through faith? God forbid: yea, we establish the law." (Romans 3.31)

> "That the righteousness of the law might be fulfilled in us, who walk not after the flesh, but after the Spirit." (Romans 8.4)

> "For Christ is the end of the law for righteousness to every one that believeth." (Romans 10.4)

> "For as many as are under the works of the law are under the curse: for it is written, Cursed is everyone that continueth not in all things which are written in the book of the law to do them." (Galatians 3.10)

> "But when the fulness of the time was come, God sent forth his Son, made of a woman, made under law, to redeem them that were under the law, that we might receive the adoption of sons." (Galatians 4.4–5)

Thus far, then, it is manifest, that when the Son of God said unto the Father from all eternity, "Lo, I come; in the volume of the book it is written of me: I delight to do thy will, O my God, yea, thy law is within my heart" (Psalm 40.8), his object was, as is immediately added, to preach God's righteousness in the great congregation, to declare his faithfulness and salvation; and there can be no doubt that the holiness of God was illustrated by the Son of Man, before the great congregation, as it never had been before; that the ends of creation were wondrously manifested, and the darkness, and gross darkness, began to be cleared away. This is done, however, as yet only to the great congregation,—that is, to the elect church; the rest of the world remaining as dark almost as before. But in the fulness of the time, the manifestation shall be enlarged to all the inhabitants of the earth, and, in the end, unto all the creatures of God who are now looking upon the progress of its accomplishment. Thus much for the justification of God's holiness, for which the incarnation of his Son was the appointed way. But much yet remaineth to be said with respect to the demonstration of his grace in the forgiveness and salvation of the sinner.[4]

4. The omitted material is summarised above and can be found in Edward Irving, *The Complete Works of Edward Irving, Volume 5*, edited by G. Carlyle (London: Alexander Strahan, 1865), 27–48.

PASTORAL COMMENTS

From the passages of Scripture which are the groundwork of the preceding remarks, it doth clearly appear that our Lord and the apostles never fail to take a higher view of the incarnation than as one of the events of time and occurrences of this fallen world; contemplating it as an act of Godhead, done from all eternity, purposed before the foundation of the world, prearranged and foreordained in all its parts, to this very end of manifesting unto all intelligent creatures the glory of God's holiness and grace in the salvation and forgiveness of sinful and apostate creatures; that it was not an act consequent upon the fall, though taking its form and character thence, but an eternal purpose, which God purposed in himself before the world was, to the praise of the glory of his grace. This view of the subject, notwithstanding that it is so constantly taken in the Scriptures, hath grown into such disuse in the church that it cannot be presented without much explanation, and without answering the most seductive question, What is the good of it? What is the use of it? And rather to be profitable unto your souls, dear brethren, than to indulge this common form of all ignorant gainsayers, I shall a little open the good use of these higher views.

Assurance

It seemeth to me, that a pious and believing soul, which desireth, with all its might, to return back again to God, and lose its will in his most holy will, can in no way be so refreshed as in studying to know the purpose of that will, into the likeness of which it hasteth to be reduced, and longeth to be transformed; and in order to satisfy this noble, desire of the renewed mind, God hath taken the veil from off the secrets of his purposes, and condescended to teach us, not only by outward appearances, and manifestations of his holy providence and gracious redemption, but also by the knowledge of the eternal principles in his divine nature, from which they proceed, and the eternal ends of peace and blessedness whereto they minister, and wherein they shall result. And this hath he done not only in gracious condescension to our desire of knowledge, and effectual furtherance of our desire of conformity to his mind and will, but also in great wisdom, to comfort and establish our minds in Christ Jesus to root us and ground us in that holy truth which he hath delivered unto us, and wholly to free us from all fear of accident, and change, and circumstance; from all fear of adversity, temptation and outward violence. There is no peace, there is no rest, there is no contentment to the soul until it is delivered from the fear of change and fluctuation; nor is there any activity, or bravery, or steady conduct in the soul, until it feeleth itself all directed, wound up, and steadfastly bent upon some great end which it knoweth to be within its reach.

Now when God purposed by his Son to deliver our souls from an oppression of the flesh, and the world, and Satan, as they presently labour under, in what way could they have been awakened to such a fearful, to such a fiery contest with all manner of oppressors, as by presenting to them the warrant of their final perseverance and success, brought direct from the archives of the Eternal and Almighty God, the covenant of their complete deliverance from sin, and reinvestment in righteousness, sealed in the blood of his only begotten and well-beloved Son? I do not say that this is effectual to rouse the deep sleep of all to whom it is made known; but I know that the deep sleep of no one was ever otherwise broken, or his active warfare otherwise maintained. For though many indeed by something less arouse men from their lethargy, as, for example, by merely preaching the free and open gospel of forgiveness and reconciliation, they shall never carry them forward against all hindrances to perfection, or against all doubts, settle them in fixed assurance, otherwise then by shewing them the divine purpose from all eternity to redeem as many as shall believe on his Son. And it is the unalterable fixedness thereof which gives the believer constancy against the moody frames of natural man, which carries him buoyant over all the billows of the adverse and tempestuous world, and gives him clear discernment through all the mists and exhalations of hell, which Satan's delusion is ever spreading over the soul. A conditional gospel can redeem no man from this conditional state of being; it would only add another puzzling perplexity to the many which the fall hath introduced.

We want a Rock to rest our weary foot upon; we want a Light in which there is no variableness or shadow of turning, whereby to guide our uncertain course; to speak without a figure, we want a Will unalterable and unchangeable, whose purposes are disclosed to us, according to which we may rectify all our errors and wanderings, and thereto conform ourselves with all our might. But if that will be not itself constant, if it also be conditional, or if it be not revealed and manifest, or finally, if it bear not tender and loving regard to us, or if it leave any doubt over the issue of the contest, no one will arise and gird himself to the battle. For it is no ordinary battle upon an equal footing; but it is a battle of the weak against the mighty; of one against a host; of a new-born child against the powers of flesh and blood, against principalities and powers, against the rulers of the darkness of this

world and spiritual wickedness in high places. If there be the shadow of a
doubt, I say again, resting over the issue of such a contest,—if its success be
not assured and pledged to us by divine power and the almighty unchangeable will, no mortal man will ever arise and take the field; or if he should
(and some certainly do take the field without the knowledge or the faith of
this eternal purpose), then mark, that he will make a poor debate with the
enemy, and come to parley and to terms of accommodation, upon being
permitted any salve to his honour, which the cunning one is ever willing to
proffer. Therefore, it is no small matter which we are handling, but the root
of the matter, the great quickening, enlivening, and conquering principle
of the warfare, even the will of God for our salvation: and for our greater
confirmation let us turn together and read a passage of St Paul where he
employs the doctrine to this very end: Romans 8.28–39.[5]

False Grounds of Assurance

But besides this, I have to observe, that if we fix not our continual attention
upon the purpose of God in Jesus Christ as the only ground of our salvation, we will be tempted to look somewhere else; and the effect of looking
anywhere else will be fatal. Of these false foundations of trust, I perceive
two especially which mislead men. The one is, to look to the outward visible
church, and the other to look to the fruits thereof themselves,—the former
giving rise to formality, the latter to mysticism.

The greater part of professors look to the outward visible church, or
what I would call the *manifestation* of God's purpose, instead of looking to
the mind and will which are manifested therein. And the consequence is,
that they are led blindly and timorously under the spirit of bondage and fear.
Instead of being acted upon in their will by the Spirit of God, they are acted
upon in their understanding, or in their natural feeling, or in their bodily
sense by those parts of the revelation which severally address the several
parts of their being. But not acknowledging the supreme purpose and will
which actuates the whole body of the revelation, their own will remains un-
subdued and entire amidst all their formality of worship, and orthodoxy of
faith, and practice of charity, and excitement of feeling. Of which formalists
there are as many separate classes as there are different parts of the natural
man to be acted upon; some of the sense merely, some of the feelings, some
of the understanding; but inasmuch as the will is unrenewed and it never can
be renewed without comprehending the purposes of God (for the meaning
of a renewed will is that its purposes are in accordance with the purposes of

---

5. Irving cites this passage in full.

God)—inasmuch. I say, as the will is not renewed and bears still according to nature, there must subsist in all such religionists a spirit of bondage; and I very much doubt whether there can exist in them the spirit of adoption, which is not the spirit of fear but of love. Into this matter I cannot enter at length; and it has been indirectly touched upon already, in what I have said concerning the submission of the will of Christ to the purposes of God, in which he delighted. There is a oneness, a simplicity of purpose in the divine acts and revelations which is as it were the soul and life of them; the uniformity in their variety. And so also in the life of a believer there ought to be the same oneness and simplicity of purpose, which may be the life and soul of all his obedience, and form the community of the Spirit in the variety and diversity of our gifts and graces. Now, I say that no one will obtain this common spirit of a son save by knowing and studying the will of our common Father. Otherwise our personality becomes lost and fritted away amidst an infinite variety of duties and engagements, of thoughts and opinions, and ever one runneth wildly after his own natural disposition, instead of submitting to the will of God; and the end is confusion, and sectarianism, and schism, and every evil work. Of so much importance is it to have our souls bent unto the contemplation of the purpose of God, by the operation of the Holy Ghost.

Besides these formalities (for I call everything a formality in which the renewed will is not) there is another object to which spiritual divines are wont to turn the attention of believers, as the ground of consolation and assurance—namely, to the growth of grace and holiness in their own souls, or to what is called Christian experience. But into this I enter not at present; for it is too large and important a matter to be dealt with slightly. Only I will say, in passing, that it is not a principle or origin, but an effect derived from something else, and therefore not depending on itself, it is therefore not fit to rest upon. Besides, it is full of imperfection, change, and cloudy uncertainty, the light having to pass through the dark and dense medium of the flesh, which doth obscure it at times and at times modify it, and at times extinguish it altogether. It is looking upon the earth for the proof and assurance of the sun's steady light, instead of looking at the sun himself. But we insist not.

Invitation to Place Attention on God's Fixed Will Accomplished in Christ

Suffice it, dear brethren, to have given you a little insight into the purpose of God to justify his own holiness in the salvation of sinners by the incarnation of his Son, and likewise to have shewn you the superlative importance of this higher theology, which they commonly stigmatise by calling it *Calvinism*, but which is in truth the theology of the Reformers, and of the Nonconformists, and of every denomination of men in whom God hath placed the testimony of his Son, and by whom he hath built up or repaired the walls of his church. Therefore I do, with the more confidence, entreat you, brethren, to meditate the purpose of God in sending his Son, and your own election in Jesus Christ before the world was; your election to be holy and without blame before him in love, and consequently your perseverance in holiness, and your full assurance thereof unto the end. This fulness of the decree and purpose which he hath purposed in himself before the world was, is the assurance of the church; and it is the overture which the church maketh to the sinful world. We wish you all to enter into this security: we hinder none, but invite all. Is the invitation less acceptable, because you are assured of salvation? Is the voyage less welcome because the vessel is well ground, and hath the blessing of God upon her, which will make her ride out every storm? Is the house less inviting because when the winds arise, and the rains descend, and beat upon the house, it falleth not, and cannot fall because it is built upon a rock? Finally, is the Saviour less welcome because he is a perfect Saviour, able to the very uttermost to save all who come unto him by faith? Because in his incarnation and death he included in the covenant not himself only, but all who should believe on his name, and on his Father which sent him? Therefore, I do invite, I do entreat as many as hear me, by the *no condemnation*, by the *no separation*, which is in Jesus Christ, by the safe-keeping of their souls, by the assurance of their salvation, by the certain victory over every sin, by the surceasing of all fear, and the engendering of all love, and by whatever other expectations and assurances are cheerful, stable and glorious, I do invite you to take refuge in this ark of their salvation, where alone is safety, that they perish not in the overwhelming flood of the wrath and indignation of God.

This freeness, and fulness, and perfect assurance of the purpose of God in Jesus Christ, which I set forth as the inducement and the encouragement, and the great argument for those weary and heavy laden with the worlds changes and disappointments, to lay hold upon him and be at rest, I do present to you who are in him, and are this day to shew forth your faith in him, and your union with him, as your privilege and passion. You are at present in the wilderness, and have neither bread, nor water, nor any rest for the sole of your foot, nor any defence against the enemies which hang about you on all sides, save this alone, your assured faith in the new covenant, which God confirmeth with you this day in the blood of his Son. These enemies look for your faltering in this faith, in order to be upon you and to destroy you. Doubt, and you are weak; disbelieve, and you perish. Remember ye the day of provocation in the wilderness, when the fathers tempted and proved him; and because they had tempted him "these ten times," they did not see what they called his breach of promise, and were not suffered to enter the holy land, but fell every carcass of them in the wilderness. So fear ye lest a promise being left you of entering in, lest a covenant having been confirmed with you, any of you should fall short through unbelief.[6] "For if they word spoken by angels was steadfast, and every transgression and disobedience received a just recompense of reward, how shall we escape, if we neglect so great a salvation?" (Hebrews 2.2–3).

SUMMARY

And for this end, dear brethren, have we endeavoured to lift your thoughts out of the visible world of manifestation into the spiritual world of divine purpose, that you might be delivered from this day from all resting upon these symbols which are to be set before you, but by them ascend into the unseen realities in the heavenly places. We have taught you that the incarnation of the Eternal Word hath for its only beginning and origin the purpose of God to make known unto angels and principalities, and men, the grace, and mercy, and love which there is in his own eternal essence; which, to bring into manifestation, he must forego for a while the love which he beareth to his own Son, and his own Son submit to become flesh, and to tabernacle upon earth, to do the will of his Father, and keep the law, and make it honourable, and render an atonement for sin, and bring in an everlasting righteousness. Whereby the eternal harmony between the Father and the Son, and the essential holiness of the Divinity, became manifest, to the delight of all intelligent creatures; and the grace and mercy of the Godhead, which yet had not been seen, but only his unrelenting severity against the rebellious, became wondrously set forth and magnified.

Now, dearly beloved brethren, forasmuch as the Lord hath promised that he will be a mouth unto his ministers, and we besought the blessed Spirit that he would lead us into all truth, and enable us to utter unto you that which was seasonable, we ought surely to believe that these thoughts, however weak the utterance, contain the food on which your souls are this day to feed. See, then, that ye meditate and inwardly digest them. And let me now help you to one or two good uses of the same.

First, it is the will and purpose of God from all eternity, that you who are called into the church of Christ should be saved. The Father hath given you unto Christ, and none can pluck you out of the Father's hands. Therefore

6. Irving appears to be referring to Psalm 95.

be assured of your election in Christ Jesus, and of your perseverance therein unto the end. Pray in faith, as those who have the spirit of adoption. Believe that "all things are yours, whether Paul, or Apollos, or Cephas, or things present, or things to come, or life, or death; all are yours, for ye are Christ's and Christ is God's" (1 Corinthians 3.22). If God could prove unfaithful, you would have a reason to doubt him; if Christ could cast you off, you would have a reason to distrust him; if the covenant depended on things created and made, you might tremble in the fall and destruction of things created and made; but if it be before the foundation of the world, that ye are chosen in him; then, though the foundation of the world were to be removed, the purpose of God, that ye should be holy and without blame before him in love, is not thereby removed, or shaken, or altered, or infringed. Therefore go on your way rejoicingly.

Secondly, as Christ did not his own will to glorify himself, but forewent the sovereignty, the divine and the uncreated liberty thereof, and learned obedience as a servant, boring his ears, as a willing slave, and delighting to be under the law, thereby to honour the will of God, which is holy and just and good; whereby he became the author of eternal salvation to all who believe: so we must in like manner yield ourselves to the holy will of God, and glorify not our own will, which is under the law of sin and death; but receiving the Holy Spirit into our hearts, to write therein God's most gracious laws, we must bring forth out of a good conversation our works with meekness of wisdom, perfecting holiness in the fear of God. For in no other way can we be sanctified, but by the will of God: "by the which will we are sanctified" (Hebrews 10.10). It is thus, by acknowledging and bowing to the will of God, that we grow into the image of Christ, and are made partakers of the heavenly gift, and grow in the increase and fruitfulness thereof, even unto the end.

Thirdly, the sufferings which in this course of obedience you have to undergo from all quarters, arising out of ignorance, error, evil inclinations, worldly temptations, satanic and spiritual influences, with all the other fruits and consequences of a disobedient and reprobate will, are to be undergone with humility and patience, yea, with a remorse and repentance at their presence; with contrition of soul and broken-heartedness, as being the fruits of your rebellious spirit, and the continual memorials of what your Lord underwent for your redemption from them; yea, there should be a certain loathing and abhorrence of all these as the sink of abomination in which you formerly wallowed. You should not fret or grow weary and impatient before the Lord. That mood belongeth to God by right, who is the party offended; not to you, who are the offenders. Brethren, in your righteousness, be patient, be not disturbed from your moderation and meekness by any inward or outward trial. Let patience have her perfect work, that ye may be perfect and complete wanting nothing. Be willing to be offered; in all your agonies, saying, "Not my will, but thine be done" (Luke 22.42). Present your bodies a willing sacrifice;[7] shew that it is not an outward act of enforcement of the members, but an inward act of the willing mind: and remember what are the signs of willingness, meekness, patience, contentment, gladness, &c. These and many other uses are to be derived from this great act of the Father and the Son, from the great revelation of grace which hath this day been set before you, and which we pray the Lord to bless to his own glory in the church. Amen.

7. Irving appears to be referring to Romans 12.1.

Introduction

to "The End of the Mystery of the Incarnation is the Glory of God"

The topic of Irving's sermon on John 13:31—as the title implies—is God's glory in the incarnation of the Son. The way in which God is glorified through the incarnation is manifold and Irving suggests a number of other ways that the topic could have been addressed. For example, he could have examined the incarnation as it stood in God's mind prior to creation, how a transcendent God manifests himself in the flesh, the humiliation of the Word in the flesh, or the power of the Word in his bodily existence. Regardless of how one examines the incarnation, the conclusion, Irving says would be the same, the might and power of God is displayed. Thus, Irving narrows down his subject to "the glory accruing unto the Father, or invisible God, from the incarnation and death of Christ." The sermon is divided into two parts. In part one, he addresses the manner in which God is glorified through the design, purpose, and nature of the incarnation. In part two, he addresses the work that Christ was given to do and how that work brought glory to God the Father.

Portions of part one are omitted. There Irving uses Scripture to demonstrate how the Father is glorified through the incarnation of the Son. Drawing upon the Old Testament he appeals to Isaiah 49 and the story of Jacob to prove this point. He also appeals to the Gospels. Four stories in particular demonstrate the God glorifying nature of the incarnation: the marriage supper of Cana, the healing of the man born blind, the raising of Lazarus, and Jesus's encounter with Greek inquirers in John 12. These appeals to Scripture show that God is glorified in the incarnation and upon the cross. The rest of part one—which is included in this volume—consists of several arguments about how the incarnation glorifies God. Before these arguments, however, Irving contends that properly speaking God's glory cannot actually increase or decrease for God is the same yesterday, today, and forever. To say that glory could be given to God would indicate that God is in some sense incomplete. So, to argue that God is glorified in the incarnation represents the kind of accommodation that God makes when communicating to us. Much like we can speak of the rising or setting sun, speaking of God "gaining" glory is an accommodation to appearances. How then is God's glory manifested to us? The manifestation is made in three ways. First, through the incarnation of the Son we see the manifestation of the divine substance in three persons, that is, the Trinity is revealed. Second, the holiness of God in governing creation is justified. Finally, God's power over darkness and sin is demonstrated.

In part two, Irving carefully examines Christ's work in realizing God's eternal purposes. The glory brought about by Christ's work is realized in three ways. First, through the incarnation the purpose of creation—and human beings more specifically—is made complete. While parts of this section are omitted, they represent Irving's arguments for what contemporary theologians have labeled "Christological Anthropology." The God-man is God's end in creation. Although the creation Adam came prior to the incarnation in the unfolding of history, Christ is in fact the telos of creation. To make himself manifest and visible, "was the first beginning, the mainspring and only end of the purpose of God, and of the Word in creating." That Christ is the telos of creation and the prototype after which human beings were fashioned—Irving explains—is demonstrated in Revelation 3:14, where Christ is called the "Amen" of God. It is further demonstrated in Colossians 1 where Christ is called the image of the invisible God, the firstborn of every creature. The second manner in which the incarnation glorifies God is related to God's eternal decrees. Here we find Irving's argument for the necessity of the fall. The fall, he argues, was necessary because only then could God's electing grace, mercy, and forgiveness be manifested. Thus, while God's creation is originally without sin, it does not continue so apart from an express act of the Creator's will. God's ultimate plan, however, is to glorify himself in the incarnation of Christ, so God withdraws the power necessary for his creatures to remain sinless. This, Irving explains, is not the same as saying that God causes his creatures to sin. The point of a God-permitted fall is ultimately that the telos of Creation—who is Christ—could become incarnate. Thus, in Irving's scheme, the incarnation is intended prior to the fall, but the fall is necessary if God is to become incarnate. The third way that the incarnation glorifies God is that through the incarnation God conquers the powers of sin, death, and Satan. Assuming a fallen human nature Christ is obedient to the Father, even to the point of death. Despite having a fallen human nature Christ resists and overcomes temptation. Christ even descends into hell to overcome the enemy and his dominion. Ultimately Christ conquers death, winning back the elect from the hands of sin, death, and Satan. The final omitted section of the sermon consists of Irving's exhortation to his audience to glorify God by putting their faith in the incarnate one.

Like the other sermons in this collection, "The End of the Mystery" presents readers with a wealth of themes that are present throughout much of Irving's theology. For example, there is a strong supralapsarian thread that runs through the entire oration. Moreover, themes of election and redemption are found throughout. The Christ-centered manner in which he approaches these doctrines is evident. Although they are less prominent than in other sermons, the themes of the Spirit's role in the incarnation and the fallen human nature of Christ are present as well. Readers are bound to find the most distinctive elements of Irving's theological convictions are present in this sermon.

CGW

2

The End of the Mystery of the Incarnation Is the Glory of God

And God is glorified in the Son of Man.

JOHN 13.31

The incarnation of the Son of God, by which the glory of the Son of Man was procured, is the grandest mystery into which angels or the sons of men can inquire. If you regard the eternity of its purpose so constantly declared to have been before the foundation of the world, before the world began, the incarnation stands before us as one of the original projects (if I may so speak) of the Creator's mind, in order to the completion of that mighty work of creation which he was about to undertake; not an expedient to meet an accident, but an original intention, more ancient than creation itself, and to which the creation of being and the permission of sin were but as it were the necessary preparation. If you regard the awful mystery of the manifestation of this purpose, that the eternal Word of God, the uncreated substance of the eternal essence, did take into consubstantial and eternal union with himself the substance of fallen Adam, or I may say the very substance of the fallen earth, even the dust of the ground, to be united with it to redeem and glorify it, and for ever and ever to be manifest therein to all the universe of

31

God; it transcendeth all utterance, and passeth all comprehension, so very great is the mystery of God manifest in the flesh. Or, thirdly, if you regard the profound humiliation and most exquisite suffering in body and in spirit, which that man endured, in whom dwelt all the fulness of the God-head bodily, while the Word was made flesh and tabernacled amongst us; this endurance and humiliation, as we shall endeavour to set forth in our next discourse, is beyond all comprehension. Or if, fourthly, you regard the exaltation far above all principality and power, and every name that is named in heaven or on earth, into which the Son of Man, the woman's seed, the glorified dust of the ground, hath ascended up on high, for ever and for ever, to manifest in himself, and in his church, in like manner humbled, and in like manner to be glorified, the manifold riches of the grace and glory of God: I say, in whatever respect you consider the work of the incarnation, in its purpose, in its manifestation, or in its completion, it is, without all controversy, the mighty power and work of God; undertaken and undergone for far higher ends than are commonly discoursed of; for far higher ends than the redemption of the elect church, who I may say, are but the lively stones with which God buildeth up the work; but the work itself is no less than the manifestation of his own glory, and the eternal blessedness of all his obedient and dutiful creatures.

THE GLORIFICATION OF THE FATHER BY THE INCARNATE SON

Wherefore our Lord, contemplating in the text, and in various other passages of Scripture, the great crisis and turning-point of this mighty work, his death, burial, and descent into hell, by which the lowest depth was sounded, and the foundation of the eternal glory laid upon the unremovable rock beneath the waters of sin, which are to be baled out; he ever speaketh of it as if it had been the commencement of his Father's glory, saying, "Now is my Father glorified" (John 15.8) "[I] have glorified thee upon the earth" (John 17.4); "Father, glorify thy name" (John 12.24), and other such expressions, which surely signify to us that the glory of the eternal Godhead was in some remarkable way to receive increase and enlargement from the work, in the accomplishment of which Christ was travailing. It is of this subject,—the glory accruing unto the Father, or invisible God, from the work of the incarnation and death of Christ, that we are now to discourse, and for which, dear brethren, we have sought to prepare ourselves with much mediation, converse, and prayer these several weeks; and we do now publicly ask your prayers, that in times of such spiritual famine, the Lord would be pleased, for your sakes, and for the sake of his church, to give us good store of wholesome and nourishing food, to the enlargement, enlivening, and edification of our souls, in the common faith.[1]

THE GLORIFICATION OF GOD IN THE HUMANITY OF THE INCARNATE SON

Having thus examined the subject of "God glorified in Christ," and shewn from Scripture the two parts whereof it consisteth, we proceed in this discourse to open the first, which is contained in these words, "Glory to God in the highest," from which we would endeavour to set forth the glory which God himself hath derived from the Son of Man; or, in other words, the glory which the Godhead hath derived from his creature man, above and beyond all other creatures; on account of which he hath smelt such a sweet savour of manhood as to have taken the nature of man into fellowship with his own nature, and will exhibit his glorious divinity in the visible substance of manhood, through the endless ages of eternity. For this is what is implied in the words, "God is glorified in the Son of Man:" whereof the point is not, that he is glorified in the divinity of the Eternal Word, but in the humanity of his incarnate Son; in the Son of Man, not in the Son of God. We are now reverently to inquire how this cometh to pass: and may the Lord help our meditation, and give power unto our discourse!

Observe, then, first of all, my dearly-beloved brethren, that the eternal power and Godhead of Jehovah neither doth nor can suffer any the least change or alteration, increase or diminution, but it is essentially one and the same, yesterday, today, and for ever; as it is written, "Every good and every perfect gift cometh down from the Father of lights, with whom there is no variableness nor shadow of turning" (James 1.17). He is the source and the fountain of all existence, from whom everything hath its being, according to the law of its being, which by him is decreed and appointed so as that it can never pass over or beyond it; but whereas other fountains are fed from their own streams, and all other causes sustained and reacted upon by their own effects, returning, as it were, for ever into the circle of that law under which they were formed; it is not so with the great original Former and First Cause of all things, who receiveth no help nor nourishment of his strength from any,

---

1. The omitted material examines a number of passages in which Irving sees a connection between the incarnation and the glory of God. This can be read in full in Irving, *CW* 5, 61–72.

or all, of the things which he hath created and made, being the self-existent, all-originating Will, which within itself, hath and all-perfect comprehension of all things which have been, which are, and which are yet to be.

Wherefore, in such passages as our text, wherein glory is said to have accrued unto God from the Son of Man, it cannot be meant that the eternal and unchangeable Majesty of heaven received any right or property in anything which before he had not possessed; but that by the peril and travail of that same great enterprise of his Son against the powers and potentates of evil, there did come forth into manifestation, that is, into the region of creation and of knowledge, some form of the divine nature and feature of the divine excellency, some secret of the divine counsels and everlasting monument of the divine power, which heretofore was undiscovered and undiscoverable, and to the creatures all the same as if it had not been. For, dear brethren, if you will but cut the cords and rise a little above the artificial structures which we raise upon the ground of God's clear and unobstructive word, you will at once perceive that, from the beginning, everything which hath been done by the Godhead, in the work of creation or of providence, or of regeneration, is but a discovering or revealing of that which was from all eternity beheld by God in his own Son, who is the express image of the person of God, in whom, as in a glass, he contemplateth all things, and beholdeth them as realities ere yet to any creature they have a being, ere yet there was a creature to whom they might be manifested.

This is the mystery of the Son's eternal and essential divinity in the bosom of the Father, that in him the Father beholdeth all things, all purposes, all possibilities, all realities, and in him enjoys them all with full and perfect fruition, ere ever they are, and while they are growing into outward being; yea, and into him shall recapitulate them all again, after they have run through their appointed transitions. Not that the things which are created shall ever again cease to be; for they were seen from eternity in the Son's fulness, and therefore must last for ever: nor that they shall be only as they were from everlasting in the being of the Son; but that they shall hereafter be outwardly existing, even as he, the Head of them all, shall be outwardly existing: they shall stand fast for ever in him, united in him, and by him preserved and protected from all encroachment and change; and by him led and directed in the worship and obedience of the Most High God.

And herein also consisteth the mystery of the Holy Ghost, that by his operation all things which from eternity have their reality in the Son become manifested in time and place, and are sustained in their outward manifestation; yea, even the Son himself became outwardly manifest in manhood by the power of the Holy Ghost, and by his power was exalted from the grave to his present supereminency. It is the mighty working of the Holy Spirit which is conducting all things through the same perilous voyage of outward and separate existence, to reconduct them back again into a condition of outward stability and unchanging reality, such as by the Father from all eternity they were really and substantially seen in the person of his own Son, in the eternal Word, and all-perfect image of himself. The only change or alteration, therefore, consisteth in revelation or in manifestation: there is nothing which hath not been eternally known to, and present in, the Son; even the possibility of sin itself, which is, as it were, the chaotic basis out of which the manifestation of holiness and righteousness cometh. These remarks I throw out for the use of those who are of a higher mood, and delight to arise into the true mystery of the doctrine of the Trinity, and to understand the higher and more precious portions of the Word of God.

God's Accommodation to Human Limitation

But the same truth may be rendered more simple, and obvious to the meanest capacity, in the following way: If we could suppose anything to be added to God which was not in him nor pertained to him from everlasting, we must suppose that before such addition he was incomplete, or is now more than complete. If we could suppose anything to be recovered which was lost, or to be remembered which was forgotten, or to be reassumed which was rejected, to be reformed which was amiss, or to be changed which needed change, we must suppose mutation, or deviation, or disappointment in him who is the Rock of ages and refuge of all distressed things, the stability and support of all being, the eternal and unchangeable "I am," the same yesterday, today, and for ever, in whom there is no variableness nor shadow of turning. So that, when words of this import and signification are applied in the Holy Scriptures unto our God, as that he repenteth, and removeth, and restoreth, and reformeth that which he hath already constituted and done, they are but significant of the changes which the mutable universe, and we a part of it, are passing through in this our outward and separate voyage, until we shall be safely brought back and reconstituted in an unchangeable union to the Lord Jesus our Head. They are the words of human language, proper to express that imperfect and unstable condition in which all things at present are, and shall continue to be, until the days of restitution; and being applied to God, they express not any change in him, but in us who behold him. As we speak of the risings, and the settings, and the revolutions of the sun, though he abideth steadfast in the heavens, or hath but a motion which to the eye is imperceptible; as we speak of his being clouded and obscured and eclipsed, though he shineth with a constant brightness; and as we speak

of the irregularities of the heavenly motions, and the unsettledness of all
sublunary things, though it be certain they do all obey a constant and in-
variable law, which neither is nor can be changed, save by the good will and
pleasure of God;—speaking in all these instances in accommodation to the
appearances which offer themselves to the sense, and against the realities
which we discover by the reason: so speaketh God in Holy Scripture concerning himself, accommodating his word so that language which is necessary to man's present condition, and presenting himself as full of repentance
towards him that repenteth, pure to the pure, and froward to the froward,[2]
and upright to the upright; yet is it most certain that within, and under,
this popular form of speech, there is also in his word a deeper revelation
concerning the oneness and unchangeableness of his being, concerning the
harmony of all his operation, and the great end of all his works; into which
revelation of his steadfast and constant being he is ever seeking to draw men
out of the changes and fluctuations in which he findeth them, and to which
he doth assimilate and accommodate himself, in the first instance, by the
only language which they are able to understand.

As any discreet man who would teach astronomy to unlettered and
ignorant people must begin from the appearances of the heavens, and
employ a language conformed thereto, until he shall have ascended with
his disciples into the great principles of things; of the heaven's rest, and the
earth's rotation; of the sun's central place, and the earth's revolution, and the
regular motions of all the planets; after which, he employeth another language derived from the facts, and not from the appearances: so the teacher
of divine truth must proceed, as indeed the Holy Spirit in the declaration of
divine truth hath proceeded, beginning by the use of the popular language
of God's repentance and changeableness towards us as we change towards
him, which is the Arminianism of divine truth, mistaken by all the Meth-
odists and the great body of our Evangelicals for the whole of it; but truly
it is only the popular accommodation thereof, in order to lead the people
into the true principles of God's unchangeableness, and the eternal sacrifice of his Son, of the eternal constitution of the church and the election of
all saints in him, of their perseverance, their assurance, and certain glory,
with all other the higher truths of the mystery of godliness, which are the
truth, and alone entitled to the name of the truth; discarded though they be
at present as high Calvinism, and ever decried as soul-destroying Antino-
mianism; yea, and all the subsidiary and subordinate language of entreaty
and promise and condition, is only adopted for the purpose of introducing
our waywardness to the knowledge of his counsels, which are one in their

2. A term to describe someone who is difficult to deal with; contrary.

purpose and regular in their progression, all leading to the one glorious end of manifesting unto his creatures the wonders of his eternal being, and securing them in the blessedness of the same. This manifestation of himself is the one end of creation, and of redemption, and of restitution; and I may also add, it is the one end of the permission of sin in the world, of an apostasy in the church, and of reprobation through eternity,—I say the chief and only end of all is the declaration of the essential glory of the Godhead.

The Irredeemable Apostasy of the Angels

Bearing these observations in mind, let us now proceed in the exposition of our doctrine, that by the incarnation glory was brought unto God in the highest, and shew how the manifestation of the divine glory did then, as it were, lift itself above the horizon, and begin to disperse the clouds and shadows of the night. From all that we know concerning creation, it appeareth, that before the human race was brought into being, sin had been permitted to enter, that through it the glory of the grace of God might more abundantly appear; for there are "angels which kept not their first estate" (Jude 1.6) and there are "elect angels" mentioned in the Scripture; whereby the glory of God's creation was in a manner marred, his majesty insulted, and the bounds of his dominions sorely troubled and infested. And hitherto there was no mention of a remedy; and, I take it, there was no possibility of a remedy according to the angelic constitution of being, which being once fallen is for ever fallen. This is a mystery which I pretend not to fathom; but the fact is not the less certain that there is no redemption for the apostate angels. I am not called at present to enter into this, but would just observe in passing, that man was created a living soul, but the angels were created spirits; "who maketh his angels spirits" (Psalm 104.4); and hence it may arise, that they are not capable of any redemption; for it is continually said, that the sin against the Holy Spirit can never be forgiven.

Now it would seem to me, that a pure spirit in sinning, must sin against the law of its being, which, in the case of the angels, being the law of the Holy Spirit, is unpardonable. But however this may be, it is most certainly revealed that sin had been manifested, and no deliverance from it had yet been manifested; no grace, no mercy, no holiness, no glory, arising from the victory over and subjection of sin. It had broken in like a mighty tempest, and swept away a whole host of the subjects of our King: nay more, it had power to awaken insurrection in their own breasts, an in obedience to their own will to carry them away. The region of pure and mighty spirits, therefore, had become darkened; God's glory in that work of creation obscured; and the enemy had obtained an active head, and a permitted power. And I may say that this former manifestation of God's being had become ambiguous and equivocal in the sight of the creatures: for what may hinder another rebellion, and another? Those indeed who fell are restrained in chains of darkness, and may deter by their example; but there is no security as yet against the breeding of the same spiritual pestilence: so that, I may say, the higher creatures lay continually open and exposed, unless some hope, promise, or assurance were given them of a time when, and of a means whereby, the activity of sin was to be destroyed, and their own security secured: which assurance, though it be not expressly revealed, yet have I no doubt, from the whole bearing of revelation, the Lord had given them; and that before man was created it was known in heaven, that through this creature man, the great mystery of the divine nature, and the great destruction of sin, were to be made manifest: yea, that it was not only known for the comfort and consolation of the elect angels, but also known among the apostasy for their terror; seeing it is written, they "believe and tremble."

Nay more, I have ofttimes conjectured, yea, and almost believed, that the apostasy and rebellion of the angels in heaven arose against the knowledge and revelation made unto them of God's eternal purpose to manifest his fulness in another type of being than their own: for it is continually written, that by Christ and for Christ all things were created; that is, for his possession as the Christ,—not as the Word, but as the Christ, or the God-man, which he was from all eternity, being "slain from the foundation of the world" (Revelation 13.8). The promulgation of this decree in heaven, I conjecture, yea I believe, was the cause of the first apostasy. It was an apostasy against the Christ, against the truth, that the divine fulness should become visible in another form of being that their own: otherwise why, as the Christ, should he judge the angels, if against him as the Christ they had not, in some way or other, rebelled; or why should they have the same portion with the apostasy amongst men in the lake that burneth, if they had not sinned as men have sinned: they, against the spiritual revelation of the Christ proper to them; we against the verbal and fleshly and ecclesiastical manifestation of him? And to the same effect, I believe, that the elect angels stood and do still stand in the Christ, by having received the decree when it was promulgated in heaven before the day of our creation, and having stood fast in their allegiance; so that we may say that the most ancient form of being was the Man-God, the Eternal Son, generated from all eternity, though not the first manifested in being, but that for which all prior manifestations did but prepare the way; and that in him all good things consist, or stand fast together, and that from him all evil things apostatise, and against him rebel: wherefore in the end all the elect shall be gathered together in him, and all the apostasy shall be cast into that passive and ineffectual condition of misery, called the second death, in the hell which he hath founded for them. Now, brethren, think not that this is a speculation; it is the orthodox doctrine of our fathers, who, in treating of the church, or in writing out their faith concerning the church, made it to consist of elect angels and elect men, chosen together in Christ; and it is the doctrine taught in our church-standards and by St Paul in his epistles. With the more confidence, therefore, let us proceed.

Adamic Humanity

The apostasy of the angels was permitted by God, or, to speak more correctly, the law of the angelic being was so constituted by God as that it could apostatise, only in preparation for the bringing in of the Christ, that perfect and all-comprehending form of being. And for this end the creature man was constituted, under a new law and condition of being, such that, if he should fall by the inroad of sin, he might rise again by the manifestation of Christ, which was, as I said above, by his being created a living soul. For though man was created in the image of God, he was not so in the same sense in which Christ is called "the brightness of the Father's glory, and the express image of his person" (Hebrews 1.3). For the two Adams are drawn into contrast by the apostle:

> It is sown a natural body, [or a body proper to a soul], it is raised a spiritual body, [or a body proper to a spirit]: there is a natural [soulish] body, and there is a spiritual body. And so it is written, The first man Adam was made a living soul, the second Adam a life-giving Spirit. Howbeit, that was not first which is spiritual, but that which is of the soul: and afterward that which is spiritual. The first man is of the earth, earthy: the second man is the Lord from heaven. As is the earthy, such are they also that are earthy: and as is the heavenly, such are they also that are heavenly. And as we have borne the image of the earthy, so we shall also bear the image of the heavenly. (1 Corinthians 15.53–54)[3]

In this passage we are taught that Adam was not a spiritual creature in the sense in which we are spiritual, who are born again of the Spirit by the quickening power of the Lord Jesus Christ: nor was he a creature in the dignity into which we are adopted by faith, and unto which we shall be admitted in the day of the Lord's manifestation. Whatever distinction

---

3. The insertions, here indicated by square brackets, are Irving's own.

there is between a soul and a spirit,—and such a distinction is continually preserved in Scripture,—that same distinction there is between the generation of Adam and the regeneration of Christ: and this distinction is declared in the passage to be equal to that which there is between the body which is sown in the grave, and the body which is raised at the resurrection.

For the further illustration of this point is to be diligently observed [in] what Paul declareth, that the natural man, or the man of the soul, which Adam in his first creation was constituted, "receiveth not the things of the Spirit of God, for they are foolishness unto him; neither can he know them, because they are spiritually discerned" (1 Corinthians 2.14). From this we learn that there is in that form of being called *the soul*, after which Adam was created, a natural incapacity for receiving or knowing the things which the Spirit teacheth, which are the same things which Christ revealeth; and that this is a form of being preparatory for a higher and more perfect one, which God might perhaps have given to our first parents if they had stood faithful unto him who created them. They were perfect in that kind in which they were created; according as it is written, "This only have I found, that God made man upright" (Ecclesiastes 7.29), but that kind was not of the perfectest, which yet awaited them, and to which they perhaps would have been translated if they had not fallen.

And this doth exactly agree with what is written by the apostle Paul in another place, where, in sketching the same parallel between the first and the Second Adam, he calleth the former a type of the latter: "which is the type of Him that was to come" (Romans 5.14). And certainly Adam, in his creation, was the fullest type of Christ, being without sin, and invested with the sovereignty of the creatures; being planted in a paradise, and having a wife taken out of his bleeding side, who might be to him for a help, and the mother of many children, having also to contend with the serpent. But he was no more than the type,—the prophet, priest, and king of the garden of Eden, typifying the Prophet, Priest, and King of the whole creation of God: and while he stood in this condition he was not capable of receiving that knowledge of God unto which we have been brought by the manifestation of Jesus Christ. He was the perfection, and as it were the fountain-head of all that knowledge which, without revelation, the soul of man is capable of: as the knowledge of nature and of natural life, the knowledge of his own being, and the knowledge of all the beings over whom he was constituted king; all natural sciences, when perfected, being but the fragments of Adam's intuition; but into the knowledge of God he could only go so far as to acknowledge him for his Creator, and the Creator of the things which were around him. Of God's spiritual being I am in great doubt whether he could have any distinct apprehension or knowledge; because Paul expressly saith, that the natural man, or the man of the soul, of which Adam was the perfect form, knoweth not the things of the Spirit of God: he could not know the Father, who is known only by the Son, who was not yet come forth from the bosom of the Father; and not knowing the Son he could not know the Spirit, whose procession succeedeth that of the Son. More than the knowledge of a Creator he could not have. His being was only, if I may so speak, preparatory to a spiritual being: wherefore the Lord God presented himself to him in some revelation proper to that state; walking, as it is said, in the garden in the cool of the day; with some attributes kindred to Adam's nature, which delighted in the garden, and loved the cool time of the day.

In like manner, Satan the tempter presented himself with like accommodation, not as a bright and powerful spirit, whirling him away whither he would, and making the round world reveal before him all its attractions, but as a serpent, one of the subject creatures; and he beguiled him with the prospect of being preferred to become as gods, knowing good and evil; whereby we perceive that Adam, in this former state of his being, was inferior to the angels, whom I understand here by the word "gods:" whereas the heirs of salvation enjoy the same as their ministers and servants. From all which I conclude, that even his knowledge of God as a Creator was very inferior to that which we now have by the revelation of Christ Jesus. But into this subject I only open a door of thought, without entering, lest I should be diverted from my great subject of God glorified in the Son of Man, having said enough for our present purpose of shewing that man in his original creation was not the glory of God, but only the type of "the Son of Man," who was prepared in the counsels of eternity to manifest that glory; and that his creation was but a step towards the introduction of the God-man into the visible universe. In which inferior form of manhood I believe him to have been created, that when he should fall he might not utterly fall, but in falling rise through deep distress, and, by omnipotent grace, into that most excellent form of being whereof paradise saw but the goodly bud.

The Fall of Adam and the Coming of the God-Man

Nevertheless, to this new creature, the expectation of the elect, and the envy of the apostate angels, was directed; the former resting assured that in it the great desire of the heavens, and the latter being assured, or at least dreading, that in it the great terror of hell, was to be revealed. And Satan, the prince of darkness, and the ruler of the powers of darkness, having set himself to destroy that creature, did so far forth succeed in destroying him as was necessary for his own destruction: he accomplished the breach which he sought to accomplish; but he little imagined that through that breach the Eternal Light against which he warred was to stream into the visible world, and revive the hearts of the elect, against whom he wageth perpetual war. He thought that if this creature should fall, as he himself had fallen, the fall would be irretrievable, and the Word of God, against which he warred, falsified for ever;—insufficient knowledge ever outwitting itself, inefficient light of falsehood always extinguished by the omnipotent light of truth. This fall of man being accomplished, the expectation of heaven, though not defeated, was again projected forward: and the song of joy which they sung over the creation was turned into sorrow and sadness, when they saw the earth also possessed by Satan, and mankind bereaved of the image of God. But their hope and faith was not utterly defeated, any more than was that of man. For a new revelation of the promise was given, and that, I doubt not, more distinct than any hint or intimation of it which had been given before. Yet were they all again suspended upon hope; and the Word of God seemed, to the eyes of the beholders, again contraverted, and his purpose again contravened: and sin to have gained another advantage over holiness; another veil to be drawn over the sanctuary, and thicker clouds to envelope the dwelling-place of God.

And now, thenceforward, all heaven and earth looked forward for the Man, by eminency called the Son of Man; that is, the child for whom manhood was created, and through whom the great secret was to be revealed, and the divine nature for ever manifested in an outward form;—which was, as it were, the great deliverance for which the womb of all creation had longed, and made an empty and abortive effort to produce it at the birth of Adam, when things were not yet ripe for the great discovery. To see God, and to be able to name his name, had been the two great desires of heaven and earth, and, I may say, must ever be the great desire of every creature. Adam did but hear his voice as he walked in the garden; and whenever any apparition or manifestation of him was given to the patriarchs or to the prophets, they expected that they should instantly die, because, as they thought, they had seen God, whom no man can see and live. The cherubim are represented as veiling their faces from the greatness of his glory; and the light in which he dwelleth is said to be unapproachable, and clouds and darkness to be around him. Hence also the exclusive honour of Moses above all men, was to speak face to face with God; which could yet be no more than the beholding of the manifestation of the glorified humanity of the Lord Jesus, symbolized in the *Shechinah* above the mercy seat, and this, we think, was granted unto the man Moses, in order that, by this solitary exception, while the mysteriousness of the thing was nowise weakened, the desire of attaining unto it might be rendered more intense, and the expectation of one day possessing it might be encouraged.

No doubt, also, herein consisteth the Lord's abomination of all idolatry, that by presenting a feigned likeness of himself, decked out with the lustrous glory of gold and precious stones, it doth attempt to open the great secret, and so far forth to destroy that one great glory of the human race, which is its distinction above all races of being, and the palladium of its safety, that in it, and through it, the great mystery of all creation, and desire of all creatures, is to have its accomplishment, by the manifestation of God-man in all his fulness and glory. And whereas the name or power of God is equivalent to his nature or being, while this lay hid the former also lay hid, and was considered to be an inscrutable secret; and a most daring profanation to this day is it held by the Jews to name the great name of God. And with us Christians also, who possess the name, the Lord Jesus Christ, there is yet a mystery drawn over this wonderful name, which will not be declared till the day of the second advent; of which mystery the opening ought to be a greater object of desire than it now is, for the Lord expressly promiseth it to the faithful as a special reward: "I will give him my new name" (Revelation 3.12).

But how can anything connected with the second advent be desired, when the very advent itself hath ceased to be desired in this all-but-apostate church? But thought that body of man, now misnamed "church," and better named themselves, "religious world," hath ceased to look forward either to the manifestation of the Godhead in a visible form, or to the revelation of his full name, it hath ever, as I said, been the desire of elect angels and elect men, and the horror of reprobate angels and reprobate men: but these "Laodiceans are neither cold nor hot; I would they were either cold or hot" (Revelation 3.15). And why hath it ever been the desire of the innumerable company of angels and the general assembly of the first-born, whose names are written in heaven? Because it was the purpose and decree of God, promulgated from the foundation of the world, and gradually growing into manifestation by slow degrees and manifold pangs of creation, according to the importance, the infinite and all-comprehending importance, of the issues which rested on it. For, brethren, it was, as I have said, the nucleus of the whole scheme, the great end and first beginning of all: and that which went before was but the germination of the seed before it appeared above the earth, or the preparing of the soil for the casting of the seed into the earth. And so God, and angels, and men, and devils, and whatever else existeth, all looked forward to the man in whose outward form the Godhead was to become eternally manifest. For that in man it was to be manifest, God himself had purposed from all eternity; and the angels, no doubt, had heard the rumour of it; wherefore the morning stars sand together, and the angels of God shouted over his birth: and Satan, with his apostasy, had also heard a rumour of it, wherefore he solicited him with his wiles to forsake his allegiance: and the knowledge was kept alive, amongst the sons of men, by every revelation made to the patriarchs and the prophets; until at length in Bethlehem, in the stable of Bethlehem,—fit emblem of the world into which he was born,—the child of infinite hopes and longings was brought into being: whereupon, instantly the heavenly host waked all their choral symphonies, and sang, "Glory to God in the highest; peace on earth, and good will to the children of men" (Luke 2.14).

I consider, therefore, brethren, that the glory which then brake through the clouds that surround the dwelling-place of God, is no less a glory than the manifestation of his whole being and attributes, which had been rather revealed in hints that it was about to be revealed than in any positive revelation. The creation lived in hope, and, I may say, is yet living in hope, till the hidden majesty of Christ shall be led forth most gloriously, from the temple of the tabernacle in heaven. But when Christ was born in Bethlehem, the hope of the elect angels in heaven and the saints on earth had its visible object: the end of the great scheme became manifest, the subject of the great decree was revealed. They could look upon and behold what they had long desired to look upon and behold: they knew that in this Second Adam the great question was again to be brought to issue; and if he stand, that the great strife will be at an end, the great question resolved, and the great mystery opened. And the Second Adam was put upon his probation as a man, having, as St Paul saith, emptied himself of his divinity;[4] in whom the divinity had of its own accord suspended itself, and by its own power kept itself continually suspended. He was man and God in one person; and during his humility the Godhead was employed in humbling or restraining itself,—which, I may say, is the highest act of a self-existent being to suspend his own activity, as it is also the highest act of grace. And thus as being man he went through the trial, out of which if he shall come unconquered then is the mystery accomplished, and the Godhead shall be for ever manifested in an outward visible condition. Therefore the Lord said upon the eve of his last trial, in the beginning of his last discourse, "Now is my Father glorified" (John 15.8).

THE WAYS IN WHICH GOD IS MANIFESTED
IN THE INCARNATE SON

And thus, brethren, you can perceive, agreeably to the idea with which we opened this head of discourse, that this glory, which the Son of Man brought

4. Irving is referring to Philippians 2.6.

unto his Father, consisteth in no less than the manifestation of the fulness of the Godhead bodily, which great manifestation to distinguish into parts is difficult, but yet for the greater clearness I do it thus: —

First, the manifestation of the divine substance in three persons, or distinct subsistences. As to the unity of God, there never hath been any doubt in the church, and out of the church there never hath been any agreement; for though the unitarians and deists pretend to worship one God, it is not the one God whom we worship, but a certain idea of perfect being and infinite power which they have from their own brain, an abstraction of certain properties of man, a generalisation of certain principles of matter, "a great first cause least understood," an all-prevailing power, and everything or anything but the true, self-existing, personal God. Alas! alas! for their miserable darkness and prostitution of holy truth, to call these conception[s] out living and true God!

But in the church, I say, whether of the angels or of men, there never was a doubt concerning the unity of God; while there was no clear knowledge of a Trinity of persons in the divine substance. It was not until the Son came into manifestation as a man, until the Word was made flesh and dwelt among us, became our Saviour, the long-expected Messiah on earth, the long-looked-for Christ and Lord in heaven, for whom all things were created, that the truth of the glorious Trinity became a grand and manifest truth for ever. Because so soon as the Son became manifest he made known the Father, to whom he always referred back as the eternal Father of the Son, and in him the great originator of all things, and principal party to the eternal purpose which the Son came forth to reveal: "No man hath seen the Father at any time; the only-begotten Son which is in the bosom of the Father he hath revealed him" (John 1.18).

By the same act also did the Spirit become manifest; for, as was said at the beginning of this discourse, Christ's becoming outward and visible was the act of the Spirit, he was conceived by the power of the Holy Ghost, he grew in wisdom by the power of the Holy Ghost, and walked by the same inspiration of the Holy Ghost, in the favour of God and man, a man under the law, yet complete before the law, and blameless; and when he passed through baptism, to become the first-begotten of the adoption, and the foundation-stone of the spiritual church, he was endowed by the Holy Ghost with baptismal gifts and graces, as he had been endowed before with circumcision gifts and graces; and by the power of the Holy Ghost he went about doing all manner of miracles, and by the mighty working of the Holy Ghost was raised from the dead to sit on the right hand of the Majesty on high, when, becoming Lord and Christ, he shed down the Holy Ghost upon the church, which is his temple unto this day. So that in Christ all the glories of the Trinity were first manifested, with all their various offices, of which I cannot now speak particularly.

Secondly, the holiness of God was justified, and I may say, for the first time manifested, in heaven and in earth by the Son of Man. I say, for the first time; because into both parts of creation, celestial and terrestrial, sin had entered, and out of neither seemeth it to have been cleansed; for even in heaven, among the sons of God, Satan had a certain right and prerogative, which more than once we find him exercising. And certainly on the earth the holiness of Godhead never been manifested or known: for though a church had been separated by special promises and privileges, and outward rites and sacraments, yet ever and aye did Satan steal in and seduce, and at length bring into open apostasy, by far the more numerous and ostensible part thereof; and holiness there was not anywhere, or at any time since the fall, separate or unmixed holiness, until the Son of God did come. And forasmuch as the holiness of the Creator must stand in suspense until there be some form or type of his handiwork which exhibiteth the same, and neither angels nor men were that form or type of being (for both had fallen), I do say that the holiness of God, which was both known and believed, was never yet demonstrated until that new type or form of being, the Second Adam, the God-man was revealed: in whose triumphant life over sin, and whose triumphant resurrection from death and the grave, in whose triumphant defeat of Satan and all his host, the glory of God's holiness was manifestly shewn unto angels and the sons of men, and an assurance given that the time was at hand when it should be established triumphant over all who had ever gainsaid it.

Now, brethren, this holiness of God is his true glory, as the white light is the true glory of the sun. The holiness of God is the unbroken beam of his glory, whereof mercy and justice, and sovereignty and goodness, are but, as it were, the refracted or broken parts; and as the green and the violet, and the orange and the red, and the other colours into which the rays of the sun are refracted in the rainbow, when mixed in their just proportions, do reproduce the colourless white: so reckon I that the glory of his goodness and mercy, and justice and sovereignty, concerning which, in the first instance, it is necessary to discourse unto fallen sinners, do as the soul clears from the mist and clouds, pass into one pure unbroken radiance of his holiness: so that when I say the holiness of God was first manifested in the Christ, it is all the same as to say, that the glory of his mercy, and of his justice, and of his goodness, and all his attributes, were then first displayed. For if there were no unbroken light of holiness, how could there be any varieties of that light?

Thirdly, the glory of God's almighty power was first manifested in Christ. For till he was manifest in the flesh, God's power stood in suspense, yea, and will never be fully cleared until hell shall receive its possessors, or, I should rather say, its sufferers. For truly the tide of sin was never turned, until the Lord did come and stem and roll it back. There was no knowing whether the darkness or the light should prevail, until the true Light appeared, which the darkness comprehended not. Then indeed the true nature of sin was discovered to be only a condition to holiness, not a thing in itself, but the state of a thing in its progress to perfection. We were sinners only that we might be sinners saved; we had fallen only that we might rise higher from our fall; and this is true of all men when as yet they were in their first head, that is, Adam. Adam's fall was permitted and ordained, only that Adam might be exalted from the condition of a living soul into the condition of a quickened spirit. And so of each one of us who fell in him, we have been brought into an outward condition out of Adam, and stand in our present peril only that we may be brought back again and recapitulated into Christ. By which great evolution of all things from the idea in the Son, back again into the outward reality in the Son, the glorious and mighty power of God had been displayed, and the evanescent, transient power of sin and its weakness have been manifested, yea, its subserviency and profitableness, and I may say even necessity, to the manifestation of the Almighty power of God, in redeeming all things from the lowest, basest condition, into the most elevated, and dignified, and mighty. For the Christ is raised above every dignity, power, and authority which is named in the universe of God: and so shall every member of Christ be for ever raised.

Whence is made the most stupendous manifestation and monument of the eternal power of the Godhead. And in these three things the manifestation of the constitution of the Godhead, of the holiness of the Godhead in the government of the creation, and of the power of the Godhead in overcoming sin, I conceive the glory brought unto the Father by the Son of Man doth chiefly consist. This was the glory in the highest, which the angels sung over his birth. This was the glory of God which moved the Father to yield him up, which moved the Son to offer himself, which moved the Holy Spirit to realise and substantiate his outward and visible existence. And here we conclude our first head of discourse, concerning the glory which accrues from the simple act, or rather from the design and purpose and nature of the incarnation. And now we come to consider more closely the work itself, and the glory with which he glorified God by his work upon the earth: "I have glorified thy name upon the earth: I have finished the work which thou gavest me to do" (John 17.4). What was this work which was given him to do? What was the glory which he brought by his life unto his holy Father?

THE GLORIFICATION OF GOD IN THE
WORK OF THE INCARNATE SON

The work which the Son of Man had to do *upon the earth,* for the glory of God, which is the second head of method, was no less than to realise the eternal purpose of God, to bring himself into manifestation. Now, in considering wherein consisteth the glory brought unto God hereby, it hath presented itself to my mind under these three particulars:—

First, he brought into existence the complete and perfect form of being which is the God-man, and for which all other beings, whether in heaven or in earth, were but the preparation, and in which they must stand as the head through all eternity; and therein he shewed forth the glory of God, in putting the headstone upon that fabric of creation, of which, heretofore, he had created the several parts. If his creation of the creatures was glorious, how much more glorious his own creation as the man ("made of a woman,")[5] the God-man, the Sovereign of them all! As the creation of man, on the sixth day, was more glorious than the creation of all the inferior animals, whose being is all a mystery, opening into, and resolved in, the being of man; so the creation of the Christ, that is the incarnation of the eternal Word, was more glorious than the creation of angels, and of men, and of all other creatures, whose being was all a mystery and a confusion until a Head was brought in to be over them all. This is the first particular in which the Son of Man brought glory to God.

The second is, by his opening the decree of election, and explaining how the elect angels of God had stood, when the rest fell, and how the election according to grace, amongst men, had been retrieved: and publishing to sinful men the gospel of the grace of God, which cometh out of, and floweth from, the fountain of the decree of electing love. This is the aspect of his mission, so continually spoken of in the Psalms: "I will declare the decree; I will preach righteousness in the great congregation. When I shall receive the congregation I will judge righteously" (Psalm 40.9); that is, he would publish and declare the true standing of every creature who doth stand in the favour of God. And thus did he open the glory of God, which had lain hidden in the eternal and inscrutable decree; and made it the basis of all preaching unto this day.

Thirdly, he wrestled with the enemies of God, and overthrew them; and shewed the glory of his power and holiness in their weakness and discomfiture; and so set on foot the redemption of the bodies of the saints from the grave, and of their souls from the place of separate spirits; and of the

---

5. Galatians 4.4.

creatures of God from darkness and sin; which redemption he shall accomplish in the fulness of time; but, in as far as the right and title is concerned, he completed it at his resurrection from the dead. These three particulars I shall now give all diligence to open; and I pray you to give all patient heed to the word which, for your sakes, the Lord may put into my mouth. And be not weary, I pray you, of the message of God, but take heed how ye hear.[6]

CHRIST AS VICTOR OVER THE ENEMIES OF GOD

The manner of this work was as marvellous as the end of it was glorious. By being created a living soul, which Paul saith, "understandeth not the things of the Spirit of God" (1 Corinthians 2.14), there was another condition of being still left from man to come into, the region of the spiritual; for the first Adam was but the type of the Second Adam; the first man being a living soul, the second a quickening Spirit. The type was broken, whose fragments we now behold in this our natural form of being; having a taste of all knowledge, save the knowledge of spiritual things; and a love of all excellency, save that of God; and making progress in all sciences, save that of theology, which we corrupt, which from time to time God doth purify, but can by no means obtain for it a seat in the world, as we behold at this day.

But this breaking of the goodly type of Christ, which Adam was, did only prepare the way for the advancement of Adam, and of all who preferred to stand in the decree of election, to the higher rank of the combined material and spiritual creature, which is the form of creation's Lord. And, in order to this preferment, Christ took of the virgin the humanity of Adam; not sinful, indeed, for he came not by ordinary generation, but by the power of the Holy Ghost; yet, though not sinful, liable to all the temptations of sin to which human nature even had been or ever could be liable: "Being in the form of God, he was made in the likeness of man; and being found in fashion as a man, he humbled himself, and became obedient until death" (Philippians 2.8). In that he truly died, it proveth that he truly was obnoxious to every human infirmity; in that he rose from the dead, it equally proveth that he had done no sin, for which he might see the corruption of the grave.

Now, it was not an arbitrary thing that the Christ should thus be brought into the world; nor was it merely to redeem man; but to become

---

6. Irving's comments on the incarnate Son as the fulfilment of creation and the preacher of God's glory and grace are omitted here and summarized in the introduction. The full text can be found in Irving, *CW* 5, 92–105.

the Lord of all, by establishing the weakness of all, and working out the stability of all. Had he been designed to be Lord of spirit only, he would have partaken of the angelic nature: but having to the Lord of matter also, he partook of the nature of man, which is composed of both. And of this he partook, not in its unfallen state, but in its fallen state, and in the fallen state of all the materialism of the world; in order that he might enter in the weakness of everything, and add to it regenerating strength, become the uplifter of its state and being, and its support throughout all eternity. Therefore it is written, "But we see Jesus, who was made little lower than the angels, for the suffering of death, crowned with glory and honour; that he, by the grace of God, should taste death for all" (Hebrews 2.9). And again, "Forasmuch as the children were made partakers of flesh and blood, he also himself likewise took part of the same; that through death he might destroy him that had the power of death, that is the devil, and deliver them who through the fear of death were all their lifetime subject to bondage" (Hebrews 2.14). And again it is written:

> He who was in the form of God, and thought it not robbery to be equal with God, humbled himself, and became obedient unto death, even the death of the cross. Wherefore God also hath highly exalted him, and given him a name which is above every name; that at the name of Jesus every knee should bow, of things in heaven, and things in earth, and things under the earth; and that every tongue should confess that Jesus Christ is Lord, to the glory of God the Father. (Philippians 2.6–11)

From which passage we rightly conclude, that there redounded unto God a great glory from the humiliation of the Son of Man unto the death, beyond that which redounded from the completion of creation's work, and the opening of the decree of election. Which glory consisteth in the extinguishing of the power of those rebellious spirits which had, by forsaking the standing of election, fallen into sin, and continued therein, fighting against God and the hope of Christ: who are exceedingly hateful in the sight of God, because they continually seek to destroy the glory of his Son, and to force themselves into a different standing from that of election, exalting their own will against the will of God.

It is a vain thing to say that God loveth sinners and ungodly creatures: he extendeth mercy and grace unto them, and loveth the election for his Son's sake; but he must cease to love his Son—that is, to love himself—when he loveth those who are rebellious against himself. He is "angry with the wicked every day" (Psalm 7.11): he cannot look upon the workers of iniquity but with detestation and abhorrence. It is one of the saying of that wretched Arminianism with which this land is overflowed, "Hate the sin, but love the sinner." What mean they? That sin is something by itself, and the sinner something by himself, so distinct from one another, that the one may well be hated, and the other may well be loved? They know nothing at all, and they will know nothing at all. But if they would open their ears to instruction, then might they be taught that sin is the condition of an apostate creature, the form a rebellious will, the very being of an enemy of God and of godliness. To make the evil of which to cease, to destroy its eternal activity against God, was the cause of our Lord's humiliation in the body and descent into hell. By which powerful and perilous ministry he did overcome and vanquish the enemy, and hath him and his dominions in his power; whenever it shall please the Father to allow him to enter in to possess them. Death and destruction have no indefeasible right in God's creatures, but only a derived and dependent one; derived from and dependent upon sin; which Christ having resisted and overcome and cast out, did win back the waste and the wilderness of this world from the occupancy and vexation of Satan and his angels and reprobate men, who ever since have stood judged and condemned, not knowing of a day's life, but expecting every day to be the last of their possession. And herein consisteth the third part of the glory which Christ brought unto the Father by the work which he wrought upon the earth; not only declaring his wrath against all the workers of iniquity, but manifesting that their power was broken, and their right destroyed, in his resurrection from the dead; whereby the glory of God was wondrously manifested in the discomfiture of all his enemies, and his holiness in their destruction abundantly manifested: as we shall shew at length in our fourth discourse.[7]

---

7. The close of this sermon is omitted and a summary can be found in the introduction. The full text can be found in Irving, *CW*, 108–13.

Introduction

to "The Method Is by Taking Up the Fallen Humanity"

Taking Luke 1:35 as his primary text, Irving addresses the manner in which the incarnation occurred. This sermon is divided into four parts. In part one he treats the constitution of Christ. From there he proceeds to speak of the universality of reconciliation and the individuality of election; which typically fall under discussion about the intent of atonement. The third part sees him addressing how Christ removes the law and puts humanity in a state of grace. Irving concludes by turning his attention to God's purposes for the elect.

As the title implies the theme that runs throughout the sermon concerns the Son's assumption of a fallen human nature in the incarnation. Christ, Irving explains, assumes a fallen human nature because it is impossible for him to assume any other nature but a fallen one. The first section of the sermon is dedicated to further developing this claim. Taking on human nature, as it actually exists, Christ has both a reasonable soul and a physical body. To deny that Christ possesses either of these parts which constitute human beings would be to fall into the trap of ancient heresies. Fallenness is manifested in both of these parts of Christ's human nature. Despite having a fallen nature, Irving stresses, Christ is not sinful. Yet, Christ's fallen human nature is not sanctified and redeemed by union with the Son alone. If the sanctification of fallen human nature occurred only in virtue of union with the Son, Irving claims, the result would be Eutychianism. Rather, the sanctification of the nature is enacted by the Holy Spirit; the Spirit sanctifies and empowers Christ. He succinctly summarizes this point in the preface of this volume:

> The point at issue is simply this: Whether Christ's flesh had the grace of sinlessness and incorruption from its proper nature, or from the indwelling of the Holy Ghost. I say the latter.

That Christ had a fallen human nature, Irving argues, was the belief of the church throughout the ages. Denying that Christ had a fallen nature, according to Irving, is a heresy, it amounts to a virtual denial of Christ's humanity. The denial of the fallen human nature "is the reappearance of that Spirit of anti-Christ, mentioned by St John." Moreover, it brings Irving much pain to see people deny this article of faith. He reflects upon the significance of the doctrine of Jesus' fallen human nature and suggests that apart from possessing a fallen human nature, the gospel would be significantly impoverished: Christ would not truly be able to wrestle with Satan and his temptations; he could not overcome the world, sin and the devil as representative, he would not be able to serve as an example for Christians to follow; and, ultimately, Christ would not be mortal.

In the second part of the sermon Irving addresses issues concerning the intent of atonement. Just like unfallen Adam represented all of humanity prior to the fall, Christ—who assumes a fallen human nature—represents all those who possess a fallen nature. Because of his universally representative role Christ redeems all of humanity from sin, the law that defined sin, death, and corruption. Christ puts all of humanity in a state of favor, forgiveness, and being loved by God. He bestows immortality and resurrection to all human beings. By his assumption of a fallen nature, Christ makes at-one-ment between God and fallen humanity. Thus, Christ's death is universal in its intent. Yet at the same time, the gifts of regeneration by the Holy Spirit, union with Christ's body, communication of his glory, and fellowship in his kingdom are gifts that the Father unconditionally gives to elect individuals alone.

Part three provides Irving's audience with his theology of the law. The law—while not evil in and of itself—acts as a sign of humanity's unreconciled state before God. Moreover it "doth awaken and fructify the passion for sin which is in the flesh." How does God deal with the problem of the law? By sending his son in the likeness of sinful flesh. Christ—who assumed a fallen nature—demonstrates God's abhorrence of sin. Additionally, Christ shows what God requires of those of us who possess fallen natures. Most importantly, however, in Christ's death, all fallen flesh died, and the law was satisfied. To those who argue that abolishing the law would lead to licentiousness, Irving responds with two arguments. First, Christ provides a model and example to follow. Again, Irving argues, that apart from possessing a fallen nature, Christ could not serve as a true example for us to follow.

Second, like Christ, who had the Holy Ghost empowering his holiness, the elect also have the Holy Spirit leading them to obedience.

In the conclusion of his sermon Irving asks what good it does for God to redeem all of humanity and yet elect only a portion of humanity for salvation and blessedness. He responds by providing three reasons. First, God created creatures to depend on him and worship him, this end is fulfilled in the redemption of all mankind through Christ. Second, God desires his creatures to know and posses a portion of his own blessedness. This he accomplishes by delivering fallen humans into a state of regeneration, power, and glory. Finally, he answers that election of all those who had been redeemed would show God's redemptive power, but it would not demonstrate his grace. Thus, to fully demonstrate his grace God elected a number smaller than the number of those redeemed.

Several key themes that mark Irving's theology appear in this sermon. For example, we are treated to one of Irving's clearest expositions of his understanding of the fallen human nature doctrine. At this point in history, there had already been controversy regarding this point of his Christology. In this sermon he presents a number of arguments supporting his doctrine and its significance for atonement and the Christian life. Moreover, we encounter his Christology which has a distinctly pneumatological emphasis. A final theme, which has not received much attention in secondary literature on Irving, that appears in this sermon concerns how Christ does battle with the powers of sin, death, and Satan. Apart from his victory over these powers at-one-ment between fallen humanity and God is not achieved. If one is looking for a sermon that captures the heart of Irving's understanding of the person and work of Christ one could do worse than to look at "The Method Is by Taking Up Fallen Humanity."

CGW

3

The Method Is by Taking up the Fallen Humanity

And the angel answered and said unto her, The Holy Ghost shall come upon thee, and the power of the Highest shall overshadow thee: therefore also that holy thing, which shall be born of thee, shall be called the Son of God.

LUKE 1:35

Having opened, in the two foregoing discourses, the origin of the incarnation, in the will of God, and the end of it, for the glory of God, we do now proceed to treat of the scheme or method of it, in the purpose of God,— concerning which, though we have frequently spoken already, we have not yet given it that large and sufficient demonstration which is needful in a matter of such vast importance to the glory of God and the good of men.

This seemeth to me the logical way of handling any act of the Godhead: first, to shew wherein it originates; then, whereto it tendeth; then, by what method it proceedeth; then, in what way it is transacted; and, finally, with what fruits or effects it is followed. The third of these steps, in the exposition of our great subject, we do now proceed to take, trusting in the

55

help of God. And to the end of opening with due order the method which God hath taken to bring about the incarnation of his Son, we shall first treat of the composition of his divine person, from his conception even unto his resurrection, observing the most notable changes which he underwent during that period: for with the resurrection I regard my present subject to conclude. It is only Christ in the flesh concerning which I have undertaken to discourse: the discourse of Christ from the resurrection onward belongeth properly to another subject, which is the church, whereof by his ascension into glory he became the Head.

After taking this view of the composition, and the successive changes which passed upon Christ's person until the resurrection, I shall proceed to open, in the second part of this sermon, how God, by uniting the person of his Son to fallen flesh, doth thereby reconcile the whole lump of fallen humanity unto himself, and is enabled, through Christ, to save as many as it pleaseth him, without any detriment unto, but rather with all illustration of, his righteousness and holiness. This will lead us to speak of the universality of the reconciliation and the individuality of the election; and to shew how harmonious and mutually co-operating are these two great truths.

From this we shall pass, in the third part, to shew how, by this same method of sending his Son in the likeness of sinful flesh, God doth remove the law, which is the form of the enmity, and bring in unto all the world this dispensation of grace under which we now stand. After which we shall conclude this discourse upon the method of the incarnation with practical conclusions and improvements of the whole.

Part 1: The Composition of the Person of Christ

With all due reverence, therefore, and trust in divine assistance, we do now proceed to open the scheme which God had purposed in himself for bringing about this most important event in creation's history, that the Son of God, by and for whom all things were created and do consist, should join himself unto the fallen creation, and take up into his own eternal personality the human nature, after it had fallen, and become obnoxious to all the powers of sin and infirmity and rebellion; in order that God might be shewn to be greater and mightier far than the creatures combined in the confederacy of sin against the Creator; and that the state of fallen sinful creation, which God had permitted to come to pass, might yield forth from its impure and unholy womb the most perfect, the most holy, the most wonderful Son of God, to be the head and support, the life, the mover, and the guide of all creation, redeemed in the redemption of that creature substance which he assumed unto himself.

THE SON'S ASSUMPTION OF FALLEN HUMAN NATURE

That Christ took our fallen nature is most manifest, because there was no other in existence to take. The fine gold of Adam's being was changed, and the divine goodness of his will was oppressed by the mastery of sin: so that, unless God had created the Virgin in Adam's first estate (which is a figment of Romish superstition), it was impossible to find in existence any human nature but human nature fallen, whereof Christ might partake with the brethren. I believe, therefore, in opposition to all fantastics, schismatics, and sectarians who say the contrary, that Christ took unto himself a true body and a reasonable soul; and that the flesh of Christ, like my flesh, was in its proper nature mortal and corruptible; that he was of the seed of David; that he was of the seed of Abraham, as well as of the seed of the woman; yea, that he was of the seed of the woman after she fell, and not before she fell. Even the time for making known the truth that Christ in human nature was to come, did not arrive till after the fall, because it was determined in the counsel of God that he who was to come should come in the fallen state of the creature, and therein be cut off—yet not for himself—to the end it might be proved that the creature substance which he took, and for ever united to the Godhead, was not of the Godhead a part, though by the Godhead sustained.

If he had come in the unfallen manhood, as these dreamers say, and had not truly been subject unto death, but, for some lesser end and minor object, and as it were by-intent, had laid aside the mantle of the flesh for a season, who would have been able to say that the manhood of Christ had not become deified—that is, become a part of the Godhead? And if so, then not only he, but all his members likewise, who are to be brought into the very selfsame estate with himself, must also be deified, or pass into the Godhead; the creature become an object of worship; the Creator be mingled with the creature; the doctrine of God the soul of the world brought in, and all the other most wicked tenets of the Eastern superstitions of the earth introduced, in the room of the most fruitful, most holy mystery of a personal God, separate from the creature, yet supporting the creature by eternal union with, though in perfect distinctness from, himself, in the person of the Son, and through the indwelling of the divine nature in the person of the Holy Ghost; to the end of worshipping the invisible Godhead of Father,

Son, and Holy Ghost, remaining hidden, and for ever to remain hidden, in the person of the Father.

I say, and fearlessly assert, and undertake to prove, that this great result and consummation of the divine scheme could not otherwise be attained than by the fall of the creature, in order to reveal its non-divinity, or prove its creatureship; so that, when the Son of God should come to take it unto himself, it might, by the very act of dying, shew itself, though of him, not to be the very God; and when, taken up into that surpassing glory with which it is now crowned, it might be for ever known to be not human nature deified, but human nature uplifted and upheld by God. The fall of all creation, spiritual and material, was but a step unto the death of the body of Christ; even as the creation of all things visible and invisible was only a step to the creation of that body. It was because the Lamb slain, as well as the God manifested, was a part of the divine purpose, that death came into the world. Death knew not what death meant, until Christ died; then the mystery of death was unfolded unto itself. If the meaning of a fall is ever to be understood, it must be studied in the cross and tomb of Christ. For if Christ had stepped at once out of the infinite and invisible into resurrection power and glory, and without dying drawn up the creatures into union with the same, the creature would have worshipped itself, so clothed with might, adorned with beauty, and with stability invested; instead of worshipping the invisible God of heaven, out of the creature, yet supporting the creature and inhabiting the creature; therefore the object of the creature's dependence, and the subject of the creature's blessedness: but yet essentially separate from and advanced above the creature's noblest state, and therefore properly the object of the creature's continual worship. And this is the first point in the mystery of Christ's constitution, his taking the substance of the fallen Virgin Mary.

THE HUMAN SOUL OF JESUS

And now, with respect to the human soul of Christ I have next to speak. That Christ had a reasonable soul, as well as a true body, is a doctrine most necessary to be believed; because, otherwise, he were not a man, but only the apparition of a man; a superior being, who for a certain end and purpose had clothed himself with human form—as was often done before in manifestations to the patriarchs and the prophets—which is the fountain of Arianism with all its poisoned streams. Besides, if Christ had not a reasonable soul, his human feelings and affections were but an assumed fiction to carry the end which his mission had in view; and his sufferings and his death were a phantasmagoria played off before the eyes of men, but by no means entering into the vitals of human sympathy, nor proceeding from the communion and love of human kind, nor answering any end of comforting human suffering, and interceding for human weakness, and bringing up again the fallen creature to stand before the throne of the grace of God: it is all but a phantasm and apparition, like that which appeared unto Manoah and his wife, and transacted wonderful things in their presence.[1]

The Proof of the Human Soul of Jesus

This was the source of the Gnostic errors in the first ages of the church. Moreover, and most of all, if Christ had not possessed a reasonable soul, as well as a mortal and corruptible body (which yet saw not corruption, by the Father's special grace), the divine nature of Christ must have been separated and divorced from his human nature during the time it hung dead upon the cross and lay buried in the tomb. If there had been but two principles, a body, and the eternal person of the Son, united in Jesus of Nazareth, then, when the body of Christ lay in the tomb, the divinity must have been separated from the humanity; and this, though only for an instant suffered, would upset the whole constitution of God in Christ. For if once the Creator and the creature part of Christ, if once the divine and human natures, have been parted, they may be parted again; and where then were the assurance of creation's stability in the Christ's constitution for ever and ever? Essential it is to the purpose of God, that when the nature of the Godhead in the person of the Son had joined itself to the creature in the substance of manhood, that hypostatical union of two distinct natures in one person should be established for ever and ever.

Clearly, therefore, doth it remain, that there must be a part of human nature capable of subsisting separate from the body, which, when the body fell into the curse of death, might maintain the continuity of co-existence with the Godhead of the Son, until the time came for the Father to send the Holy Spirit into his mortal and corruptible body, and unite it in a glorified state unto the Godhead of the Son; which hath the while preserved its creature-condition in connexion with the separate soul. And as I said above, that the fall is to be understood by meditating that for which it came to pass—to wit, the dead body of the Lamb slain from the foundation of the world; even so say I now, that the twofold nature of man, soul and body, invisible and visible, is both to be best understood, and most surely believed, by meditating upon the same great key of creation—to wit, the divinity of

1. Irving is referring to Judges 13.1–23.

the Son subsisting in hypostatical union with the invisible soul of the man, while the visible body of the man was lying uninformed with any conservative or vital principle, truly dead, truly corruptible, but not to corrupt, until it pleased the Father to raise it, in reward of Christ's faith and strong cryings, with supplications and tears, that he might be delivered from death; wherein, because of his piety, he was heard.

Yea, more: this is to me the great assurance of a spiritual world of separate souls in life, though invisible at this time, and in all times since death began his work; and it is to me the defeat of all those fantastics[2] who dote and dream concerning the sleep of the soul from death unto the resurrection; and, moreover, of that more common, but at the bottom not less pernicious, opinion, that the soul receiveth upon its being disembodied some aërial vehicle, some house of habitation, some tabernacle of very subtle matter, wherein to act and to discourse over God's creation: which I hold to be no better than refined and disguised materialism: making void a spiritual world, and also the doctrine of Christ's coming with glory, in visible, sensible humanity, to reign with his saints, in the like humanity, over a purified kingdom of flesh and blood. Moreover, I can see how, for these great ends of putting to silence such manifold fanciful and heretical notions, it should have been so distinctly declared, and so prominently brought forward in the Apostles' Creed, that the action of his incarnation did not terminate at his death; but that he descended into the place of separate spirits, and did a work therein—concerning which I do not now enter, but only recognise it as a great head of doctrine, by means of which those doters concerning the sleep of the soul, and the new clothing of the soul during its separate estate, are to be baffled and befooled.

The Timing and Means of the Son Assuming a Human Soul

Now, concerning the time and manner of our Lord's receiving this reasonable soul, I believe it to have been at the same time, and after the same manner, in which the rest of the children receive it; in opposition to those who hold the pre-existence of Christ's human soul, or that it was made before the creatures, for the Son of God to possess and unite himself to, and with it and by it to create all things visible and invisible, and afterwards to come in it and join himself to the substance of the Virgin Mary. I hold, with the orthodox church, that this is a pestilent error, which hath its origin in the confounding of a divine purpose with a divine act, and endeth in various evil consequences, which I shall in a few words expose.

2. Those whose perspective is remote from reality; dreamers.

With respect to its origin: That the Creator had himself, and his own appearing in creature form, fully and mainly in his eye from the first beginning, and through the several actings of creation, there is, and can be no question, among those who meditate such matters, or read the Holy Scriptures—for example, the first chapter of Colossians, the first chapter of Hebrews, and the eighth chapter of the Proverbs. Everything that hath been done by God out of himself, was done in the contemplation and to the end of himself becoming unto creatures manifest in creature form; and that creature form was the form of risen God-manhood. But to suppose that to the effecting of this purpose it was necessary that the Creator should first create a human soul, in which and by which to create all things, is a gratuitous hypothesis to represent a purpose by an act, and to destroy altogether the beauty, harmony, and order of the divine idea, developing itself by slow and sure progression, and at length manifesting itself in the birth of Immanuel the Virgin's Son.

Moreover, if the human soul of Christ was thus before creation hypostatically united with the divinity of the Son, we have an in-spiritual before we have an in-carnate God; we have God in union with spiritual creation subsisting, and therefore unto spiritual creatures manifest, before we have God in union with flesh subsisting: now this is to destroy the whole tenor of the Scriptures and scheme of God, which represent the angels and all creation hanging upon the lips of promise, and looking with faith unto the symbols of the man about to be, and travailing with hope until the great end of all things should appear. Besides, it wholly destroys the continuity of things, and casts them back again upon themselves, to say that a soul which had known and effected the creation should pass into infantine ignorance and childhood simplicity, and ascend through all the stages of a human life. Moreover, then creation hath not fallen wholly, for this pre-existent soul hath never found a fall; and, being united with the body of Christ, is still the creature in the unfallen state; and so the better half of the man Christ is unfallen, and the other half of him is fallen. Strange conjunction! and heterogeneous mixture! Believing, therefore, and holding it to be a point of great importance to believe, that the human soul of Christ came unto him just as the human soul of another man, we proceed a little further to open the nature of the person thus constituted.

God at first, when he had created man, breathed into his nostrils the breath of life, and he became a living soul. Such a living soul is, therefore, the definition of man: "The first Adam was made a living soul" (1 Corinthians 15.46). Again, it is said, "The body returneth unto the dust, and the soul to him that gave it" (Ecclesiastes 12.7). Man, therefore, is a body of dust and a soul given by God, in a state of living union. Man is not a body of flesh, nor is man a disembodied soul; but these two in living union constitute a man. From the time that Christ was conceived by the Holy Ghost in the womb of the Virgin was he both body and soul of man. He was not soul of man before he was body of man; but he was soul and body of man from the same moment of his conception. From which moment also the Holy Ghost abode in him and sanctified him; so that he was in very deed a holy thing from the beginning of his creature being: which distinctly to understand it is necessary to have clear views of the divine purpose, as it is contained in these words, "The Holy Ghost shall come upon thee, and the power of the Highest shall overshadow thee: therefore also that holy thing which shall be born of thee shall be called the Son of God" (Luke 1.35). In these words we have all the direct information which Scripture affordeth concerning this great act of God, which was the end of all the promises of God from the fall onwards; and we are told that it was an act done by the Highest in the person of the Holy Ghost.

THE COVENANT OF THE FATHER AND THE SON ENACTED BY THE SPIRIT

Now every act of the Holy Ghost is an act of the Father and the Son, from whom the Holy Ghost proceedeth. The Holy Ghost worketh nothing of himself, but worketh the common pleasure of the Father and the Son. In the creation, therefore, of this body of Christ of the woman's substance, there is an act of the Father's will and a word of the Son assenting thereto. The word of the Son is given unto us by St Paul: "A body hast thou prepared for me. [. . .] Then said I, Lo, I come; in the volume of the book it is written of me, to do thy will, O God" (Hebrews 10.5, 7). In which words are contained both the will of the Father, that it should be so done; and the word of Christ consenting so to do. And what is the thing thus willed of the Father and assented to of the Son? It is, that he should take the body which the Father would prepare for him. This was the covenant between the Father and the Son: this was the purpose in the Christ: the Father willing it out of very goodness, that he might manifest himself unto creatures which were to be made, and support the creation in blessedness for ever; the Son consenting to it out of very dutifulness unto his Father, together with the same goodness unto the creature; and thus the covenant between the Father and the Son being willed and worded, the Holy Ghost, of very delight in the communion of the Father and the Son, to execute what their pleasure is, and likewise of very goodness to the creature, consented to prepare that body, so willed and so worded by the Godhead.

Creation and Incarnation by the Power of the Spirit

And with this view, of preparing a body for the Son of God and acting forth the eternal covenant, the Holy Ghost created all things out of nothing, and began as it were the collecting of materials, and the putting together of scaffoldings, for the construction of that body in which, as in a holy temple, Godhead should abide, and shew itself for ever; and by which, as the great head of intelligence, heart of love, and right hand of power, the Godhead should for ever perform the pleasure of its will, and bring forth the harmony of its purpose. And now, when a spiritual world had been created, and by its fall demonstrated that it was not an end in itself; and when a visible world had been superadded thereunto, and by its fall shewn that neither was this the end of the purpose; the fulness of the time being come, forth proceedeth the Holy Ghost to lay the foundation-stone of that temple of the Divinity, to bring into being that right-hand Man of God, to form that body (bone of our bone and flesh of our flesh) which had been the great end of God in coming forth at all by creation to give existence beside himself. And the instant that act of the Holy Ghost began, in the very beginning of it, in the instant of life quickened before the sight of God, did the Son, in his independent personality, once and for ever join himself to the holy thing, which by that conjunction became properly named the Son of God. And such I conceive to be the mystery of this conception of the child whose name is Wonderful, Counsellor, the Everlasting Father, the Mighty God, the Prince of Peace.[3]

And as his conception was, such also was his life; his constitution never changing; being in the embryo what it was in the man of stature; being in the humiliation what it was in the exaltation, what it is now, and what it shall be for ever and for ever. The constitution of his being is unchangeable: the development of its power and glory being the only cause of apparent change. And what is this wonderful constitution of the Christ of God? It is the substance of the Godhead in the person of the Son, and the substance of the creature in the state of fallen manhood, united, yet not mixed, but most distinct for ever. And is this all? No: this is not all. With humility be it spoken, but yet with truth and verity, that the fallen humanity could not have been sanctified and redeemed by the union of the Son alone; which directly leadeth unto an inmixing and confusing of the divine with the human nature, that pestilent heresy of Eutyches. The human nature is thoroughly fallen; and without a thorough communication, inhabitation, and empowering of a divine substance, it cannot again be brought up pure and holy. The mere apprehension of it by the Son doth not make it holy. Such a union

---

3. Irving is referring to Isaiah 9.6.

leads directly to the apotheosis or deification of the creature, and this again does away with the mystery of a Trinity in the Godhead.

The Sinlessness of Christ by the Power of the Spirit

Yet do I not hesitate to assert, that this is the idea of the person of Christ generally set forth: and the effect has been to withdraw from the eye of the church the work of the Holy Spirit in the incarnation, which is as truly the great demonstration of the Spirit's power and manner of working, as the incarnation itself is of the Father's goodness, and the Son's surpassing love. This comes from the omission of the third part in the composition of Christ, which is, the substance of the Godhead in the person of the Holy Ghost: to whose divine presence and power it is that the creation of the body in the womb of the virgin is given, the mighty works which Christ did ascribed, and the spotlessness of his sacrifice attributed, in the Holy Scripture. The Holy Ghost sanctifying and empowering the manhood of Christ even from his mother's womb, is the manifestation both of the Father and of the Son in his manhood, because the Holy Ghost testifieth of the Father and of the Son, and of them only: so that in the manhood of Christ was exhibited all of the Godhead that shall ever be exhibited, Father, Son, and Spirit; according as it is written, "In him dwelt all the fulness of the Godhead bodily" (Colossians 2.9), or in a body. The time was not come for manifesting it gloriously, because the heat of battle was then going forward, when the warrior is all soiled with sweat, and dust, and blood. He was wrestling with sin, in sin's own obscure dwelling-place; against the powers of darkness, in their dark abode: he was overcoming sin in the flesh. And therefore was it that he appeared not in the glorious raiment of a conqueror, or in the full majesty of a possessor, as he shall appear when he cometh the second time. Nevertheless, he was the person of the Eternal Son, manifesting forth the will of the Father and the work of the Holy Ghost, as well as the word of the Son, in manhood, yea, in fallen manhood. He took up the creature in its lowest estate, in order to justify God therein, by proving how good even that estate was; verily to prove that it was holy; a part of the scheme of him whose name and style is Holy, Holy, Holy; yea, moreover, that it was a state of the creature necessary for the knowledge of God, as the God of grace, mercy, and peace. Christ in fallen manhood redeemed, Christ as the Lamb slain, is, let me tell these silly dreamers, a necessary exhibition of the Godhead, to the end that its love, its grace, its pity, its compassion, might be known, as well as its goodness and might and majesty and power.

The Three-Staged Anointing of the Incarnate Son by the Spirit

For my own satisfaction, and for the satisfaction of all unsophisticated orthodox members of Christ's church, I should conceive the foregoing opening of the subject to be quite sufficient; but, what with the malice of Satan,
the ignorance of men, and the multitude of those who malign the truth
which I preach, holding me for a speculator or a fool, or even a madman,
I deem it good to argue this matter a little, in order to put to silence the
gainsaying of foolish men, and to establish the church in so fundamental
a point of doctrine. And therefore, at the risk of being thought tedious by
the enlightened and the believing, I shall enter a little more particularly into
this question, and endeavour to set the matter in a still fuller and clearer
light, by opening those successive anointings with the Holy Ghost which
our Saviour received, those apparent changes through which his humanity
passed, before he became High Priest in full degree, and did receive that
glorious body which was prepared for him by the Father.

There was this peculiarity in Aaron's consecration to the office of the
high priest, that he was anointed with the holy oil of consecration upon the
head, which flowed down his beard, and unto the skirts of his garment. The
rest of the priests were not thus anointed, but sprinkled with a mixture of
blood and oil, as was Aaron also. But this anointing over his whole person,
like his birthright and his garments, was proper to Aaron as high priest; and,
being so, is a point of much importance towards understanding Christ's peculiar anointing with the Holy Ghost; for that most holy oil of consecration
is everywhere used as the emblem of the Holy Ghost, with which Christ was
anointed above measure: "I have found David my servant: with my holy oil
have I anointed him" (Psalm 89); "The Spirit of the Lord God is upon me,
because he hath anointed me" (Isaiah 61.1).

Spirit as Agent of the Son's Reception of Fallen Human Nature

Now, of this anointing there is a threefold act to be noticed in Christ's life;
the first being from the time of the existence of his body,—indeed, it was
this anointing with the Holy Ghost which gave his body existence: "The
Holy Ghost shall come upon thee, and the power of the Highest shall overshadow thee; and the holy thing which shall be born of thee shall be called
the Son of God" (Luke 1.35). It was not with Christ, in this respect, as it
was with Jeremiah and the Baptist, who were filled with the Holy Ghost
from the mother's womb: he was not merely filled with the Holy Ghost,
but the Holy Ghost was the author of his bodily life, the quickener of that

substance which he took from fallen humanity: or, to speak more correctly, the Holy Ghost uniting himself for ever to the human soul of Jesus, in virtue and in consequence of the second person of the Trinity having united himself thereto, this threefold spiritual substance, the only-begotten Son, the human soul, and the Holy Spirit—(or rather twofold, one of the parts being twofold in itself; for we may not mingle the divine nature with the human nature, nor may we mingle the personality of the Holy Ghost with the personality of the Son)—the Eternal Son, therefore, humbling himself to the human soul, and the human soul taken possession of by the Holy Ghost, this spiritual substance (of two natures only, though of three parts) did animate and give life to the flesh of the Lord Jesus; which was flesh in the fallen state, and liable to all the temptations to which flesh is liable: but the soul of Christ, thus anointed with the Holy Ghost, did ever resist and reject the suggestions of evil.

I wish it to be clearly understood—and this is the proper place for declaring it—that I believe it to be necessary unto salvation that a man should believe that Christ's soul was so held in possession by the Holy Ghost, and so supported by the divine nature, as that it never assented unto an evil suggestion, and never originated an evil suggestion: while, upon the other hand, his flesh was of that mortal and corruptible kind which is liable to all forms of evil suggestion and temptation, through its participation in a fallen nature and a fallen world: and that thus, though at all points assailable through his flesh, he was in all respects holy; seeing wickedness consisteth not in being tempted, but in yielding to the temptation. This, I say, I consider to be an article of faith necessary for salvation: and the opposite of it, which holdeth that his flesh was unfallen, and not liable to all temptation by sin, nor conscious to it, I hold to be a virtual denial of his humanity; a removal of us from the fellowship of his mediation; a removal of him from the sympathy of our sufferings and temptations; and a bringing in of many ancient heresies which the church condemned; and, if I err not, it is the reappearance of that spirit of Antichrist, mentioned by St John in these words, "Every spirit that confesseth not that Jesus Christ is come in the flesh, is not of God" (1 John 4.3).

I foresee, moreover, that if some one will not stand boldly forth to bear the odium of this point of orthodox faith, and to redargue[4] the gainsayers of it, to such a pitch of sickly sentimentalism are we come, that a confirmed system of heterodox doctrine and pharisaical life will be the fatal issue. For, is it not a thing clear as noonday, that if you are ashamed to think the holy soul of Jesus should inhabit mortal and corruptible flesh, which must first be

4. An archaic term meaning "to demonstrate" or "to prove."

a little purified before the divine glory will consent to tabernacle in it, then you will be also ashamed, after you have been sanctified of the Holy Ghost, to confess the sinfulness of your own flesh, but will think and believe, with the Arminians, that it hath received a purification? and, thus purified, you will loathe to mingle again with publicans and sinners, lest you should be tainted anew; and you will say, "Stand off: I am holier than thou."

While Christ carried about with him this mortal and corruptible body, which lay open and assailable to the assaults of the devil, the world, and the flesh, he was able to meet the demands of the law, Thou shalt not do this, Thou shalt not do that; because he was tempted to do it, and yet did it not. But unless he had been liable and obnoxious to do the evil, there would have been no merit in refraining from it, and keeping the commandment. He did ever, therefore, prefer the Creator unto the creature, the glory of his Father to the glory of things seen and temporal, the law of the Spirit to the law of the flesh, his Father's will unto his own will; and so was fitted to be the sacrifice, holy and blameless, without fault in the sight of God and in the sight of man. "He did no sin, neither was guile found in his mouth; [. . .] he was holy, harmless, undefiled, and separate from sinners" (1 Peter 2.22); and yet carrying about with him a tabernacle of flesh, into which our mortal enemies had poured all their poisoned arrows. This fallen creature substance, thus preyed upon, thus wrestled for, by him that had the power of death and of corruption, our Lord and Redeemer must redeem out of the hands of the enemy, and carry into the acceptable and honourable place of the right hand of the Majesty on high: which being accomplished, it was proved that a created substance, in which sin and Satan had power, might yet be wrested out of their hands, and presented blameless and faultless in the presence of God; which I take to be the one great thing to be demonstrated.

But if Christ's flesh was never obnoxious to Satan's power as mine is, but in some lesser degree, or not at all, what proof have I received by his resurrection that I also am capable of resurrection? The saints who rose with him might, indeed, afford some hope to me, but his rising could afford none. I say, then, that Christ's flesh was as mine is, liable to all temptation, that through it he might be tempted like as we are; but that his soul, though brought into consciousness and feeling of these temptations through its union to his body, as my soul is to my body united, was yet, through its having been taken possession of by the Holy Ghost, and that in consequence of its having been taken up into union with the second person, prevented from ever yielding to any of those temptations to which it was brought conscious, and did reject them every one—yea, did mourn and grieve, and pray to God continually, that it might be delivered from the mortality, corruption, temptation, which it felt in its fleshy tabernacle; and was heard in that it feared. Now, no one was ever thus anointed with the Holy Ghost. For though Jeremiah and the Baptist are declared to have been filled with the Holy Ghost from their mother's womb, yet their souls came not possessed with the Holy Ghost, for they were born by ordinary generation; and therefore they must have been capable of regeneration; which implies that they were in their creation-state sinful, seeing they needed the washing of regeneration and the renewing of the Holy Ghost. It is not the time during which we are unregenerate, nor is it the number of sins which we have committed in our unregenerate state, but it is the fact that we need regeneration, which constitutes our original sinfulness in the sight of a holy God.

The Son Anointed High Priest by the Spirit

Now, though I have thus fully discoursed of the birth-holiness of our Lord Jesus Christ, I do not think that this anointing of the Holy Ghost is that which constitutes him High Priest; which office, as both Peter (Acts 2) and Paul (Hebrews 5) declare, he took not upon him until after, or rather by virtue of, his resurrection, when he proved himself to be the first-begotten. And what, then, is this first anointing of the Holy Ghost answerable to under the law? It correspondeth to the seven holy things of the sanctuary, which were anointed with holy oil, before there was a high priest to minister thereat. By virtue of this anointing, his body became the holy altar, the holy laver, the holy shew-bread, the holy lamp, the holy golden table, and the holy ark of the covenant; but he was not the High Priest as yet, who is to minister thereat.

Neither did he become the High Priest in virtue of his anointing with the Holy Spirit upon the occasion of his baptism; which, if I err not, was his anointing to the prophetical office, answering to the anointing of Elisha by the hand of Elijah. For John the Baptist, which is Elias, expressly declareth, that the reason of his coming to baptize with water was, that the Lamb of God should be made manifest to Israel: as it is written "And I knew him not, but he that sent me to baptize with water, the same said unto me, Upon whom thou shalt see the Spirit descending and remaining on him, the same is he which baptizeth with the Holy Ghost" (John 1:33). Yet that Christ did not baptize with the Holy Ghost until after his resurrection, is expressly declared by the evangelist John, in these words, "For the Holy Ghost was not yet given" (John 7.39), that is, was not manifested as the Spirit of Christ— "because that Jesus was not yet glorified" (John 7.39). Meanwhile, therefore, John the Baptist, by the baptism of water, did make Jesus manifest as the Prophet of Israel, about to become the Baptizer with the Holy Ghost: as

Elias anointed Elisha to be prophet in his room, so the Baptist anointed Christ. And yet it was not the Baptist's sprinkling or anointing with water, but the Holy Ghost descending in the form of a dove, which manifested Jesus as the Son of God, in whom he was well pleased. But this is a nice point, upon which it may be necessary to discourse a little before going forward.

The first question is, What connexion the baptism by John had with the manifestation of Jesus unto Israel? I answer, it was not the very manifestation, but a necessary step to it. The Holy Ghost, being minded to connect himself with the ordinance of washing with water, would not manifest himself unto the people as the property of Christ ever after to be holden and dispensed by him, until that same ordinance of baptism had been done on him also.

By this divine arrangement two things are, moreover, taught,—that baptizing with water is not in itself the substance of the ordinance, but needeth to have joined therewith the baptism of the Holy Ghost. For not only were these two things separated in the baptism of Christ, but in the Acts of the Apostles we read of some who had been baptized into the baptism of John and had not received the Holy Ghost, nor even known that there was a Holy Ghost. So that John's baptism was a baptism unto expectation; but Christ's baptism is a baptism unto possession. And, methinks, in these times they believe themselves to be baptized only into the expectation of receiving, and not into the actual receiving, of the Holy Ghost; into John's baptism, and not into Christ's baptism; which will be followed with the forgetting that there is a Holy Ghost.

Another question, arising out of this special anointing of the Holy Ghost, is, Whereto did it profit? and for what end was it given? I answer, That it did profit unto the information of Christ's mind with all prophetic wisdom and with all prophetic power of signs and wonders; and it was unto the end of fitting him for the office of preaching the gospel unto the poor, of binding up the broken-hearted, of proclaiming liberty to the captives, and the opening of the prison to them that are bound, of proclaiming the acceptable year of the Lord. But it may be asked, Was not Christ furnished with this power even from his mother's womb? I answer, No: he "grew in stature and in wisdom, and in favour with God and man" (Luke 2.52). He truly passed through the various stages, from childhood up to manhood, not merely as to his body, but as to his mind; and in order to enable him to speak as never man spake he must have a special power of the Holy Ghost, as well as to enable him to heal all that were oppressed with the devil. But on this point let the apostle Peter speak, who said unto Cornelius and his company:

The word which God sent unto the children of Israel, preaching peace by Jesus Christ; (he is Lord of all;) that word, I say,
ye know, which was published throughout all Judea, and began
from Galilee, after the baptism which John preached; how God
anointed Jesus of Nazareth with the Holy Ghost and with power;
who went about doing good, and healing all that were oppressed
of the devil; for God was with him. (Acts 10.35–38)

It may be asked further, And what signification could there be in washing Christ with water, who had done no sin? I answer, Just the same reason
as there was for the purification of his mother, and for his own circumcision; because he possessed the same flesh with other men, and therefore
needed, like other men, as he said unto John, to "fulfil all righteousness."
For when John said, "I have need to be baptized of thee, and comest thou
to me? Jesus, answering, said unto him, Suffer it to be so now, for thus it
becometh us to fulfil all righteousness" (Matthew 3.13–15). These are great
visible demonstrations of the truth which we have argued above, that Christ
took flesh and blood with the brethren: as it is written, "Forasmuch as the
children were partakers of flesh and blood, he himself also took part of the
same" (Hebrews 2.14). It was signified, by his baptism in Jordan, that he was
clean from the sins and defilements of flesh, through the Holy Ghost dwelling in his soul. His baptism with water signified that he was the washed,
cleansed, and holy one; and the baptism of the others signified that through
one, whom John testified of, they also should be washed and purified, when
he should come who would baptize with the Holy Ghost. John's baptism
was for the manifestation of Jesus as the baptizer with the Holy Ghost; and
when the Holy Ghost had manifested Jesus from amongst the baptized with
water, John's baptism did point to this one as its end; did, as it were, hand
the people over to him, as the Lamb of God which taketh away the sin of
the world, and baptizeth whom the Father pleaseth with the Holy Ghost.
They had, therefore, to believe upon Jesus, as the Lamb of God about to be
sacrificed, and as the quickening Spirit, the Second Adam, about to beget
sons unto God. John's baptism did point the respects of men unto Jesus the
Prophet, and unto Jesus the Lamb slain, and unto Jesus the risen Christ and
Lord, who received power at his resurrection, and on the day of Pentecost
put it forth in baptizing with the Holy Ghost.

There is yet another and a higher mystery, in that baptism with the
Holy Ghost which Christ received at his baptism with water, besides that
which we have opened above: It did not only constitute him the Prophet and
possess him with all prophetic gifts, and shew him as the Prophet the seal of
all the prophets—from whom they had derived their light, as the morning

star deriveth its light from the sun, whose rising it doth herald unto the earth—but, moreover, this baptism with the Holy Ghost was to him truly and literally that same baptism of power and holiness with which he was afterwards to baptize his church, when he should have ascended up on high. The baptism which he received in his conception enabled him to keep the law, and to fulfil all the righteousness of the law: but it did no more: and to this completion of the legal work he alludeth, when he said unto the hesitating Baptist, "for thus it becometh us to fulfil all righteousness."

But after his baptism with the Holy Ghost he began to live the life above law which his church, that should be afterwards baptized, was to live until his second coming. God testified that Jesus of Nazareth was the person whom he had by the Baptist foreshewn, as about to baptize with the Holy Ghost, by baptizing him then and there upon the spot. Thus giving him the precedency of all the baptized spiritual church, as in his resurrection he hath the precedency of all the resurrection church. In his life, anterior to John's baptism, he fulfilled the law, and made it honourable, and gathered up its authority and its righteousness into his own person, to do with it as he might see good; but from John's baptism he began to set it aside, as we Christians are required to do, and to live a life in the power of the demonstration of the Holy Ghost, as we also are required to do. From that time forth, accordingly, began his conflict with the spirits of darkness, such as we unto this day have to maintain: from that time forth also began his power of casting out spirits, of preaching the gospel, of forgiving sin, of healing infirmities, of liberty and of power; in which spiritual course also all that have been baptized with the Spirit are required to walk. Thus he shewed us an example that we should follow his steps; and hereby he became the great prototype of a Christian, as he had been the great antitype of all the holy men under the law. And this continued, as I judge, until he fell into the agony and the pangs of death; when the power of the Spirit, through which he had enjoyed the light of his Father's countenance, was for a season removed away, that he might know the hour and the power of darkness; and so become the great example unto his church of patience, resignation, faith, and every grace of suffering, under those desertions of the divine presence, and oppressions of the powers of darkness, to which his church was again and again, and very often, to be subjected, by the sovereign will and disposal of God.

In thus pointing out the successive changes of condition which Christ underwent in the days of his flesh, I am opening the wisdom of God in bringing our Great High Priest unto perfection. I am unfolding no change in the eternal and essential divinity of the Son, which is unchangeable, being very God of very God; but I am unfolding certain changes which passed upon the humanity, and by virtue of which the humanity was brought from the likeness of fallen sinful flesh, through various changes, unto that immortality and incorruption and sovereign Lordship whereunto it hath now attained, and wherein it shall for ever abide. For to me it is most manifest, that the eternal Godhead of the Son did not despise the Virgin's womb, but was in deed and in truth united personally with the embryo of a man—was born into the world a babe, and laid in a manger. So that what the Virgin bore is to be called very God; what was laid in a manger is to be called very God. What was circumcised; what sought knowledge of the scribes and doctors in the temple; what grew in wisdom and in stature, and in favour with God and man; what was in subjection to his parents; what was baptized in Jordan; what was tempted of the devil; what went about doing good, healing all that were oppressed with the devil; what was crucified; what died—all these actings and sufferings are proper unto God in that human nature, which is as much of him as the divine nature is of him.

There is a double operation, a twofold will—as we shall hereafter explain—one with the Godhead ever consubstantial, and out of the absolute unto the manhood condescending, in order to suffer and to act: the Godhead ever emptying itself into the manhood: the manhood not containing the Godhead, but consenting with harmony to the mind of the Godhead. And not until these two operations have taken place is any act of Christ's complete. The person, the *I* who speaketh, acteth, suffereth in Christ, is not the divine nature, nor yet is it the human nature, alone; but it is the divine nature having passed into the human nature, and therein effecting its will and purpose of acting or of suffering.

I totally reject—for reasons which will appear in the sequel of this discourse—the language of those divines who say, "Now the divine nature acteth, now the human nature acteth" language which I hold to be essentially Nestorian, making two persons in Christ. I say, on the other hand, that in every act of Christ the divine nature acteth and the human nature acteth; the former, by self-contraction unto the measure of the latter; the latter, by coming into harmony with the former through the mighty power of the Holy Ghost. In therefore pointing out the successive changes which passed upon the humanity of Christ, and shewing him, first as a man under the law; then as a man under the Spirit, enjoying the joy of God's chosen ones; then under the hour and power of darkness, suffering the agonies of God's chosen ones, when it pleaseth the Father for their sins to chastise and rebuke them; I am doing no more than shewing the gradual progress unto perfection through which the body, the humanity, of Christ came, that it might be, during the days of his flesh, the perfect thing, the all-exemplifying thing, the beginning and the ending, the alpha and the omega, the first and the last; both the Jew and the Gentile, the circumcised and the baptized, the living and the dead, and the living for evermore. And it doth but remain that we proceed a little onwards to speak of the dead body of Christ while it lay in the tomb, yet saw not corruption.

The Anointing of the Corpse: Christ's Flesh Kept from Corruption by the Spirit

The true doctrine, therefore, of Christ's body, as to its mortality or immortality, seemeth to be rightly expressed thus: The flesh he took of the Virgin was mortal and corruptible, in the same manner, to the same degree, and for the same reason, that the rest of her flesh which was not taken, that all flesh whatsoever of Adam and Eve descended, is mortal and corruptible. Which attributes of mortality and corruption flesh deriveth not from the manner of its propagation, nor from its propagation at all, but anterior to all propagation, from that very word of God which saith, "In the day that thou eatest thereof thou shalt surely die" (Genesis 2.17). When the fruit of the forbidden tree had been eaten, from that time forth flesh—that is, the body of man, the bodies of all men, in our first parents contained, as all trees and plants were contained in the trees and plants which God created and made—the body of flesh, I say, became mortal and corruptible from thence; and shall so continue, until all flesh shall have passed into death, anterior to the universal resurrection and common judgment. And I may observe, by the way, that the universality, the stability, the unchangeableness of this, the law of all body of Adam descended, doth raise into a very high and vast importance those exceptions of Enoch and Elias, the only ones which have ever been permitted—and undoubtedly not without the gravest causes and greatest ends permitted; which I think are, to shadow forth the great mystery which Paul teacheth "we shall not all sleep, but we shall all be changed" (1 Corinthians 15.50).

This change of the living God was not to shew in the person of his own Son, who before the foundation of the world was destined to be slain: therefore it was necessary to shew it forth in some one or other of the types and forerunners of his Son. And yet, to the end that in this also he might have the pre-eminence, the transfiguration upon the Mount was given, and Elias made to attend upon the changed Lord; in order to signify and shew, that not only did the resurrection stand in Christ, but likewise the changing of the living, the rapture of the saints, which was foreshadowed in the rapture of Elias. But whether there be any speciality in the translation of Enoch, besides and above that which was in the changing of Elias, and what that speciality is, I confess myself at present unable to say. Seeing then that the law of flesh, undeviated from save in those two exceptions, is to be mortal and corruptible, I hold, that wherever flesh is mentioned in Scripture, mortality and corruption are the attributes of it; and that when it is said Christ came in the flesh, it is distinctly averred that he came in a mortal and corruptible substance: and, though I would judge no one, yet would I warn the church to take care how they undervalue or contradict the mortality and corruptibleness of Christ's body, which I hold to be no less an error than to deny that the Son of God is come in the flesh.

Well then, Christ, having taken to himself mortal and corruptible flesh, the work of the Holy Ghost consisteth in making that flesh immortal and incorruptible; but first it must be proved to be *mortal*, before it can be proved to be immortal. Immortal, Christ is to become, by overcoming death, and him that had the power of death; not by escaping and never seeing death, but by seeing it, tasting of it, and overcoming it. He died, therefore, because he had taken flesh and blood with the brethren; because he had taken true flesh. And the man who says that Christ did not die by the common property of flesh to die, because it was accursed in the loins of our first parents, that man doth deny that Christ was under the curse; he doth deny that Christ was made a curse at all; he doth deny that Christ was made sin at all; yea, he doth deny that the Word was made flesh at all. Christ came to death, in order to prove himself to be of the seed of Adam, of the seed of Abraham, of the seed of David, and of the substance of the Virgin; bone of our bone, and flesh of our flesh. For, if flesh, in the Holy Scriptures everywhere else meaneth that substance from Adam generated under the law of sin and death; then, where it is said that the Word was made flesh, it must be meant that he was made this very same substance; or else the Holy Spirit doth speak an enigmatical, yea, and a deceptious language.

But, besides this, the establishment of Christ's very and true manhood in the fallen state thereof, which could only be unequivocally and indubitably demonstrated by death, it was necessary, moreover, to demonstrate that he differed from all men in this respect, that he never sinned; for, if he sinned, atonement and reconciliation are made void for ever. It must be shewn, that the death which he died he died not for his own sins, but for the sins of the world; that it was vicarious, and not in his own deserving; that it was for the Father's glory, and not for his own punishment; that it was with free-will acting of the second person unto the fulfilment of an eternal purpose of Godhead, and not a necessity induced by any cause or for any sake. Yea, I will go a little higher, and say, it was necessary to prove that death itself, and sin itself, were only servants unto the glory of the divine purpose in Christ; and that a fallen world was only the stage between a created world and a redeemed world; and a stage as necessary to be gone through, for the manifestation of the divine purpose, as creation itself.

And how is the subserviency of sin, and the subserviency of death, unto the great purpose of God and the glory of Christ, to be demonstrated? I answer, By his dying, and yet not seeing corruption. To corrupt, is for flesh to change its form, and dissolve again into its primeval dust. Corruption is the great proof of a creation fallen. Creation out of the dust composeth flesh: corruption, the antagonist of creation, into dust resolveth flesh again. If Christ, therefore, was in very flesh; nay, if Christ was not an angel, or an archangel—that is, if he wore visible and material form; that is, if he had a body—then he must be liable to corruption, as well as to death. And why, then, seeing he saw death, saw he not corruption? This question let the Holy Ghost himself answer, as it is written: "I have set the Lord always before me: because he is at my right hand I shall not be moved: therefore my heart is glad, and my glory rejoiceth: my flesh also shall rest in hope" (Psalm 16.8). Why, I ask, shall his flesh rest in hope? For the same reason for which his heart is glad, and his glory rejoiceth,—because he hath set the Lord always before him, because the Lord is at his right hand. Therefore his flesh resteth in hope; therefore also, he continueth, "Thou wilt not leave my soul in hell, neither wilt thou suffer thine Holy One to see corruption" (Psalm 16.10).

This deliverance from seeing corruption he received, because he was God's Holy One; because he had set the Lord always before him; because he had listened to the counsel of the Lord; because he had made the Lord the portion of his inheritance and of his cup; because he had not offered the drink-offerings of bloody idolaters, nor taken up their names into his lips; because his delights had been with the excellent in the earth, and the saints; because Jehovah he had declared to be his Lord; because in God he did put his trust: or, in one word, to sum up the various descriptions of his life by the Holy Ghost in this psalm, because he had lived a life of faith, and of prayer, and of holiness undefiled. This is the reason why he saw not corruption. This is the reason why he could not be held by the pains of death (Acts 2). This also is the reason why he was saved from death, because "He had offered up prayers and supplications, with strong crying and tears" (Hebrews 5:7) in the days of his flesh.

In order, therefore, to put a difference between this man, who had lived and died like other men, and all others who had in like wise lived and died; in order to prove that his life was blameless and sinless, though at all times and in all respects under the conditions of fallible, yea, and of fallen men; his body was not suffered to see corruption. The not suffering of it to see corruption was the beginning of the Father's work in honouring and glorifying his Son. I may say that it was the resurrection begun: not indeed the activity of God's pervading Spirit to transmute the matter of his body into a glorious and unchangeable substance, but the activity of his Spirit to resist the decomposition, the corruption, and inherent tendencies to decay and change, which have been proper unto all matter since the fall of Adam, who was created matter's lord. That Jesus's body saw not corruption, when the life was gone forth of him and it was an inanimate lump, is demonstration and consolation unto the inanimate world, that the Holy Ghost is able, when it pleaseth him, to stay that corruption which is in it, and to take it out of the power of that word of God which was spoken in Eden, and hath been since fulfilled in all material substances, save only the inanimate body of Christ. If sin had been in that flesh of the Lord Jesus—that is to say, if it had ever been an instrument unto sin; if sin had not been efficiently resisted and mightily expelled out of that flesh of Jesus—then, rest ye assured, it would have seen corruption. For what else is corruption but the consequence of sin? In Adam, in the paradise of Eden, in the world unfallen, there was perpetual health, and no vestige of decay; no autumn with its yellow leaf, no winter with its naked desolation, but one continued fulness of life, without any indications of change: and because corruption was not able to touch with its destroying finger the body of Christ, all dead and lifeless in the tomb, and separate both from animating soul and sustaining Godhead, it was proved that the substance which he took of a sinful woman he had been enabled to preserve pure and spotless, and from it to expel the powers of corruption which were in it by nature, which were now proved to be in it no longer.

Mighty act of Almighty power! comfort of all material creation! foundation-stone of an incorrupt and incorruptible world! Ay, true it is, and of verity, that had the Lord's body remained years and ages in the tomb, it had never seen corruption; because he had lived without sin, and so had redeemed the corruptible into incorruption. But that it was a corruptible which he redeemed, is manifest from all the infirmities unto which he was liable; from his weakness, his weariness, his faintings, his wounds, his death. But with death the demonstration of the corruptible endeth. Thus far was he one with me; thus far took he part with the children, and no further: for while his soul, descending into the abode of invisible spirits, wrestled there, through the might of the Holy Spirit and the personal union of the only-begotten Son, against all spiritual wickednesses, all invisible enemies of God, his body was laid up, in order to be proved impervious to the infirmities of the dead inanimate matter. Oh, there it lay, the trophy of the great conquest which in flesh had been achieved for flesh, and for flesh's monarchy, the visible world. There it lay, to prove that all which had been created for Adam in the beginning—sun, and moon, and stars, and earth, the palace of Adam the monarch of all; and which had all fallen; being shorn of its glory, driven from the presence of its God, reflecting not his perfect image, ministering not his holy purposes, but overwhelmed with sin and possessed with corruption—that all this material fabric, from the body of man downward to the worm which crawleth upon the earth; and from the earth upward to the utmost bound of the starry sphere, wherever matter subsisteth, and in whatever form; beyond the utmost reign of telescopic vision, and within the inmost penetration of microscopic vision; that all life, and all life's tenement and habitation was now redeemed, was now rescued, was now delivered from corruption, and for ever wrested out of the power of death. "He was made a little lower than the angels, for the suffering of death, that by the grace of God he might taste death for every man;" "that by death he might destroy him that had the power of death, which is the devil" (Hebrews 2.14).

So much, and no less, do we derive from the great work of God, that Christ's body saw not corruption. He gave him up to death—or rather, I should say, the Father separated between his soul and body—that he might shew forth that there was a power in Christ's body greater than corruption. In his life, God shewed that there was a power greater than sin; in his death, he shewed that there was a power greater than corruption. His body in life was all-liable to sin, as the body of every fallen man; but the fulness of the Godhead in that body preserved it from sin: the same body in the tomb was liable to corruption, like the body of another man; but the power and favour of the Godhead unto that which had not sinned, preserved it from corruption. This did God even when his Son was separated from it, and the living one was no longer in it, in order to shew that the Eternal hath as great a love and care over that matter which the Holy Spirit hath sanctified, as he hath a hatred against that which sin hath defiled and the Spirit hath not sanctified. So that, as Christ's sinless life in sinful flesh, as Christ's triumphant conquering life in flesh, oppressed and tempted by all the powers of darkness, is the assurance unto every believer of his own personal triumph over the sinfulness which is in him; is the assurance unto the church militant of her triumph, sinful though she be, and obnoxious to the devil, the world, and the flesh; so is the incorruption of Christ's body in a corruptible grave, the assurance unto the church, both in glory and in tribulation of the power of God, greater than that power of corruption which is now revelling in the bodies of the saints.

If Christ had sinned through the infirmity of his flesh, there would have been no assurance unto the church of attaining unto holiness in the flesh through faith in Jesus Christ. If, again, Christ's body had tasted of corruption after death through its corruptibility, then there would have been no proof unto the separated souls of believers, nor unto us daily expecting the same, of a power greater than the corruption which our bodies shall underlay; but, as it hath been set forth above, and ever been believed by the orthodox church, we, who are in sinful flesh, have knowledge of a power able to produce holiness by prevailing against sinful flesh; and they in the Jerusalem above, whose bodies are mouldered in the grave, have in the body of Christ, which prevailed against corruption, an assurance of a power in the Godhead more powerful than that corruption which they underlay. Now if Christ's living flesh had not been liable to all sin, if Christ's dead flesh had not been liable to all corruption, this demonstration of a power able to sanctify actually sinful living flesh, and to prevail against corrupt flesh, would not have been given; and more than this I consider it unnecessary to say, except that those who will not receive these things, can never have a full and legitimate ground of hope, either for holiness, or for incorruption. All which is briefly, but divinely, stated: "But if the Spirit of him that raised up Jesus dwell in you, he that raised up Jesus from the dead shall also quicken your mortal bodies by his Spirit that dwelleth in you" (Romans 8.11).

THE RESURRECTED BODY, THE CHURCH, AND THE GIVING OF THE SPIRIT

Thus have we opened the composition of the person of Christ, in tracing out the successive steps through which his flesh passed until the very instant of its being raised into glory and immortality by the resurrection. And here, as hath been already said, we consider that our present subject doth cease and determine, and a new subject begin; which is not the incarnation, but the church: for then Christ became Head of the church: concerning which, his risen glory, though I be not at present called upon to discourse, reserving it for some future occasion, if God should give me permission and opportunity, yet will I add one word in this place, for the sake of completeness. The body which the Father had destined his Son to subsist in, and of which he gave such glorious notices in the Old Testament, is not the body of his humility, suffering and dying, but the body of his glory, reigning and rejoicing in unchangeable power and majesty. All concerning which I discourse, that took place between the conception and the resurrection, is but a state of transition or passage unto the state of fixed permanency. The embodied Christ whom the prophets commonly spoke of, is the mighty and unchangeable one, now on the right hand of the Majesty on high. I say not that they forgot or omitted the mention of his sorrowful travail to his joyful crown; but I do say, and will never cease to insist, that the Father in his purpose, and the prophets in the unfolding of that purpose, do most chiefly, and most

principally, contemplate that which is the end, the consummation, and the
eternal persistence of the embodied God.

Therefore, the incarnation, whose importance I am thus setting forth
at length, is—all-important as I make it—but the porch to that temple of
glory which God shall for ever inhabit; is, I may say, but the foundation of
the temple,—is, I may say, but the conception, the bringing unto the birth,
of the God-man. We must proceed forward beyond the incarnation, in order to come at the knowledge of the full anointing, and perfect preparation
of the body of Christ; which was done at his resurrection: for until the resurrection Christ's flesh continued unchanged: the Holy-Ghost did not till then
expel Satan out of that region: who had room to come and go, and with all
enlargement to play his evil part, until the hour of Christ's death, yea, until
the hour of his resurrection. His death proved well of what kind was his flesh
up to that time—namely, that it was mortal. Its being laid in the grave and
buried, proved that it was of the corruptible. Now, that which is mortal and
corruptible is not yet taken possession of by the Holy Ghost; and therefore I
hold, that up to this time the holy ointment had not anointed him from the
crown of the head to the skirts of his garments. But when the Holy Ghost,
inhabiting his separate soul, which was united unto the Godhead, did come
unto his dead body that was kept from seeing corruption, and quicken it
with eternal and immortal life, instantly all mortality and corruption were
thenceforward expelled from it for ever; and the seed of woman, of mortal,
sinful woman, the seed of David, the seed of Abraham, was manifested in
immortal and incorruptible life and glory; the true Adam was born; the
Beginning of the creation of God was made known; the Foundation-stone
of the building was laid; the body prepared for him in the purpose of the Father was possessed; the fore-birth of creation's child was ended; and the Son
of God was manifested in his glory and in his beauty: and from this time
forth creation in the form of regeneration began to be unfolded; the Holy
Ghost was given, because Jesus was now glorified: and now the High Priest's
anointing was completed—one thing only excepted, which is his garments
(the anointing went to the skirts of the high priest's garments);

> when the disciples went unto the sepulchre, he whom Jesus
> loved stooping down, and looking in, saw the linen clothes ly-
> ing, yet went he not in: then cometh Simon Peter following him,
> and went into the sepulchre, and seeth the linen clothes lying,
> and the napkin that was about his head not lying with the linen
> clothes, but wrapped together in a place by itself. (John 20.5)

These wrappings of his dead body the Holy Spirit altered not; but his
body itself was wholly absorbed in the change; as the logicians say, it was

numerically the same body: nothing was left but the raiment which surrounded it: no film, no slough, no particle dropped away from it. It was
regenerated with a new life; it was changed into a glorious body. It was no
longer under the ordinary laws of matter: it rose into the heavens at its pleasure; it passed into the invisible at its pleasure, and at its pleasure became
visible again; it passed through barred doors; it partook of meat when it
pleased, and when it pleased it partook of none.

But its former life it laid down for us: the blood, which is the symbol
of life; the blood, which is the life of the natural body, fell upon the earth,
and was not resumed again,—that is, he gave a life for us, though he liveth
still: he died, who had done no sin; he died for our sins; his blood was shed
for us. That life lost is life gained to the world. And to demonstrate beyond a
doubt that the life lay in the blood, and to shew us that when Christ's blood
was shed his life was truly taken, was the meaning of the consecration of
blood in Noah's time, and its continuing consecrated until that great end had
been accomplished. And after all this pains which God hath taken to shew
us that Christ was truly mortal, I wonder that any one should entertain a
doubt upon such a matter. The subject we have opened fully; and here we do
but observe, that his bloodless body was anointed with the Holy Ghost, and,
instead of its blood-life, received a spiritual and eternal life; and now, in very
truth, was both Christ's soul and body, his human nature, completely, thoroughly, and fully anointed with the Holy Ghost. And for the garments with
which he shall come arrayed, they shall be forthcoming when the elements
of nature, the earth and the heavens, have been purified to furnish them. The
garments of his glory are to be fitted out and furnished forth from nature's
various chambers; and when the creatures, when the whole creation, shall
have finished with their long protracted travail, and brought forth the incorruptible forms of matter, they shall be the vestures and the glorious drapery
of his person who is Priest and Lord: Priest, to sanctify and purify all things;
and Lord, to command all things to serve and obey him.

And be it further observed, that that blood of a blameless life which
fell from his cross upon the ground, and which the earth greedily drank up,
is to her the assurance of hope, and speaketh out from the ground better
things than the blood of Abel, crying, not for vengeance, but for redemption. It is her baptism of blood; one of the witnesses which witnesseth of
glory yet to come. For what the Holy Spirit is to man, the blood of a holy
man is unto the ground: because man is the life of the earth, as the Holy
Spirit is the life of man. So that that blood of Christ, being his mortal life, is
truly the redemption of the mortal creature, the seal of the new testament
of blessings. And thus was our High Priest anointed with the Holy Ghost,
as Aaron was anointed with the holy anointing oil; thus, by the operation

of the Father, the Son, and the Holy Ghost, was the High Priest and Lord of all creation anointed. This is truly the work of God, which was wrought in and upon the human nature of Jesus Christ, to bring a clean thing out of an unclean, and to begin the work of regeneration in the fallen world.

And from this time forth beginneth the procession of the Holy Ghost from the Father and the Son, through the man-soul of Jesus Christ. So that now we receive the Holy Spirit as the Spirit of Christ. The Holy Ghost doth now come through one in human form, and with human sympathies invested, in order to work in the chosen ones of the Father that same mind which is in Jesus Christ; and we, who receive the sanctification of the Spirit unto obedience and sprinkling of the blood of Jesus Christ, are from that time forth of the same royal priesthood, kings and priests unto our God: we are filled with the Spirit of a holy Priest and King, even Christ: we become possessed with the desires and inclinations of the holy God-man; we become the members of the holy God-man; and are renewed, after the image of God, in righteousness and true holiness. Meanwhile our fleshly nature becometh restrained, but not changed; it longeth still after wickedness, it suggesteth wicked thoughts, it is assailable to every evil seducer, and tried with every seduction: and thus it ought to be; God thus bringeth us into trial. Arrayed on one side are all the powers of nature, unto which he leaveth us obnoxious through the flesh: while, on the other hand, the spirit, apprehending our glory and excellency in Christ; seeing there also the love of God manifested, and his grace shewn forth; apprehending likewise the hope of a sanctified body in the resurrection, which is Christ, contendeth against the flesh, with the world, which is visible: and, between these two contrary and opposite influences placed, the saint doth glorify God, by preferring him in Christ, to the wicked world, lusted after by the flesh and by the eye. So that verily we do receive a present sanctification in the soul, which holdeth in check and prevaileth over the degradation and corruption of the flesh; until at death the body descendeth with a good hope into the grave, being conscious to the Spirit of God which had dwelt in it; and well knowing that, "if the Spirit of him that raised up Jesus from the dead dwell in us, he that raised up Jesus from the dead shall also quicken our mortal bodies, by his Spirit that dwelleth in us" (Romans 8.11).

Part 2: Universal Reconciliation and Particular Election

THE AGENCY OF THE FATHER IN THE SUFFERING OF THE SON

Besides these good effects, necessarily resulting from Christ's taking our fallen humanity, and of which not one would have resulted had he taken humanity in an unfallen state, there is another, to which divines of this age will be more alive; which is, that there could otherwise have been neither reconciliation nor atonement between God and man. Those, indeed, who consider atonement as a bargain, of so much merit on Christ's side against so much demerit on ours; so much suffering in his person, instead of so much suffering in ours; will see little or nothing in the line of argument which I am now about to pursue. But those who consider, as I do, that this is a most insufficient, and, when taken for the whole, a most prejudicial view of the mystery; and who understand atonement in its only scriptural sense, of at-one-ment, or reconciliation between the holy Creator and the unholy creature; that which I am about to argue will appear of the greatest moment, and unanswerable. With respect to that bargain-and-barter hypothesis, I observe, that in order to make out of Christ's sufferings an infinite quantity to cover the infinite delinquency of his elect, the reason that: It was an infinite person that suffered and therefore his sufferings must be of infinite value.

Now, with all sound theologians, and with all doctors, I deny the possibility of the divine nature suffering. The Godhead cannot be tempted, and how should the Godhead suffer? The human nature of Christ alone suffered; and that is not infinite, but finite. Therefore there is no infinite amount of suffering to balance against the sufferings of the elect through eternity; and so the account will not balance, and the base theory falls to the ground. Besides being illogical, how degrading is it to represent the great mystery as shut up in this, that the Father would have so much punishment, get it where he could, and so he took it out of his own Son! That the Father did hide his face from his son; that he did say, "Awake, O sword, against him that is my Fellow" (Zechariah 13.7); that it pleased him to bruise him, and to put him to grief, there can be no doubt—and any view of the mystery which will not give fair interpretation to these vindictive expression of God's holiness cannot be received;—but that orthodox and enlarged view which I have given of the Father's act, as bringing Christ into the conditions of fallen humanity, doth well and truly appropriate every utterance which the Father hath uttered, and every act which the Father hath done against sinners, to be spoken and done against Christ also: not by substitution merely, but by reality; not by imputation merely, but in very truth. This, indeed, is what they cannot understand who consider imputation as containing the whole mystery of God; whereof it is only a part, though a very important part: and it will prove utterly unintelligible, confusion worse confounded, to all those who consent to the sufficiency of the debtor-and-creditor theology; or have been sucked by Satan into the heresy that Christ had a humanity in some way diverse from ours. This most unsound view of the matter, as the other is most insufficient, doth in effect make altogether void the Father's activity in the sufferings and death of Christ, which we are at such pains to preserve. If as the adversaries of truth allege, Christ in his incarnation did apprehend an immortal and incorruptible substance, and not the very same mortal and corruptible which you and I inherit under the curse; and if, by a mere act of power or will, he brought it into death, and laid it in the grave, and as it were, rid himself of it for a season, then why may he not, by the same act of will and of power, rid himself of it again for another season, and another, and another? and why not rid himself of it for aye, and use it as a mantle, according to occasion? and where is the security of the redeemed creature, that it may not again altogether fall out of union with the Godhead?

But if Christ took upon himself our fallen and corruptible nature, and brought it up through death into eternal glory, then is the act of the will of Christ not to lay down, but to assume or take up humanity into himself; and the continuance of his act is to keep it in union with himself, and not for any sake to dismiss it from himself. He takes it, he loves it, he strengthens it, he sanctifies it, he immortalizes it, he glorifies it. For his part he doth nothing but embrace it, and hold it fast unto himself. It is the act not of the Son but of the Father, which makes the flesh drop off from his immortal being into death and the grave. This, I say, is the Father's act; and it is the Father's act again to bring up that body in its changed and glorified state: not, indeed, without Christ's consent, but that consent given, when he consented to join himself to the mortal and corruptible seed of the woman. He consented to be brought into the possession of an enduring body through the transition state of a mortal life, through the passage of death and the grave; to which consenting, he consented therein to the act of the holy Father, which required the corruptible and mortal creature-substance to fall off from his immortal soul and divinity into death and the grave. And this is the meaning of the remarkable saying: "Therefore doth my Father love me, because I lay down my life, that I might take it again. No man taketh it from me, but I lay it down for myself: I have power to lay it down, and I have power to take it again. This commandment have I received of my Father" (John 10.17–18).

In these words Christ asserteth three things: first, that no one whatsoever, man or angel, had power to take his life from him; the second, that it was by himself laid down; and the third, that this was done by the commandment of the Father. These three things concur in his act of dying: a commandment of the Father, his own free will to obey that commandment, and his total independence of any third power or influence. Every act of his life was of the same kind; done of free will, without constraint, in obedience to the absolute will of the Father. I say, therefore, Christ died because the Father had said, "Wake, O sword, against the Man that is my Fellow." No one could take his life from him. He had but to look, and they became as stones; he had but to speak, and they staggered and fell; he had but to pray the Father, and twelve legions of angels would have succoured him; but "how, then, would the scriptures have been fulfilled?" (Matthew 26.54). His Father's commandment alone could take that life from him; his Father's commandment alone could make him suffer and die. It was his Father's commandment, and his filial obedience thereto, which brought him into the condition of suffering and dying. It pleased his Father to bruise him, and to put him to shame, and to make his soul an offering for sin; and why so? not surely because the Father had ceased to love him, for of love there is no suspension between the persons of the Godhead.

What is it, then, for which the Father chastiseth Christ? and for what offereth he his Son upon the cross? The Son surrendereth himself unto the Father; giveth himself up wholly unto the Father; and is in the Father's hands, to be disposed of according to the Father's mind. In one act of willingness are included; his Father may do with him thenceforth after his good pleasure. The act from thenceforth of his incarnation, suffering, agony, death, resurrection, glorification, is the Father's forthshewing of his own mind upon his willing Son, unto the instruction and edification of all by whom it is witnessed, and to whom the tiding of it, the fruits of it, shall reach, far and wide, for ever. Blessed, ever blessed Son! who thus made himself of not reputation, emptied himself of his own inexhaustible fulness, and yielded himself to his Father, like clay in the hand of the potter. Marvelous lesson unto every creature to do likewise! and for this very end designed, that we might yield up that rebel independence which we falsely feel, and pass into the conditions of the Father's will; and by faith deliver ourselves over to be crucified, sacrificed, and brought down to dust; yet never doubting, but aye believing, that out of the dust we shall be exalted unto glory. Christ, from the day of his self-surrender, is no longer his own master; a servant evermore, in subjection evermore, suspending himself from the Father's will evermore; and so exemplifying faith and obedience for ever unto all the creatures; and acknowledging his honour, his glory, and his power to proceed from the invisible Father, and teaching all creation to do the same. Great Head of subjection! great High Priest of Worship! great Heir of God! great Conveyancer of the inheritance of God unto all the children! O my soul, honour him, as honourest the Father.

Now, then, having Christ in the Father's hands, that the Father might demonstrate through him his own being and his own perfection, and through him communicate to the creatures whatever can be communicated, what doth the Father make of him, make with him? he maketh use of him, first, to shew what is the enmity between himself and the fallen creatures; what is the nature of sin, and what the nature of holiness. Therefore joineth he him unto the sinful thing; and, lo, what follows? exhaustion of Divinity! For its blessedness, suffering; for its infinity, narrow limitation; for its power, weakness; for its glory, shame; for its life, death! And there endeth this first act of the mystery of the Father's will, which amounteth unto this awful truth: That God, even the mighty God, being personally joined to the fallen creature, cannot hinder, cannot help, that it should not suffer and die; be dark, and need faith; be oppressed, and need comfort; be borne down, and need the Holy Ghost's sustenance continually. Was ever the weakness of flesh so proved as by this, that the personality of the Son joined to it could not strengthen it, without the continual energizing of the Holy Ghost? Was ever the sinfulness and mortality of the flesh so proved as by this, that the Holy One could not keep it from sin and from corruption but by operation of the Holy Ghost? Was ever God's alienation from the sinful creature so proved, as that the union of Godhead with it could not hold it to himself, or hinder it that it should not drop away into death and pass into corruption, had not the Holy Ghost changed its form, purged out its sinfulness? after which it can abide, and doth abide, in union with the Godhead for ever; but until which it was as it were, but an abortive attempt at a thing which could not be. Doth not this prove, that, let the creature believe in Christ to the uttermost, and let Christ incline to the creature in the uttermost, they cannot come together, stay together, and be one, otherwise than through the power of the Holy Ghost changing the creature's form, drawing it through death, and out of corruption regenerating it?

So that the act of the Son to redeem all mankind doth not suffice to deliver any from death and corruption, or to unite any with himself in infallible and inseparable union; like withering leaves, we shall drop off from him; like fruitless branches, be pruned away; like his own body of sin, drop into death and the grave; unless we shall have partaken of that regenerating power of the Holy Ghost which he partook in the tomb; which saved him from corruption, which shall deliver the regenerate out of corruption; which united his body, that was mortal and corruptible, unto his immortal part, consisting of soul and second person of the Godhead, and fixed it there in immortal union for ever and ever. So, likewise, doth the Father hereby make it manifest, that of all living and dead flesh, of all flesh together, which cometh into death, no more shall be united for ever unto to the glorious person of Christ, save so much only as shall have partaken the regeneration of the Holy Ghost;—that, though all flesh be now under him as Lord; though he be, as it were, united unto all flesh, by virtue of what he did in flesh; yet only so much of it as the Father by the Holy Ghost regenerated shall be brought up in the fashion of his glory, and all the rest shall be brought up in the fashion of the mere and unmixed sinful creature, to inherit for ever the estate of the second death. Behold how, in the sufferings and death of Christ, the Father openeth his mind and purpose!

IMPUTATION OF SIN TO CHRIST

Thus, have I shewed the Father's activity in the sufferings of the blessed Lord, and that these sufferings come not by imputation merely, but by actual participation of the sinful and cursed thing, I proceed further to express my views of imputation, before entering into the full exposition of the reconciliation which is wrought in flesh by the method detailed above, of uniting the Godhead to fallen humanity. The view of his humiliation and death in common use is, that the sins of all the elect were imputed to him, and all of the suffering which through eternity they should have borne laid upon him, and that his death had no relation whatever to any but God's elect. Let us take this scheme in its best form, and give heed to these questions: First, how then hath Christ purchased to himself a right over the reprobate as well as the elect, for his action toucheth them in nowise? and how is his finished work to be preached to the reprobate as well as to the elect, for it hath no application to them? To this it is no answer to say, That we know not the one from the other. If we preach to all, we preach to all; if we preach to a part, preach only to a part. Christ must have brought some benefit to all, that the gospel should be preached unto all; not the benefit of salvation, as the universalist damnably believe, but the removal of the law, and the introduction of grace, and the condemnation of sin in the flesh, and the spoiling of Satan, and the lordship of the fallen creation; to lead them unto the Father, that through him they may transact with the Father, and the Father transact with them, according to the new relations of grace. This much we preach to all, as having been really wrought out for all; and there leaving the general and universal question, we are ready to enter upon the additional and special question of the election and the regeneration.

We have Christ in his earthly work doing a common good for the fallen creatures, but in his risen work doing a particular good for the election of the Father; and we say again, that upon the scheme of mere substitution for the elect in his sufferings, and for them alone, this great end of preaching a gospel unto all, of preaching him the Saviour of all men, especially them that believe, cannot be attained. These two things, Christ concerning himself for the elect only, and the good of Christ preached unto all, are contrary to one another, and will never fail the one to destroy the other: but Christ's doing in the flesh a work for flesh in general, and in the spirit a work for the spiritual or elect in particular, are two truths which be consistent with a freely preached gospel, and likewise with an elected church; consistent also with the present lordship of Christ over all, and the future resurrection of all in Christ, and with their separate eternal destinies of heaven and hell, likewise in Christ. This way of viewing Christ's death as a compensation in kind for the elect only, is not peculiar to those who hold the heterodox view of Christ's humanity: but, being commonly found in company with it, and indeed being the only view possible on such a scheme; and moreover, being, as I conceive, partly the occasion of its revival in these times; I have thought it good to remark upon it here though regarding it with far more respect than I do the doctrine of Christ's immortal and incorruptible body, which I utterly detest and abominate. Indeed, this view of Christ's death, so far as it goes, expresseth the truth; for Christ is indeed the substitute for his people, and it is the elect only who realize the benefit of his death; but it falleth short, in not pointing out the relation which Christ's work hath unto the reprobate; and for this defect, rather than for any heinous error, we have at this time alluded to it, and do now proceed to explain the true doctrine of imputation.

As it seems to me, the meaning of imputation of our sins unto Christ consisteth in these two things:—First, that nothing constrained him, as the Son of God, but he did of his own free will take unto himself the body which the Holy Ghost quickened of the Virgin's substance, and in this body did commit no sin, but in all things did the Father's will, and was holy and blameless. Whence it follows, that, whatever he suffered, and, which is far more, whatever he forewent of infinite glory and blessedness in order to suffer, is all to be placed of the account of mankind, and not to his own account. By imputation I understand, that his humiliation and suffering were not for anything which he had done, but for what mankind in Adam had done. And to the end he might suffer for the kind, and not for individuals of the kind, he came not by ordinary generation; but the Holy Spirit did take up a portion from all the fallen substance before him, out of which to make his body, as he had taken up a portion of the earth to make Adam's body in the beginning. He did not now take up a portion of the earth to make of it an unfallen creature, because the work which was now to proceed was not the work of creation but the work of redeeming creation. Not, therefore, inorganic dust, but dust changed by creation's word into flesh and blood he took, and formed of it the body of Christ. The substance of created manhood in an unquickened state he took, as I may say, at random, and formed of it the body of Christ. So that, as the whole earth stood in Adam's body represented, with the fate of Adam's body implicated, in it to stand and fall and be redeemed; so likewise the whole substance of organized flesh and blood, living, and dead, and to live, stood represented in the body of Christ which the Holy Spirit had formed from the Virgin's substance, to stand or to fall according as this man newly constituted, this new thing created of God, should stand or fall. As unfallen creation stood represented in Christ and as in Adam's fall all together fell, so in Christ's resurrection shall all be made alive again.

This is the first part of imputation: that he freely came under, without any obligation of whatever kind, the load and burden of a fallen world's infirmity and sin—or, if you please to speak in the language of the covenant, the Father laid it upon him; charged him with it; imputed it to him; treated him as the guilty one; and, as Luther said, the only sinner: so that by his suffering and death justice should be appeased, and sin for ever done away with. There may be other depths here that I cannot fathom—such as the proportion between the suffering of Christ by which the sin was atoned for, and the eternal suffering from which his atonement delivereth his people. I cannot tell how this is, and I do neither say nor gainsay it, being minded only to speak what the Lord hath made me clearly to know.

I do indeed perceive this much, that no creature could pay the price of sin but by eternal separation from God, because I see it to have been so in the fallen angels; and if so, then the recovery of man must be accomplished by an act of power of an infinite measure; which act Christ's was, by that two fold will or operation which was in him—one conversant with the Godhead, and enlarged to its infinite bound; another conversant with the manhood, and restricted to its humble and suffering conditions—these two wills, or operations, as the orthodox fathers termed it, being necessary to compose any act of the person Jesus Christ. The *I* in him, embraced the infinite and the finite also; which gave to every action and feeling of his a character of infinity. When he suffered, though the divine nature suffered not, yet came he out of that delectation, and down from that elevation, into the human nature, which did suffer. And this, not of suffering only, but of feeling and of acting; which he did always as a man; and in order to do as a man, must first condescend form the infinitude of the Godhead in order to do it. In this twofold operation, in this twofold will, consisteth the one personality of the natures of Christ; his God-manhood, the hypostatical union, his identity of substance with the Godhead, his identity of substance with the fallen manhood. And in this I perceive everything which I want,—the infinite goodness of God, the infinite merit of Christ, the exceeding sinfulness of sin, and the glory of God shewn forth in our deliverance from it. And I see that there is an infinite ocean of merit here, to counteract an infinite ocean of demerit in the creature, if in that way the question is to be viewed; which, however, I freely confess, my mind approveth not, to the degree in which I find it current amongst some orthodox and pious men.

APPLICATION OF CHRIST'S RIGHTEOUSNESS TO US

Now, besides this view of imputation, there is a second part, which seems necessary to complete the whole; and this is, the applying of Christ's righteousness to us, as the sins of others were applied unto him. For he "is made unto us righteousness" (1 Corinthians 1.3); we are "the righteousness of God in him" (2 Corinthians 5.21). This, also, I know they are wont to bring out of what I may call the theology of infinities; but for my part, I am inclined to look upon it as an original part of the purpose of God; or, if you please, an original condition of the covenant between the Father and the Son; of which nothing more can be said, than that it was according to the good pleasure of their will. But with respect to the thing itself, it consisteth of two parts: the first universal, the second elective, in its application. The universal being that which Christ in the flesh did for flesh—to wit, redeeming it from sin, and from the law which defined its sinfulness, and from death, and from corruption; and instating it in God's favour, forgiveness, and love; bestowing upon flesh immortality and resurrection. These things together constitute the gospel, and are a free bequest unto men, which we ministers are appointed to tell them of.

The other part, which is elective, Christ did not in the flesh, but received from his Father in gift and reward for that which in the flesh he had done: it is the gift of the Holy Ghost, by which to bring many sons unto glory. This latter, being the gift of the Father unto Christ, must be regarded as the Father's fulfilling his part of the covenant; and being given for the sake of as many as the Father pleaseth, and no more, doth constitute a peculiar people, a holy nation, an inheritance of Christ in the saints, and election in the midst of the redemption. Here, then imputation of Christ work is twofold: one, grace and peace unto all; a thing revealed and that may be proclaimed, yea, that ought to be proclaimed unto all. The other, regeneration of the Holy Ghost, union unto Christ's risen body, communication of his glory, and fellowship of his kingdom: a thing not to be preached unto all; a secret thing belonging to the Father; which men must be told they have not received, but have yet to receive, if the Father pleaseth; which men are to be told God the Father hath placed no interdict[5] against their receiving, while he hath continually revealed that it is a special gift and favour; which moreover, men cannot receive but in the faith and use of that common gift which they have all receive in Jesus Christ.

Now, as the extent of this higher imputation resteth with the Father, and is, indeed, that very right of his which maintaineth him Sovereign in the redemption, first Originator there as he is in creation, yea, as he is in the Godhead itself; so were I willing, and do incline to believe, that nothing more ought to be said upon this subject, save that it is the pleasure of the Father to extend it unto whomsoever it pleaseth him to extend it: and I do rather think it to be of evil consequence for men, similitudes derived from the market-place, to say that there is just so much merit as will cover the demerit of so many persons. But into this matter I enter no further; and having fairly, however, lamely, explained my view of imputation, the way is now clear for opening my views fully and fairly upon the subject of the reconciliation and atonement.

RECONCILIATION AND ATONEMENT

Of the doctrine taught in the first part of this discourse this is the sum:—That there was united in Jesus Christ, the Godhead, in the person of the Son, and the manhood, in its fallen state; and that the subsisted together in one person, in suchwise as that he was wholly without sin, holy and blameless in the sight of God. Now, by the grace of God, I will shew you how, in this incarnation of the Son of God, thus incarnate, in the fallen, and not the unfallen creature, is shewn forth and demonstrated the truth of the text—"God was in Christ reconciling the world unto himself; not imputing unto them their trespasses" (2 Corinthians 5.19). And to make this demonstration the more complete, I pray you to look back unto the beginning.

See the substance of mankind, now innumerably divided into living and dead persons, all shut up and contained in Adam, in a state of goodness with which the Godhead was well pleased. See it again, by the fall of our first parents; all brought into a state of sinfulness, most abhorrent unto the mind of a holy and righteous God; offending all his commandment, refusing him worship, and giving it unto stocks and stones, and four-footed creatures,

---

5. A prohibition.

and in all possible ways shewing forth a most hideous and irreconcilable enmity in the creature unto God. The question then is, How is this enmity of fallen man to be taken away? How is the world to be reconciled unto God? How is this sinful and sin-possessed creature to be delivered, sanctified, and brought into favour with God? As in an individual, even Adam, the enmity came, so in an individual, even Christ, the reconciliation came. And as from the first individual the enmity was propagated to many, yea, to all, so from the latter individual is the reconciliation propagated unto many. As is the fall, so is the remedy.

And how, then, was the reconciliation accomplished in the man Jesus Christ? and afterwards is it propagated from him unto other men? In the man Jesus Christ, there was the Godhead of the Son, which is the same in substance with the Godhead of the Father and of the Holy Ghost. There was also the manhood; the same in substance with the manhood of the other men, otherwise it is not manhood: "Verily, he took not on him the nature of angels, but he took on him the seed of Abraham" (Hebrews 2.16); "Forasmuch as the children are partakers of flesh and blood, he also himself likewise partook of the same" (Hebrews 2.14). Consider now attentively this the person of Christ. If the human substance which he hath taken be of a piece with mind and with yours as we are all of a piece with Adam, and can, through the union with the Godhead, be preserved pure, and blameless, and carried through death incorrupt, and brought into the presence of God perfectly holy, then it is made manifest that a fallen creature can be reconciled unto God, for it hath been done, it was done in the person of Christ; and the only question which will remain is, How is it to be done in other persons? How is to be propagated abroad unto many, as Adam's declension was propagated?

But if, on the other hand, Christ took not our substance in its fallen, but in its unfallen state, and brought this unto glory, then nothing whatever hath been proved with respect to fallen creatures, such as we are. The work of Christ toucheth not us who are fallen; there is no reconciliation of the fallen creature unto God; God is not in Christ reconciling a sinful world, but he is in Christ reconciling an unfallen world, which hath no sin, which is never fallen out with God? If God in Christ reconciling something to himself, that something must be, In Christ, reconciled with God. And what is there in Christ, but God and man? These two, that met in him therefore, and were reconciled, must be the same two between whom enmity had come. Do I say, then, that Christ was sinful, or did any sin, or that his temptations led him into any sin? If there was sin, how could there be reconciliation? No; he was holy. But was he liable to sin? Yes; he was tempted in all points like as we are. How could he be tempted like me, unless he were like me?

His Godhead could not be tempted; as it is written, "God cannot be tempted with evil" (James 1.13). Only, then, his manhood could be tempted. And how can any one be tempted or tried, unless he be liable to sin? Even Adam, before he fell, was liable to sin. If any one, therefore, say that Christ was not liable to sin, he doth say he was not a man; he doth say he is not come in the flesh; "for all flesh is grass, and the glory of it as the flower of the grass" (1 Peter 1.24); and if any man say that Christ is not come in the flesh, he is not of God. "This is that spirit of antichrist, whereof ye have heard that it should come, and even now already is in the world" (1 John 4.3).

Be it so then admitted, that Christ is come in the flesh, and was tried with all our infirmities, and tempted in all points, like as we are—which is a doctrine the most necessary to salvation, albeit now set light by, nay, and even reproved—you have at once redemption and reconciliation made sure. You have original sin taken away in him by the manner of his conceptions. He is not, as it were, an individual of the sinful individuals; he is not a human person; he never had personal subsistence as a mere man; he sees the whole mass and lump of fallen, sinful flesh; he submits himself unto his father to be made flesh; his Father sendeth the Holy Spirit to prepare him a body. This is done through means of a rational soul, which the Holy Spirit possessing doth therewith take up, from anywhere in the lump of existing flesh, a part; and when so forming a body the eternal Son of God humbleth himself to apprehend it, for ever to unite it to his own divine person; and thus, by creative act of Father, Son, and Holy Ghost, not by ordinary generation, Christ is constituted a divine and human nature in one person. He hath taken part with the children, with the fallen children; but he came by that part, not through connexion with Adam, but by his own free will, and his Father's free will, and the free will of the Holy Ghost; and thus original sin is avoided, though yet the body he took is in the fallen state, and liable to all temptations.

Now, then, consider ye how the reconciliation between these two most contrary and irreconcilable things is accomplished. Most people never think at all about the matter, and would fain not be troubled to think about is; but woe be to the minister, and woe be to the people together, who are content to lie sunk in such sloth, in such indifference to God's most principal and most glorious work: Hear me, then, patiently, and give diligent heed, while I explain to you this matter distinctly. The divine nature of Christ hath continual communion and identity with the Godhead, is of the Godhead, is the Godhead; dwelling with the Father, and in the Father, not the less because it acteth towards the creatures, through this body, and through it shall for ever act. By his divine nature, I say, with the Godhead he transacteth, and by his human nature he rendereth the will and purpose and action of the Godhead intelligible, visible, and perceptible to the creature. But before two instruments will render the same harmonious sound they must first be brought into tune with one another; and the question is, How shall human nature, in the fallen state, be brought to be in harmony with the acting of the holy Godhead? Ever since the fall, God and man have been at variance. The thing was not, that ever the human will had acted in harmony with the will divine; and how then is it now to be? How is a human nature to respond, truly and justly, and in all things to a divine nature? This is the reconciliation of which so much is made mention in Scripture. This is the atonement of which they make so much discourse, without knowing what they say or whereof they affirm. Atonement is not reparation, is not the cost or damage, but the being at one. It should be pronounced "at-one-ment."

What are the two things to be brought at one? Are they not God and sinful man, fallen man? And where are they to be brought at one, but in the person of Christ, where we have them now brought together without any original sin? If human nature be in itself so contrarious, so sinful, so very sinful, how shall it be brought in Christ to tell truly, for ever and ever, the mind, and will, and purpose of God unto the creatures? There is the difficulty: solve me this, and redemption and reconciliation are resolved. It is the work of God the Father, and of God the Holy Ghost, so to operate in and upon the fallen humanity of Christ, as that it shall be ever harmonious with the Godhead of Christ. This is what is meant by these words, "Thou has prepared a body for me" (Hebrews 2.14). The Son is willing to act through a body: the Father by the Holy Ghost expresseth his satisfaction with his Son's condescension, by preparing that body and making it fit for him to act through, so as to open unto the creatures the mystery of God; and through the body thus attuned unto divine harmony, the Son doth humble himself to act all his Father's mind, all the Godhead's mind. The preparing of the body is, I say, the great work of the Godhead working in the person of the Holy Ghost: the acting through it, whatever pleaseth God, is the great work of the Godhead, in the person of the Son; and the effect is, God reconciled in Christ unto a fallen world.

THE ENABLING OF THE SPIRIT

It now remaineth to examine how the Holy Ghost bringeth the body into this harmony with God. This difficulty must be met again, and not avoided. A sinful world, sinners such as those around me, want to know how they are to be reconciled, how their reconciliation hath been accomplished in Christ. "We are in earnest, and we are not to be shuffled out of our salvation by any subterfuges: therefore tell us plainly, how this great work was accomplished." By the grace of God, I will tell you. The Holy Ghost took up his residence in the soul of Christ: God had given the world unto the devil, and the devil had his residence in the fallen world around. The flesh of Christ was the middle space on which the powers of the world contended with the Holy Spirit dwelling in his soul. His flesh is the fit medium between the powers of darkness and the powers of light. And why fit? Because it is linked unto all material things, devil-possessed, while it is joined in closest, nearest union unto the soul, which in Christ was God-possessed, in the person of the Holy Ghost. His flesh is the fit field of contention, because it is the same on which Satan had triumphed ever since the fall.

Here, then, in the flesh of Christ, is the great controversy waged. Through this, Satan presented his temptations of appetite, of sight, of pride, trying him with the lust (desire) of the flesh, with the desire of the eye, with the pride of life. This did he at the very outset of his ministry, not that he had not done it before, or was not to do it after, or did not do it ever, but that it was then done in a manifest and notorious manner, that it might be capable of record and of tradition; and that such dreams might be prevented as I am now reproving, and that it might be for ever manifest and indubitable, that the Son had no favour, and that Satan had no let or hindrance in this great and terrible conflict. And when, at the end of his ministry, he said, "The prince of this world cometh, and findeth nothing in me" (John 14.30). He solemnly declareth, that during the whole of the fiery conflict which he had endured, and unto which he alone was conscious, Satan had never been able to make a lodgment, or gain a hold in his flesh; that though free to come in all his might, he had ever been repelled, as he was repelled in the wilderness; that his flesh thus oppressed, thus hideously oppressed, had never been able to sway his will, upholden in its steadfastness by the Holy Ghost; that the might of the Holy Ghost in his soul had been able to reconcile unto God the inveterate obstinacy and stubborn rebellion of flesh and blood; that for once the law of the flesh had not been able to drag down a soul unto perdition; that for once a soul had been able to draw up the flesh into reconciliation with the will of God; that all his life long the will of the flesh had been successfully withstood by the will of the Spirit, yea, that the will of the Spirit had enforced the flesh to do it unwilling service.

All this is signified by the expression which he used immediately before his agony, "Satan cometh, but findeth nothing in me." And it is signified, moreover, that Satan was then coming with an assault of a more dreadful and terrible kind, which is emphatically called "the hour and power of darkness" (Luke 22.53); and which, beginning from his agony, continued till his resurrection, partly without and partly within the veil, partly in the body and partly in the separate soul, partly upon earth and partly, as the Creed saith, in hell, understanding thereby the place of separate spirits. Which conflict being over, it was pronounced, not merely by word of man, "Satan hath nothing in me," but it was pronounced by the word of God, and that not by the word of God syllabling airy sounds in the vault of heaven, but by the word of God working through the Spirit that change of state which his body underwent in the hollow tomb.

Then indeed, when the Spirit had taken hold of the body also, when the divine glory and holiness struck its beams through the body also; then when matter stood purified by the Spirit: then when sinfulness, and corruption, and defectibility forsook flesh and blood, and incorruption and immortality, and infallibility, and holiness untemptible, and strength and almighty inhering and inhabiting, shone forth in that which heretofore had been human, fallible, temptible flesh, it was demonstrated by the finger of God, that reconciliation was accomplished between the Creator and the creature. And now was the body prepared, and not till now was the preparation of the body accomplished: and through that body, with harmony ever perfect, with variety of harmony infinite, with indubitable certainty shall the Godhead, in the person of the Son, express through the redeemed, risen, glorified manhood, all its purposes, and accomplish all its effects. So that the reconciliation begun in the Virgin's womb, between God and creation, is perfected in the womb of the earth, is acknowledged in the height of heaven, is honoured of the Father, as his chiefest work, with the chief place of the right hand of the throne of the Majesty on high. And thus, do you behold in the resurrection the reconciliation or at-one-ment accomplished between God and man, in the person of the Lord Jesus Christ, through the union of the Godhead to fallen humanity.

RECAPITULATION

Let us pause here, and see what we have attained unto. Of the whole fallen substance of manhood considered as one thing in Adam summed up, and in Adam assuming its present form, law, or condition, we have the Godhead, in the person of the Son, taking up a part, an integral part, with the same properties as all the rest. And this part is so empowered by the Holy Spirit, as to be in concert with the Godhead always, and at length is crowned of the Father, and seated on the throne of his majesty. If this had been any favoured part of the fallen material, then might the law of its redemption not have applied to the less favoured parts. If it had been a part that had never fallen, the law of its redemption would not have applied at all to the fallen substance of manhood. But seeing that it was the same of which all the brethren are partakers, it follows that what is accomplished in the whole; that reconciliation being made between God and one part of the fallen thing, reconciliation is made between God and the whole fallen substance. And therefore we may go about and preach reconciliation unto all the world, as it is in the text, already quoted, "God was in Christ reconciling the world unto himself, not imputing unto men their trespasses." We preach the resurrection unto all who have partaken of the death which came by Adam. We have a right to say, that as in Adam all have died, so in Christ all have been recovered from death, or made alive. And doubt can there be none, that Christ hath purchased unto himself right and lordship over all the fallen creatures; and in virtue of his resurrection shall raise them all from their graves,—some unto the resurrection of life, and others unto the resurrection of judgement. His resurrection makes him Lord of heaven, and Lord of hell. He hath purchased back the possession, and in doing it, he hath asserted likewise his lordship over the usurpers of the possession. Here then is redemption and reconciliation purchased for fallen mankind, by the incarnation of Christ, as truly and completely, and as extensively as in the fall by one man, even Adam, death and alienation were procured.

THE TWO WILLS IN JESUS CHRIST AND "AT-ONE-MENT"

To make this a little more manifest and forcible, it will be necessary that I speak here a little concerning the two wills or operations in Christ,—a subject which for several centuries agitated the church. The orthodox doctrine, and a doctrine it is of the most vital importance, holdeth that there were in Christ two wills or operations, which the Monothelites (who hold only one will in Christ), a class of heretics that grew out of the Eutychean stem, denied, asserting that there was only one operation, Theandric or Godmanly. Sergius proved, or attempted to prove, that it was proper to speak neither of one nor of two wills or operations; and Honorius, bishop of Rome, approved this course: but Sophronius, patriarch of Jerusalem, stoutly maintained that one ought to profess his faith to be, that there were two wills in Jesus Christ; which dogma was confirmed by the Sixth General Council of Constantinople, and the opinion of the Monothelites was condemned by the Catholic church;—as it hath likewise been condemned by the Church of England, in the acts of her convocation; and by the Church of Scotland, in her condemnation of the doctrine of Eutyches, which these single-will heretics always favoured, as they abominated the Council of Chalcedon, in which Eutyches was condemned. Now, I am well aware that the unbelieving spirit of this age, like the Emperor Heraclius, will be for imposing silence upon such questions as unimportant; and I confess they are altogether unimportant to those who see in Christ's work only the barter of so much suffering against so much suffering, of so much merit against so much demerit. But to those, who consider the atonement as the deeper mystery of the reconciliation of the holiness of God to the unholiness of the fallen creature, and the taking out of the way the law of commandments, which is the expression of the enmity between God's holiness and the fallen creature, it is a question of the utmost importance, and most necessary to the complete exposition of the reconciliation or at-one-ment.

Those who say that there is but one will in Christ, either make him only God, or only man. There is the absolute will of the Godhead, and there is the limited will of the creature. These two may be consentaneous with one another, which is holiness; or they may be dissentient from one another, which is unholiness in the creature; but the one cannot be the other without confounding two most opposite things, the Creator and the creature, and introducing the doctrine of Spinosa, the doctrine of the Eastern sophists and Western savans; that God is the soul of the world; that he is diffused through the creatures, and that the creature is of him a part. If, again, you say with Sergius, that the operation in Christ is neither divine nor human, but a mixture of both, as he called it, Theandric or Godmanly, you do confuse the two natures of Christ, and make one between them, which is neither God's nature nor man's nature, but an unknown something lying between them both, with which man hath no sympathy, or rather no consubstantiality; with which God hath no consubstantiality, and therefore, which cannot be Mediator between God and man. This also leads directly to the confusing of the Creator with the creature, in the person of Christ, and therefore to everything evil besides; and again bringeth out God to be the soul of the world, and the world a part of God. It is therefore, however little apprehended by our debtor-and-creditor divines, no less than to confuse and confound all things, thus to permit such points of doctrine as this to remain in error, or even under silence.

Now the orthodox doctrine is, that there were two wills in Christ; the one the absolute will of the Godhead, which went on working in its infinite circles, the other a man's will, which was bounded by the limited knowledge, the limited desires, the limited affections, and the limited actions of manhood; a divine nature, and a human nature, God and man. The orthodox doctrine holdeth, moreover, that from the incarnation onwards, and for ever, the Son of God never thought, felt, or acted, but by condescending out of the infinitude of the divine will, into the finiteness of the human will;

in which condescension, the self-sacrifice, and humiliation, and grace, and goodness of the Godhead are revealed: without which condescension these attributes of the Godhead could never have been known unto the creatures. This condescension it is which giveth an infinite value to every act of Christ,—in the Father's sight, inasmuch as it makes him know and obtains his great purpose of self-manifestation;—in the creature's sight, inasmuch as it shews unto the creature the great free-will condescension of the Son, by which the Father is made known, and the Holy Spirit communicated. Moreover, the attributes of thought, feeling, and action, under which the Godhead is represented in the Old Testament, before the incarnation, appertain not to the absolute will of the Godhead, which hath no limitation of space or time, no creature mind, nor creature will, but appertain to the Godhead, contemplating itself as about to be united to the manhood by incarnation of the Son; so that all revelation is truly an anticipation by word, like as all creation is an anticipation by act of the great thing which was accomplished by the union of two wills or operations in Christ; or, to express this truth in Scripture language, the Spirit of Prophecy is the testimony of Jesus. It is not to tell out the truth fully, to say that such expressions as God changeth, God repenteth, are accomodations to man's way of speaking: they are anticipations of God's way of shewing himself, by taking the nature of man into the personality of the Son, and through that nature acting the purposes of the Godhead by the creatures. And human language itself is a great, and, next to creation, the greatest, work of God unto the same great end; and Christ the Creator is only worthy to be expressed by Christ the Word.

Be it so, then, that unto every thought, word and act of Christ, there concurreth two operations; an operation in the infinite Godhead, and an operation in the finite manhood; and that these two operations are not the operations of two persons, but of one person only; and what result and inference have you, but this most sublime, most perfect one, that the actings of the Godhead, all the volitions, purposes, and actings of the Godhead, are consentaneous with, are one with, all the volitions, all the actings, of the manhood of Christ? For the Godhead never acteth but by the Son; and the Son never acteth unto the creatures, but by the manhood, which with his Godhead, formeth one person. Wherefore, this sublime, this perfect truth is for ever incorporated in the person of Christ: that Godhead and manhood are not in amity merely, not in sympathy merely, not in harmony and consociation merely, but in union, unity, and unition, hypostatical or consubstantial. I would not give the truth expressed in these words of the Catechism, "Two distinct natures, and one person for ever,"[6] for all the truths

6. This appears to be a reference to the Westminster Shorter Catechism.

that by human language have ever been expressed. I would rather have been the humblest defender of this truth in the four ecumenical councils of the church than have been the greatest reformer of the church, the father of the Covenant, or the procurer of the English constitution. But we must bridle our spirit, and yoke our strength again unto the argument.

At-one-ment, or reconciliation, is a mere notion, figure of speech, or similitude, until it be seen effected in the constitution of the person of Christ, under these two wills or operations. I object not to the similitude taken from paying debts, nor to the similitude taken from redeeming captives, nor to the similitude taken from one man's dying in the room of another, nor to any of the infinite similitudes which St Paul useth most eloquently and most fitly for illustrating and enforcing this most precious truth of the at-one-ment, or reconciliation; but the similitudes are, to my mind, only poor helps for expressing the largeness, fulness, and completeness of the thing which is done by the Word's being made flesh, and which is exhibited as done, by the placing of the God-man on the right hand of the Majesty on high, visible Head, effective Ruler of the created worlds, and of the intelligent creatures which possess them. This head actor of all things enacted, this being comprehensive of all beings created, great fountain of life, full ocean of animation, is in every thought, in every act, God and man, God's will and man's will, in one person united. Everything, therefore, thence flowing, circling wide as creations utmost bound; every occurrence, every accident, every attribute, every act, every relation, every change, every position which together constitute the variety of life in the creation redeemed and ruled by Christ, is in very truth a demonstration of manhood at one with Godhead, because it is all thought, spoken, and done by the person, the one person, who is all his thoughts, words, and doings, is God and man. What reconciliation like this reconciliation, what at-one-ment like this at-one-ment?

From this great head of orthodox doctrine, that there were two wills or operations—the one absolute divine, the other the limited creature will, between which perfect unity in one person was preserved, and so reconciliation between God and the creatures established, not upon the conditions of a covenant merely, or by the commutation of suffering merely, but by the very being of Christ, and in his being, and in every one of his actions, and in all his eternal government, of all creation;—from this only fit and only sufficient demonstration of that atonement and reconciliation which the creature languisheth, dieth, to know and be assured of, even from this truth of truths, the two distinct natures of God and man in one person, Satan, as his custom is, hath deduced one of the foulest and most culpable heresies which he hath ever at hand, to hinder fearful and ignorant people from listening to the subject, and so to remove them away from the knowledge of the hidden mystery, and most blessed consolation of the truth in Christ. The heresy to which I allude is part of the Borigninian heresy against which our church beareth continual testimony in the questions which she putteth to every preacher before giving him license, and again before ordaining him over a flock. The heresy is, that the human will of Christ was unholy, or contradictive of the divine will, which is an abomination so much to be abhorred, as the truth of their harmony and unity set forth above is prized. For the at-one-ment or reconciliation, effected by the two harmonious consenting wills, divine and human, in the one person of Christ, would be distinctly and flatly denied, avoided, and destroyed, if it could ever be said that the human will aboded not in, and assented not to, and set not forth, the will divine. The atonement, the redemption, the reconciliation, standeth or falleth with the personal unity of the two distinct natures of Christ.

Now this error cometh from the Nestorian stem which maintained two persons to be joined together in the Christ, harmonizing with each other by friendship, consociation, and sympathy, and not by personality: but by what manner of malice, by what blindness of malice, dare they to affix such a tenet upon the orthodox, who maintain the very contrary, and rest all Christian doctrine upon the contradiction of it? It is, for I know it well, because we say and will maintain unto death, that Christ's flesh was as rebellious as ours, as fallen as ours. But what then? is Christ's flesh the whole of his creature-being? No: it is his humanity inhabited by the Holy Ghost, which maketh up his creature-being. And, through the power of the Holy Ghost, acting powerfully and with effect to the resisting, to the staying, to the overcoming of the evil propensity of the fallen man, it is, that the fallen manhood of Christ is made mighty, and holy, and good, and every way fit to express the will of the Divinity. Be it known unto these gainsayers, that in Christ, and in the soul redeemed by Christ, and in the world redeemed by Christ, we can do as ill without the divinity of the Son. We have a fallen world to redeem, we have the Son of God to redeem it: but these two must not intermingle or be confused with each other; and therefore, in order to make that fallen creature harmonious with the Godhead of the Son, and so to obtain one person, we must also have in it the life of the Holy Ghost, overcoming the death of sin.

THE TRINITARIAN GRAMMAR OF REDEMPTION

Ye may be able to state out the redemption, without a Trinity of persons in the Godhead: I lay claim to no such ability. Your trinity is an idle letter in your creed; but it is the soul, the life of mine. Your Christ is a suffering

God; I know it well; my Christ is a gracious, condescending God, but a suffering man. In your Christ, you see but one person in a body. My Christ is the Trinity manifested; not merely the Trinity told of, but the Trinity manifested. I have the Father manifested in everything which he doth; for he did not his own will, but the will of his Father. I have the Son manifested, in uniting his divinity to a humanity prepared for him by the Father; and in making the two most contrary things to meet and kiss each other, in all the actings of his widest, most comprehensive being. I have the Holy Ghost manifested in subduing, restraining, conquering, the evil propensities of the fallen manhood, and making it an apt organ for expressing the will of the Father; a fit and holy substance to enter into personal union with the untempted and untemptible Godhead. And who is he that dares stand up and impugn these eternal truths? Be he whom he may, the devil himself, with all his legions, I will uphold them against him for ever; and I will say moreover, that in upholding these, I am upholding the atonement, the redemption, the reconciliation, the regeneration, the kingdom, and the glory of God.

Doth any one doubt that there was in the flesh of Christ a repugnancy to suffer, a liability to be tempted in all things as we are tempted, and which was only prevented from falling before temptation by the faith of his Father's promises, and by the upholding of the Holy Spirit? Then I ask that man, What is Christ? a man? No—for fallen manhood doth nothing but sin. A creature? No—for defectibility is the very thing which distinguisheth creature from Creator. None whatever, save, as these heretics hold, some preexistent heavenly humanity, which passed through the virgin unto the earth, as by a canal, without partaking of her substance. And then, to what amounteth the history of his life? whereto serveth it? For imitation, for consolation, for assurance? What model have we of the Holy Ghost's manner of working? What proof that the Holy Ghost is able to prevail against the fallen creature's evil functions; what at-one-ment or reconciliation is there between God and fallen creature? An at-one-ment indeed there is between God and this sublimated and super-celestial humanity of yours; but what is that to me, who am earthly, sensual, and devilish? And what is Christ's intercession to me, and what his mediation, and what my love and obligation to him? for to me it was not that he condescended, but to some other creature, of some other kind.

The whole life of Christ is a demonstration of this one thing, that the second person and the third person of the Godhead, conjoined, after their proper modes, with the creature, are able through the creature to make manifest unto the fallen creatures, and in the fallen creature, the manifold wisdom of God. His hunger, his thirst, his weariness, his temptation of Satan, his shrinking from the cup which his Father gave him to drink, his saying in so many words, "not my will, but thine be done," his grief of spirit, his zeal, his sympathy, his tears, his love, his pity, his every affection and action shew that his flesh had the same, the self-same dispositions and inclinations as the flesh of other men, which yet in him were restrained, were withstood, were overcome, attained not unto a volition, attained not unto an action; and if they attained unto a word, it was not a word of purpose or of wish, but only a word for our information, to tell us that he was of our very substance, and had the fellow-feeling of all our pains. And he lived by faith as we do, upon God's written and recorded Word; as Paul solemnly declareth, quoting from the Old Testament, what occureth not in one place, but in a hundred places, yea, I may say, wherever Christ is spoken of, "I will put my trust in him" (Hebrews 2.13). But is faith dishonourable? Ye fools, it is most honourable and holy. Doubt is that which is dishonourable and sinful. Now, like as Christ teacheth us, by his agony, how his flesh shrunk back in the prospect of that which it was to endure; not infinite measures as they say of human suffering, but simple, single, human suffering; even so doth he teach us by that word which he spake at the grave of Lazarus, how truly he lived by faith, and how desirous he was that this great head of doctrine should be acknowledged and believed. "Jesus lifted up his eyes, and said, Father, I thank thee that thou hast heard me; and I know that thou hearest me always, but because of the people which stand by, I said it, that they may believe that thou hast sent me" (John 11.41–42).[7]

JESUS AS UNIVERSAL REPRESENTATIVE

We may say, therefore, that in the flesh of Christ, all flesh represented;—that, in the flesh of Christ all the infirmities, sin, and guilt, of all flesh was gathered into one; and in the great triumph which the Godhead attained over the confederate powers of darkness and of wickedness in the holy, blameless life of Christ, that sin was vanquished and condemned in the flesh, and Jesus became Lord of living flesh by right of redemption; and that he hath conveyed by his victorious life unto all men a redemption from the slavery and bondage of sin, which Satan had obtained for himself, and over which he held power. And to this agrees the word of the apostle, "for what the law could not do, in that it was weak through the flesh, God sending his own Son in the likeness of sinful flesh; and for sin condemned sin in the flesh"

---

7. Irving illustrates his case by a lengthy extract from a letter he received from an unnamed correspondent. This extract can be found in Irving, *CW* 5, 172–74.

(Romans 8.3): that is to say, the law could not get the better of sin; and to accomplish this, the incarnation of the Son of God was necessary, "not in the likeness of angels, not in the likeness of sinless flesh, but in the likeness of sinful flesh" or as it is in the original, "in likeness of flesh, of sin, and about sin," that is, "with a view to sin, condemned the sin in the flesh."

This having accomplished, the law was made bootless. The law had revealed the weakness of the flesh, and proved that when a being should in flesh, and keep the law, that being was more than man. The law did serve to establish Christ God, by differencing him from every other being in flesh and blood subsisting. He took the weakness, he took the sinfulness; in one word, he took the fallenness of flesh; or, to use the Scripture language, "God made him sin for us" (2 Corinthians 5.21); and being thus constituted by might of holiness divine, he strangled the serpent in his very cradle, and triumphed over him until his death; so that flesh is not any more heir to sin; sin is not any more imputed unto men. Our infirmities and our diseases are borne. Sin may skulk about us like a condemned thing, or abide in us like an imprisoned thing; but it hath no law nor liberty. We are heirs to righteousness, to justification, to power, as it is written, "him that knew not sin he hath made sin for us, that we might become God's righteousness in him." God's righteousness, therefore, are we become in Christ; and if so, then Christ was made the offering for sin, and in him sin is swallowed up, and out of him floweth an everlasting righteousness, which is called God's righteousness, because it is the only righteousness God accounteth such.

We fondly think that there is a righteousness in us. We fondly think that if Adam had stood, there would have been nothing but righteousness, never believing that Adam's fall was as necessary to the bringing in of Christ as Adam's creation;—necessary for this very end, of shewing that there was, and could be, no righteousness of God, but that which flowed from his own Son in the creature-form; and therefore, until he came, creation went on lounging deeper and deeper into sin. Christ therefore is the fountain of righteousness, as he is the fountain of everything else, and thus he standeth unto the creatures; bright Sun of light, life, purity, and goodness. Moreover, Christ was made sin for us, and weakness for us, and a curse for us, that he might be able to taste of death for every man, and to overcome him who had the power of death. Death proved the creature not to have life in itself; in order that he who had life in himself, might be proved more than the creature, that he might be proved the Life. Satan had this power over death given to him, that by taking it from him Christ might be proved the more powerful, the living one. And all men had been brought under Satan's dominion of the grave, in order that by the resurrection of all from the grave,

Christ might be demonstrated Lord of all, Lord of life, the Resurrection and the Life.

By his death, moreover, the infirmity of all flesh dies; and in his resurrection the life of all flesh arose; and in his ascension to the right hand of God flesh ascended above angels, and principalities, and powers. And in the descent of the Spirit, God-manhood bestowed God's righteousness, God's life unto manhood in the flesh; and thus in Christ is God's glory unto the creature manifested, is God's glory in the creature vested, is God's glory by the creature communicated, is God's work through the creature accomplished. And all that was done at creation by God, under the assumed limitation of creature-form, is done over again, or rather is perfected in its doing by Christ, in whom that assumed form was realised. And what is the preaching of Christ? Is it not even the forth-setting of him unto all men; as having wrought for all men this unspeakable redemption; as having delivered flesh from the power of sin, and from the power of death; as having purchased for us the good-will and favour of God, which we had lost and forfeited; as having attained unto the undisputed lordship over us; as having the keys of hell and of death. This is the glad tidings, this is the good news, this is the gospel of the grace of God, this is the ministry of reconciliation through the faith of Christ. And when thus freely, fully, intelligently, and unequivocally preached, it is that the gospel proveth to be the power of God, and the wisdom of God. And when this message is believed, I will now shew you the standing into which it brings the creature unto God

This unspeakable and inestimable work of Christ in the flesh for every man, as it is written, "That he, by the grace of God, should taste death for every man" (Hebrews 2.9); and again, "Who is the Saviour of all men, especially of them that believe" (1 Timothy 4.10); and again, "That through death he might destroy him that had the power of death, and deliver them who, through fear of death, were all their lifetime subject to bondage" (Hebrews 2.15);—this ineffable benefit wrought for mankind; this redemption and resurrection of its estate, all done, all accomplished, and all freely presented unto the world through Christ, and in Christ, is God's argument against the argument of Satan, is faith and hope's good against the good of sense, is Christ's plea against nature's, made, and by preaching proclaimed, unto the four quarters of the world. And wherever this is proclaimed rightly, men are brought under the penalty of having rejected, or under the benefit of having received God's Christ,—of having rejected or of having received God himself. And now it is, when the gospel hath been preached unto him, that man discovereth what is the true dignity and use of his reason,—namely, for the sake of weighing and deciding between these two claimants; the world as it is seen out of God, lying in the evil one, and the world as it is believed by faith to lie in Christ, the Holy One. Reason is able to apprehend the good, as well as the evil. The fallen man is not one who knows only evil, but one who knows good and evil: as it is written, "And the Lord said, Behold, the man is become as one of us, to know good and evil" (Genesis 3.22).

In Christ risen, having wrought his work, and achieved his conquest, the good to be perused, to be known, to be believed, is held up to fallen man. Blessed object of hope! blessed object of holiness! blessed object of all goodness! This is our office as preachers and ministers of the reconciliation, to hold it up before you, to lay it open unto your various faculties of desire, of hope, of faith, to instate you in the possession of it by sacramentary seals, to enfeoff[8] you in its holiness with sacramental washing of water, to enfeoff you in its bodily substance, with bread and wine, and in every possible way which human wisdom can devise to secure man in the assurance that Christ's reconciliation and redemption is as truly the common inheritance of the race, and will as truly be proved so by the resurrection of all, as sin is proved to be the common inheritance of the race, by the death of all.

Thus, then, men are brought into a strait between two. On the one hand, the devil's world of sight, dressing out to them its blessedness, its dignity, its heaven: on the other hand, Christ's "world to come, the habitable world to come, whereof we speak" (Hebrews 2.5), dressing out to them, by the minister's voice, its true blessedness, its true dignity, its true heaven, to be enjoyed and possessed after the resurrection. Both these worlds, Satan's and Christ's, are capable of being known and apprehended by every man; but the knowledge and apprehension of a thing is not the possession of it. Reason, God's creature, unto which Christ is addressed by the preacher, even as Christ in flesh was addressed unto sense, likewise God's creature; reason, being thus dealt withal, straightway discovereth the bondage of the will. She would put forth her hand and take also of the tree of life, and eat and live for ever. But she findeth that she cannot; and if we preach no more than this reconciliation, we would agonise men, and not bless them. We see it, we would possess it, but the devil is too mighty for us. Then he saith, Cast yourselves upon God, for that help which you truly need. He sent not his Son to tantalise, nor yet to agonise, but to bless and save you. You have apprehended those good things that are in Christ, even life and immortality; that is God's argument for you to trust in him. He hath sent out his Son, in reason's form arrayed, with man's perfectibility and with man's perfection, as his boon to man, in order that thou, O creature man, might know how merciful a Creator thou hast, how good, how gracious; and that thou mightest bless him for the reason thou possessest to apprehend these things—for the

---

8. Archaic term meaning to invest someone with a possession

capacities thou possessest to inherit them—for the inheritance itself, for the life itself, which now is brought out unto thee, from the purpose of the eternal, in the person of Christ. Thou sayest truly, that there is a mighty work yet to do. That work is with the Father; and if thou wilt not trust the Father to do it—him who is thy rightful Creator, and who now hath manifested himself thy reconciled Father, if thou wilt not trust—then assuredly thou art proved twice dead, twice rebellious. To thee Christ hath indeed died in vain. Thou preferrest present death and future resurrection unto judgement and eternal death; thy perdition thou preferrest to the Creator's authority and a Father's love. Thou tramples upon Christ, whom he hath sent, and in whom he hath vested all power, visible and invisible. Thou shalt be brought up to judgement out of thy grave, by the voice of him whom now thou wilt not hear; and by virtue of his death thou shalt receive power of resurrection, and shalt bear up in thyself through eternity the righteousness and justice of his lordship, as the blessed shall bear up the grace and mercy of the same. Thus it is, holy brethren, that the universal reconciliation which Christ's death hath wrought, and the universal restoration unto life which his resurrection hath wrought, instead of being the support of universal salvation, is the support of universal right and lordship over all the creatures, which for the present doth constitute the world in him to stand, and for him obligated unto the Father; and hereafter shall constitute the world in two estates, of eternal and infallible blessedness, or eternal and unchangeable misery—the one in virtue of his lordship honoured, the other in virtue of his lordship dishonoured; the one vessels unto honour, the other vessels unto dishonour.[9]

Part 3: The Removal of the Law

Having thus explained how, out of the union of the God-head and fallen manhood, in the person of Christ, there cometh perfect and complete reconciliation and atonement between God and the fallen creatures, I have now to shew how this is accompanied with the removal of the law; not any particular law, or part of the law, but law in general, as proceeding from the mouth of God unto his fallen creatures. The grace of God, the goodness of God is, I may say, hindered from being known and communicated where the law is present, which is the expression of God's holy indignation against sin. The law is the form of the enmity between God and the fallen creatures,

9. The omitted material can be found in Irving, *CW*, 179–202.

which came not into existence from the beginning; for the promise was before the law, in order that it might be seen that grace, and not severity, was the end of the fall. Therefore, God pronounced upon Eve and Adam, and the earth, certain judgments, under the hope of a redemption from them; which judgments still continued to afflict the condition of men. But as yet he gave not the law; and long before he brought in that excessive bondage, he had given the covenant unto Noah, and the promise unto Abraham. And then, for greater manifestation, and for further punishment of sin, he imposed the law, which came by Moses, and was removed by Christ. The law, therefore, is the great sign and standing monument of God's unreconciled mind towards men. Most necessary therefore it is, that I should set forth, under this head of the atonement and reconciliation, how we are delivered from law, and placed under grace. In the course of which demonstration, it will appear how futile, how idle and profitless, are the notions of those who will not receive the method of the incarnation, by the personal union of the divine nature and fallen human nature; and new strength will be brought to the orthodox doctrine which we maintain.

THE FALL AND KNOWLEDGE OF OUR CREATUREHOOD AND THE GRACE OF GOD

To open this subject fairly, it will be necessary to go back a little in the history of creation and redemption, of which I have demonstrated, in the former discourse, the great end to be the glory of God. And into that general subject I mean not to inquire further, but am willing to discourse somewhat particularly concerning the scheme, as it hath relation unto the law. The very end of the fall was to put the proper difference between the Creator and the creature; and to shew the creature that the source and the continuance of its being was from God, and not in any way from itself. If any one ask me, "And could not this, without a fall, have been accomplished?" I am ready to answer, As to that I cannot tell; but I believe that this was the best way of accomplishing it. The creature being put to silence, and its pretensions to power and being, in itself, entirely negatived by sin and death, God proceeded by demonstrations of his grace to make known, even from the beginning, his own Son incarnate in the creature, as the only object of its hope for deliverance, and the only source of its strength for endurance; or, in one word, as the life.

Of this grace the promise, and the possession also, was first given unto Abraham; wherefore he is emphatically called by the apostle, "He that had received the promises." Anterior to Abraham, the world was not without witnesses; yet Abraham is called the Father of the Faithful, and from him the dispensation of righteousness imputed unto faith, is always in the Holy Scriptures made to begin. Abraham is the head of the church, or election, and answereth in his circumcised person unto the baptized persons now in the world; but before Abraham, the world, the whole race, had been brought under covenant in the person of Noah, whose preservation in the ark, with all his house, and with all the creatures of the earth, is significant of that common preservation of mankind, and deliverance from the power and thraldom of sin and Satan, which Christ purchased by his death, whereby he is said to be the Saviour of all men, and the propitiation, not for our sins only, but for the sins of the whole world. And that sanctification of blood, which was part of the covenant with Noah, giving unto sacrifice its peculiar sanctity, doth point unto the blood of Christ, as the propitiation and purchase of man's life, and the life of the world he dwelleth on, from the just and righteous indignation of God; so that, as in Abraham you have the election according to grace standing represented, in Noah you have the redeemed race likewise standing represented; and therefore the present constitution of the world and the church, which hath obtained since the coming of Christ, had its existence in promise and expectation, even from the deluge;—sacrifice being unto all men the proclamation of the one sacrifice, which taketh away the sin of the world; and circumcision, or the putting away the filth of the flesh, being the proclamation unto the church, of the work of the Spirit to crucify the flesh, with its corruptions and lusts. Here, then, from the deluge, we have the world under a dispensation of universal redemption, with a church in it under the dispensation of particular election; and the only difference between our condition and theirs is this, that theirs was prospective, or prophetic—ours partly retrospective, and partly prophetic; they looking forward unto him that was to come; we looking backward unto him that is come, and forward unto the same one that is to come again.

THE LAW AND THE GOSPEL

Thus, then, the world stood, under general and particular promise of grace, until the time that the law was given. Now, be it observed, that the law was not given unto all the world, but only unto the church, the circumcised church. It went not to the bounds of the covenant of Noah, but was confined within the limits of the covenant of Abraham. And why this limitation? For many reasons, but chiefly for this, that the Jew might have no reason to boast himself over the Gentile, that they who had the covenants of promise might also have the condemnation of the law; that, their sins being made to abound through the law, they might be preserved as much as possible from self-righteousness, and taught to prize the special and peculiar grace which they had in the covenant of circumcision. And the world which was without law was left to the law written on their hearts, to the excusing or the accusing of their own thoughts; they that are without law being judged without law. Hence it is, that the apostle, in the Epistle to the Romans, being minded to prove all men under sin, and the whole world guilty before God, doth make his case out against the world, in the first chapter, by shewing their sins against conscience and against nature; but against the Jews he maketh out his case by shewing their sins against the law.

The Law, Human Infirmity, and Sin

The law is the voice of God, telling us of the evil. When man fell, he came to know both good and evil, whereas formerly he had known only good; this goodness, being all departed out of the physical world, had its visible object only in hope of seeing Christ, and being goodness unto the undeserving, it hath the name of grace. Unto the knowledge and desire of good in man, Christ therefore was addressed, and God in Christ. Unto the evil that is in man, the world which is seen was addressed; and thus religion came into controversy with worldliness, and the future into controversy with the present—the object of good being in the future, the object of evil being in the present visible world.

Now, with which of these doth the law rank? Holdeth it of the conscience of good, or of the conscience of evil? I say it holdeth of the conscience of evil. If the gospel be the voice of God addressed unto the conscience of good, then, I say, the law is the voice of God addressed unto the conscience of evil. And out of this opposition, between the law and the gospel arose that heretical notion in the primitive church, that the law was created by the evil principle, and the gospel created by the good. The law is by the apostle absolutely called sin, even as Christ, when under the law, is likewise called sin. And that the law hath sin, and not righteousness, for its object, is well declared: "Until the law, sin was in the world; but sin is not imputed where there is no law" (Romans 5.13). And that it hath not righteousness for its object is declared in that passage, "If righteousness could come by the law, then is Christ dead in vain" (Galatians 2.21). The law, therefore, was added, that the offence might abound, and that sin might be shewn to be exceeding sinful.

But before entering at large upon this subject, I would have it confirmed under sanction of the written word; and to this end, I ask you to turn with me to the 7th chapter of the Romans, from the beginning.

> Know ye not, brethren, [for I speak to them that know the law,]
> how that the law hath dominion over a man as long as he liveth
> [or, it liveth]? For a woman which hath an husband is bound by
> the law to her husband so long as he liveth; but if the husband
> be dead, she is loosed from the law of her husband. So then if,
> while her husband liveth, she be married to another man, she
> shall be called an adulteress: but if her husband be dead, she is
> free from that law; so that she is no adulteress, though she be
> married to another man. Wherefore, my brethren, ye also are
> become dead to the law by the body of Christ; that ye should be
> married to another, even to him who is raised from the dead,
> that we should bring forth fruit unto God. (Romans 7.1–3)

In these verses, the church is set forth as a wife who hath been twice married: in the first instance, to the law; in the second instance, to him that is raised from the dead; of whom the former husband must be dead before she can be wedded unto the second. But seeing that we are wedded unto the risen Christ, the apostle affirmeth that either the law is dead or the church an adulteress. Now, how doth the law become dead to us, and we dead to the law? [Paul] himself answereth the question,—By the body of Christ, which nailed the law along with himself unto the cross, took it into the grave, and left it there, along with his body of sin and death, when he took his body of life and righteousness. And so, bridegroom-like, in beautiful garments he went forth from his chamber, like a strong man rejoicing to run his race of glory and of might. Unto him, then, not in humanity under the law, but unto him in glory above all law, Lord of all, the church is now married, to the end that we should bring forth fruit unto God. Wedded unto this Husband, branches of this Vine, the church bringeth forth much fruit unto God, whereby the Father is glorified.

But being wedded unto the law, what is the fruit that she bringeth forth? A fruit unto death, in direct contrast to the former. For is it not written in the next verse, "When we were in the flesh, the motions of sin (or as it is in the margin, the passions of sin), which are by the law, did work with energy in our members, unto the end of fruitbearing for death?" (Romans 7.5). What a word is this to those who will live under the law! It is here expressly declared, that the law is the seed of sin, which doth quicken the substance of sin, already in our flesh, and make it bring forth fruit unto death; not unto God, but unto death. Now, this is the reason for which I am setting my face steadfastly against the law; because it is the masculine parent of sin, and doth awaken and fructify the passion for sin which is in the flesh. It is the life of the flesh, the joy of the flesh; and where works are preached, the natural man is glad.

Now what saith the apostle further in this most wonderful and curious discourse, concerning the law? "Now, however, are we delivered from the law, that being dead wherein we were held; that we should serve in newness of spirit, and not in the oldness of the letter" (Romans 7.6). Can anything be more explicit to declare our deliverance from the law, and the law's deadness to us, and our deadness unto it? Can anything be more joyful unto the uncarnal and spiritual man, than such a deliverance from that which engendereth in the flesh only sin and death? "We are delivered from the law, that being dead," or, as it is in the margin, "being dead to that wherein we were held." And what is the fruit of this deliverance? Is it license? No; but it is liberty. Is it adultery? No; but it is honourable and fruitful marriage. Subjection unto the spiritual Parent of good in our spirit, and deliverance from the parent of sin in our flesh. Yes; there is a service still: but it is service not known until the Spirit was given, or but dimly known by those who being under the law, yet forgat not that they were under the promise,—service in newness of spirit, and not in oldness of the letter. The willing obedience of the law of liberty, "written, not with ink, but with the Spirit of the living God; not in tables of stone, but on the fleshly tables of the heart" (2 Corinthians 3.3).

Hear the divine apostle, still farther, upon his favourite theme; hear the great law-breaker, the great law-destroyer, and magnifier of the grace of God, who boasteth that he had destroyed the law, and looketh upon himself as a most heinous transgressor, if he should lay a stone to rear it up again, saying, "For if I built again the things which I destroyed, I make myself a transgressor" (Galatians 2.18). [He continues] "What shall we say then? Is the law sin? Be it not spoken, but sin I had not known except by means of the law; for covetousness had I not seen, except the law had said, Thou shalt not covet. Sin, however, taking occasion by the commandment, wrought in me all covetousness; for without the law, sin were dead" (Romans 7.7). This is marvelous exceedingly. The apostle acquits the law of the sin, which he had asserted was bred between the law and the flesh: he will not allow the law to be sin in itself, though the occasion of sin in him, as it were awakening it from its dormancy; yea, he saith, quickening it from its death; for without the law sin was dead, even as unto a wicked lustful person the most virtuous object is the occasion of sin, without any sin in itself, but contrariwise haply the greatest aversion to it.

So the apostle doth set forth the pure and holy law, the beautiful and perfect law, the chaste virtuous and severe law, as the occasion of all sin in the weak and sinful flesh of man. And as an instance of it, he quoteth the Christian commandment, which forbiddeth covetousness of everything that is our neighbour's; and he declares not merely, that he would not have *known* the sin of covetousness, but that he would not have *seen* it, had it not been for that commandment which said, "Thou shalt not covet:" but so soon as he knew that same commandment, sin in him stirred up all manner of covetousness and concupiscence, spiting as it were the commandment of God, shewing herself to be mistress of the flesh, and more powerful than the commandment. As an usurper, Pharaoh, for example, rageth more against his slaves, when the idea or hope of liberty stirreth amongst them; so sin, potent empress of the flesh, kindleth into fury, and violently rageth, and worketh all manner of contradiction and contravention of that holy law, which the flesh knoweth to be good, but skilleth not to keep, because it is overruled by another, and by a greater than itself. Great idea! blessed God, and likewise favoured man, from whom, and through whom, this great idea came! Let my soul learn to embrace it, and to possess it. Let me forget the law that I may remember my risen Lord, for I cannot be married unto them both. Let me cease from the commandment, that I may cease from sin. Let me die unto the law, that I may live unto Christ; for, as saith the blessed apostle, "I through the law am dead to the law, that I may live unto God!" (Galatians 2.19). Now, brethren, tell me whether you think the language of such divines as Luther, the language of such preachers as myself be, or be not, consentaneous[10] with the language of the blessed apostle.

The Law and the Holiness of God

Taking this text for our warrant, we would now set ourselves to discourse concerning the law and its removal from the church; for the law is the form of the enmity which came by Moses, between the holiness of God and the wickedness of the fallen creature.

There is in the law such a purity and fitness for producing human well-being; there is so much good sense in the Ten Commandments, so much right feeling, so much beauty of virtue and righteous judgment, that every good and wise man seeketh earnestly and desireth fervently to put himself under such a goodly system of morality, which is at once the perfection of moral philosophy, the code of justice, the guide of affection, the sum of religion, the bulwark of society, and the stay of life; insomuch that I know

10. Suited; expressing agreement.

not what preternatural power is required to separate a man from this form of wisdom, which is all redolent with humanity, and with humanity's noblest forms. The only thing capable of divorcing between the moral law and human nature is the inexorable holiness of God, which will not be satisfied with anything short of its complete obedience. If the law would relax a little to the infirmities of the flesh; if it would be gentle, and tender, and gracious, and look not so much to our shortcomings as to our attainments; or if it would tarry a while and wait the gradual progress of virtue; or if it would forget the past transgressions in our present endeavour to do our best; or if, moreover, it would quietly stand like a Grecian temple, or a Grecian statue, as the ideal, the beau ideal, of moral beauty and perfection, and suffer us poor sculptors to carry on the work of moulding ourselves the best we can after the model of its beauty, then indeed it might stand and receive the homage of all virtuous and well-disposed men.

But it hath such a tongue of iron, and doth ring out again such thunders of revenge against every transgression, and every shortcoming it doth gauge with such exact rule, and such a mighty omniscient eye doth watch sleepless over its virgin purity, that while, on the one hand, it doth solicit and attract with its perfect form, on the other it doth repel with its chill and icy coldness. God's inexorable holiness, I say, is that which maketh the very beauty of the law, and its perfection, to be most horrible and most revolting unto the heart of a believer. But if we could but persuade ourselves that God's holiness would relent, and that he would soften and accommodate the law to our infirmities, all might yet be well; and this truly is the hope and belief of all those who are making shift with the law for a rule of life. They do, in very deed, believe that God is not so holy, but that he is able to forgive a transgression of the law, and to overlook our shortcomings from its obedience. And this notion is so firmly rooted in men's minds, that nothing but a great demonstration to the contrary could overcome it. Men have no right estimate of the evil of sin, of the holiness of God, of the inexorableness of the law; and before you can wean human nature from the contemplation of its own perfection, and perfectibility in the law, you must have to offer unto them some indubitable demonstration and stupendous monument of the unalterable holiness of God, the irreducible demands of the law, and the hideous nature of sin. If such a demonstration and monument of a lasting kind can be given, and established in some grand and conspicuous way, it may be possible; but otherwise it never will be possible to divorce human nature from the high-minded affections which it beareth to the good, and just, and honourable law, and the easy hope with which it flattereth its good nature, that God will never require of his poor creatures more than they are able in this state of sin and infirmity to perform, especially when he beholdeth in them a devout aspiration after the perfect and blameless righteousness of the law, together with a continual sorrow and repentance because of our many shortcomings and positive offences.

But if, I say, it can be made to appear, beyond doubt and question, that he that offendeth in one point of the law is guilty of all; that heaven and earth may pass away, but one jot or one tittle shall not pass from the law till all be fulfilled; and that God cannot forgive a transgression, the slightest as the heaviest, without a recompense of an infinite price; and that as one transgression brought the world and all its inhabitants into this misery and death, out of life and blessedness, so any one transgression will condemn the soul into the lowest hell for ever; and that this is God's unalterable, unchangeable being and attribute;—if this, I say, can be made clearly apparent, and undoubtedly true and unchangeable for ever, then men may be brought to see the law in another light, and to abhor it as a living man abhorreth the dagger of the assassin, or the axe of the executioner, or the grim face of death, or the corruption of the grave, or the pit of hell.

Now, I ask, where, by what, hath God made this eternal demonstration of sin's horrid guilt, and his own inexpressible abhorrence of the sinner? I answer, By sending his Son in the likeness of sinful flesh; by making the Word flesh; by making him consubstantial with the sinner, and shewing how under this form God hid his face from his own Son, and bruised him, and put him to grief, and called for his sword to slay him, and covered him with the pall of death, and brought him into the humiliation of the grave;—all this, though he was without sin, and saw not corruption, merely because he had become consubstantial with the sinful creatures. Thus, and no otherwise, was that great demonstration made. And I stand in my place, as a preacher of truth, and say, that there is no demonstration of all this, if Christ did not become bone of our bone, and flesh of our flesh; if he were in any other state than the fallen humanity; if he were in the likeness of sinless flesh, and not in the likeness of sinful flesh.

The Fallen and Suffering Humanity of Jesus Christ

Let us for a moment suppose that Christ came in an immortal and incorruptible body; that is to say, in the nature of man before he fell; I have then to ask, in addition to all that hath been said above, what demonstration would be given of God's holy indignation against a fallen sinful creature, if so be that Christ was in the immortal and incorruptible state of manhood? A demonstration indeed is given of God's wrath against an unfallen creature, bearing a fallen creature's sin; but we want the demonstration of God's wrath upon a fallen creature himself. We are not unfallen creatures bearing another's sin; but we are fallen creatures, bearing our own. And the thing to be demonstrated unto us is, that God will take vengeance upon our iniquities, without making any, the least abatement for our fallen state.

This is the very shelter which human nature constructs for herself; and out of this shelter she must be driven, before she will forsake self-righteousness and self confidence. For hear what the natural man saith, "Will God require of me, born in sin and infirmity, and dwelling in this sinful world, perfection? And say you that he will visit my slightest transgression with eternal death?" The thing which we want is to be able to say to the natural man, "Yea, verily, thine every sin eternally separates between thee and God, and eternally doometh thee unto wrath." Now this answer cannot be given, if Christ had not a fallen humanity; verily our humanity; verily the natural man; for an unfallen humanity, or a redeemed humanity, is not the thing in question. "True," the natural man saith, "an unfallen man may be, ought to be perfect; but there is the widest difference between an unfallen and a fallen man. And by loading an unfallen man with ever so much sin of another, you do not make him a fallen man; and that he should bear it, and that he should keep the law without offence, is no proof to me that I shall be called to keep the same law, with the same strictness, or that I shall be visited so fearfully for every transgression of the same. Besides, we want no demonstration of what God requires of unfallen manhood, or what visitation its sins are to be visited withal, for we have it already in Adam. We are the monuments thereof; the world is the monument thereof; but is there to be no allowance for the wide difference between our state and Adam's? Are you to expect from a 'miserable sinner' the same straitness and completeness of holiness as from a being whom God created good, and constituted lord of the lower earth?" These are the questions to be resolved, as I have said above, before you can drive men from trusting in the law, and in their own keeping of the law; and these are questions which can be resolved only by a demonstration made in our fallen manhood. They understand nothing at all of the problem to be resolved, who say that it could be resolved in the unfallen manhood, or in the angelic or in the archangelic form of being.

Furthermore, I confess myself unable to perceive how it is possible for suffering to reach an unfallen creature without subverting the fundamental principles of the divine purpose and administration. I do not mean the principle how the eternal Son should consent and condescend to the suffering and humiliation; for this, indeed, he doth in the plenitude of his own divine freedom; but the difficulty, and impossibility as I think, is, how the suffering should reach him otherwise than by a fallen body. This is the very end of the fall, that Christ might come at suffering. The Godhead cannot suffer, because it cannot change. Those sufferings which Christ underwent reached him through his creature-part. Now, if that creature-part of Christ was in the unfallen state, how should it suffer? If the unfallen creature can suffer, then is there no difference between the unfallen and the fallen; for suffering and death are the signs and the wages of the fall. The answer which they make to this question is, he suffered for the sins of others. That I say also, because he had no sin of his own wherefor to suffer. On this we are agreed; but my question is, How can suffering for another reach an unfallen creature? I know of no way by which suffering can reach an unfallen creature, but by the way in which it reached Adam—namely, by his committing sin; and if it be said, that without committing sin, suffering can reach an unfallen creature, then the only difference between the unfallen and fallen is taken away, and the very nature of sin, as an act of the will, is abrogated.

But that suffering can come to a fallen creature, without any sinful act of his own, is manifest in every child that is born; and that death can come to a fallen creature, without any sinful act of its own, is manifest in every child that dies. And, therefore, there is no difficulty whatever in believing that, without any sinful act of the will, Christ in a fallen nature should both suffer and die, because this very thing is the universal experience of every fallen creature. But there is not such a thing in the records of being, as that an unfallen creature should suffer. The will must fall first by sinning, before suffering can be felt. But that, in the fallen state, the just should suffer for the unjust, and the innocent for the guilty, is the great truth experienced of all; seeing God visits the sin of the fathers, and the sin of Adam especially, upon those who have as yet no power of will whereby to commit a sin; so that I may truly say the whole history and constitution of man's estate, under the fall, is to the very end of schooling us into the method of the incarnation, of teaching us how, without evil actings of the will, suffering and death may be experienced by a creature in the fallen state.

If Christ therefore took our fallen nature; if the eternal Godhead, being purposed to extirpate sin and death from flesh for ever, and to bear up through his almighty and divine strength, the lapsed creation: it is easy to perceive how, by taking part of flesh and blood with the fallen children he might do so: but if, by taking an unfallen nature, he could do so, then I have no demonstration whatever that I myself am fallen. For what proveth me to be fallen? suffering and death. If it be added, Positive transgression of my will? I answer, No; that should not enter into the definition of a fallen creature; because it applieth not to all fallen creatures, nor indeed to any fallen creature in all its being. Children, and all men while children, are incapable of acting good or evil by the will, and yet they are fallen. And how know we them to be fallen? because they suffer and die. But if an unfallen creature can likewise suffer and die, then the only definition, and the only proof, of a fallen creature is taken away; and if this be taken away, then redemption is likewise taken away. Now, it only makes this conclusion stronger, if they say that the difference between an unfallen creature suffering and a fallen creature suffering is, that the one suffereth by imputation and the other suffereth not by imputation but for his own sin. Then I say, that by this definition children are unfallen; for they suffer not for any sin of their own, but by imputation of the sin of their fathers, and most especially the sin of Adam. Here, then, is another great foundation subverted—to wit, the difference between the unfallen and fallen creatures; and Socinianism marches straight in at the breach, which says that we are just in as good and perfect a state as Adam, and as able to keep the law as he was; and then where is the redemption, when there is no fall? It is completely avoided, and made of no effect.

Oh, it relieveth my heart, in the midst of these painful studies and deep meditations, to find that I am fighting the battle which the apostle John began, and which the holy fathers of the church, for seven centuries, ceased not to wage. This heresy of the immortal incorruptible body of Christ, of his supernatural humanity, was broached by Cerdon, the disciple of that Simon Magus who is mentioned in the Acts: from him it passed to Marcion, and Valentine, and Manes, all great heresiarchs: in Eutyches it took a more generic form, which was condemned in the fourth general council at Chalcedon. It revived in the Emperor Justinian, who held that Jesus Christ had not a corruptible body, but was resisted by the patriarch of Constantinople, and the patriarch of Antioch, and all the orthodox church, who said, "It cannot be called incorruptible in any other sense than as it was always unpolluted with any defilement, and was not corrupted in the grave." It revived again under the new name of the Monothelites, concerning whom it is written in a former head of this discourse; and after surviving for nearly a century, it was condemned again, in a general council, the third at Constantinople, held in the year 680. And now, again, behold it is upon the field; and here I am, a poor despised minister, contending, day by day, for the faith for which holy martyrs and apostles contended; of whom it is reported that one, even Polycarp the disciple of John, when he met one of these heresiarchs—I think Marcion—on the streets of Rome, and being asked of him, "Knowest thou me?" the martyr answered, "Yes; I know thee to be the eldest born of the devil."

Now, abandon these heresies, and look at the demonstration as it is in truth, and you will see how grand it is. The eternal divinity of the Son, who inhabited the fullness and the dearness of the Father's bosom, to the end of shewing how holy, and good, and gracious his Father is, and knowing well the divine hatred against sin, as being himself divine, and the eternal contradiction between God and the sinful creature, as being himself God, doth nevertheless take up into his person human nature in its fallen state, and is as truly a fallen man, as he is truly God; and thus the Eternal and Absolute One enforceth the recreant and rebel nature of man to keep the holy law of God: and the Father, though loving him beyond love's utterance, in the infinite degree, as being of one substance, doth not the less exact from him the utmost measure of a sufferer's sufferings unto death itself; a death of disgrace, of agony, and of torture. He had no exemption because he was God, but suffered because he had taken part with the brethren of the suffering and doomed thing. If God would ever have relaxed, for any sake, the extreme rigour of the law, and the imperious curse of death, would he not have relaxed now, when the sufferer was his own Son, holding, by his divine nature, indissoluble communion with himself?

That person, who suffered in his human nature, did by his divine nature maintain all the while perfect unity with the Father. There was between them perfect oneness of substance; and yet the person of the Son suffered as a man suffereth, was a man of sorrows and acquainted with grief. He who made the law, he whose absolute will is the parent of all laws, did come under the law, in all respects, and did keep it in all points. After this, can any one doubt that God will exact, to the uttermost jot of that law, from every fallen creature? Why should he spare another who spared not his own Son, his only-begotten and well-beloved Son? Beyond this, methinks, demonstration of holiness cannot go. Oh, what an awful spectacle unto creation for ever, to see such love as the Father had unto his Son postponed unto holiness, set aside for the manifestation of justice, suspended for the honour of a broken law! What a word, then, is law! the pillar of ages, the stability of worlds, the very word of God! and who, understanding this, will dream of the frangibility,[11] or the changeableness of law? It may not be any longer thought or spoken, that the adamantine law will divide into parts: it dieth by the loss of the least jot; it cannot die while God who spake it endureth. Inflexible law, inexorable law, thou art honoured indeed; very venerable art thou become. Woe, woe to him that toucheth the hem of thy skirt, or meditateth the infringement of thy integrity. I cannot express, and never shall be able to express, the sanction which Christ hath given to the law. Truly he hath made it honourable. Behold also what demonstration there is of the sinfulness of sin. That sin should poison life's fountain, in a creature created so noble as Adam; that sin should poison the streams of life in all their branches; that one sin should engender from its venomous drop enough of suffering to steep a world in misery, is indeed an awful truth;—but that sin

11. Capable of being broken

should be able to struggle with Godhead itself, that a fragment of the perilous stuff, being assumed into the personality of the Son, should weigh down
the Almighty One, from his delectation in the bosom of the Father, and
make him say, "Why hast Thou forsaken me?"—that a fragment of the perilous stuff being taken into the person of the Living One, Life of life, should
agonise him with hunger and with thirst, and oppress him with weariness,
and tempt him with the round world's idle state; should make the divine
person groan, and weep, and sweat great drops of blood, and be passive to
all suffering which flesh is heir to; this is the mightiest demonstration of
sin's iron gripe and deadly hold, proving it to be all but the mightiest power
in being.

The Power of Sin in the Flesh and the Power of Divinity in New Humanity

This, according to the view I have given of it, is not, as it were, the accumu-
lation of the sins of all the elect; but the simple, single, common power of
sin diffused throughout, and present in, the substance of flesh of fallen human nature. Such power hath sin in my flesh, in the flesh of every one who
heareth me. They greatly err who make this humiliation of the Son's person
to arise from many thousand measures of sin, as it were, poured into the cup
of one man. No, verily; that which a fallen human nature in Christ prevailed
to do against a divine nature, it prevaileth to do in me, and in every single
man; and no power whatsoever, but the divine power which prevailed over
it in Christ, can prevail over it in me.

This scheme of supposing Christ to have been laden, as it were, with
a body that had the sins of many bodies imputed to it, doth take him out
of our sphere again, and destroy the application unto us, of those things
shewed forth in him; for the sinner might turn upon us, and say, That example of the sinfulness of sin, which you educed from Christ, is not applicable to me, who have but my own sin to bear. Do I speak herein against
imputation of our sins? God forbid. I believe that he bare our sins in his own
body on the tree; and this is a point which I have sufficiently handled in my
first discourse. It was all our sin, and none of it his:—it was the sin of flesh
in general, in common, which he freely undertook to extirpate. But what is
sin? Reflect what sin is. It is not a thing, nor a creature, but it is the state of
a creature,—the second state of a creature, in which it is not subject to the
law of God, neither indeed can be. Sin, therefore, is common to us all: it is
the creature man working against the Creator God. And the Creator God,
to shew that he neither had been nor would be baffled by his own creature,

took it up into himself, and, having sanctified it, brought it through the passage of death without seeing corruption, to see immortality and unchangeableness. And the measure of the potency of sin, and of its evil in one man, in any man, in all men, in the region of humanity, is the degree unto which it humbled and reduced one of the persons of the eternal Godhead. I wonder what men mean who will not look at this, and be astonished: it passeth comprehension, it passeth utterance. Holy men are lost in the adoration of it; angels desire to look into it; sinners are saved by it; and none but [. . .] heretics withstand it.

It is very painful indeed to me, but nothing new, as you can testify, to witness the obstinacy and perverseness with which men contend against this truth, that Christ came in the likeness of sinful flesh, to condemn sin in the flesh. What mean they by their ignorant gainsaying? Is it not the thing which is to be done in you and me, sooner or later, by God, that we should be sanctified and redeemed, this very flesh of ours, by the indwelling and empowering of the Holy Ghost? If there be something so shocking in the Holy Ghost's abiding in sinful flesh, let those that think it so shocking do without it, if they can, and go down into the pit for ever. Whether is it more honourable unto God, that he should recover his creature, or lose his creature? And if sinful flesh is the thing to be sanctified and possessed of the Godhead, shall not Christ in this also have the pre-eminence? or shall it be done in us, without being first done in him? But whence this abhorrence? Is it dishonourable to vanquish sin? Doth the man become a serpent who graspeth the serpent in his grip, and crusheth him? Do I become a devil, by wrestling with the devil and overcoming him? And doth Christ become sinful, by coming into flesh like this of mine, extirpating its sin, arresting its corruption, and attaining for it honour and glory for ever? Idle talk! They know not whether they drive. They are making void the humanity of Christ, and destroying his mediation as virtually as if they denied his divinity. A mediator is not of one: how truly he is consubstantial with God, so truly is he consubstantial with me, or he cannot be mediator between me and God. The Daysman must be able to lay his hand on us both.

The Strength of the Law Is the Holiness of God

These demonstrations of the unalterable holiness of God, of the inflexible rigour of the law, and the exceeding sinfulness of sin, which are no demonstrations at all unto us availing, unless Christ be come in our just and exact nature, are, so far as they bear upon us, profitable in the highest degree by destroying all hope of salvation through the relentings of God, through the yielding of the law, through our obedience of the law, or any other method which buildeth upon God's facility of disposition, or our own self-righteousness. For if God would not relent on behalf of God, but obliged his own Son, when made flesh, to bear the rigours of the law, then how should he relent towards another? And if it required the informing Godhead of the Son, and the sustaining Godhead of the Spirit, to enable the man Jesus Christ perfectly to keep the law, how should any mere man expect to keep it? And if no one may expect to keep it, how should any one expect to be saved by it? Whosoever, therefore, rightly apprehendeth the incarnation of the Word, doth dread the law, with revoltings of soul, and cry out, Oh, thou inexorable law! how shall I escape thy most certain sentence? Oh, thou most holy God! how shall I find acquittal from thine offended law? If thou art strict to mark iniquity, as it appeareth by thy Son's experience in the flesh, then how shall I answer for one of ten thousand of my transgressions? I am a lost man—a man lost and undone, unless that awful law be taken out of the way for ever. If it stand, I fall; for I am sold under sin. Oh, wretched man that I am! who shall deliver me from the body of this death?

Such is the agony of a man who is enlightened by Christ, in God's character as a sovereign Lord. He is at his wit's end: yea, it would drive a man out of his wits, as at times it threatened to do for poor Luther, whose ideas of God the Lawgiver became at times so insufferable to himself, that he would run howling from the hideous thought, and seek to hide himself from the fear of God. Paul, in like manner, in the seventh chapter of the Romans, seemeth to have been all but undone, by his reflections upon the holiness of God the Lawgiver. And I would that every one who heareth me, and I myself, were in likewise amazed and astonished. There would then be no need of argument to drive men from the law; they would avoid it as they do consuming fire. There would be no need of arguments to persuade men to take refuge in grace: they would snatch at it, and fasten such hold upon it as the drowning man doth upon the lifeboat which hath arrived just in time to save him from the yawning waves. Then would the world know what that word meaneth, "The law came by Moses, but grace and truth came by Jesus Christ."

The Law Satisfied in the Life and Death of Christ

What, then, is to become of that inexorable law? and what is to become of us, whom it damneth to the lowest hell? Christ, for his part, hath kept the law, and made it honourable; but we in weak flesh, what can we do to keep it? Nothing whatsoever. We do but mangle it; we do but dishonour it;

we do but enrage it, and deceive ourselves. Will it not call out against us then? Yea, and it doth. And what, then, is to be done? We must die, and see corruption. Our natural man must die, and the law will be satisfied; for the law hath claims upon the natural man alone. If my concupiscence die, if my covetousness die, if my destructiveness die, what more would the law? In one word, if my flesh be crucified, what more would the law?

Now this is what taketh place in every one that believeth in Christ, according to the principle of imputation laid down above; that, as by Adam came the weakness of the flesh, so by Christ came deliverance from its weakness: or rather, in Christ's death all flesh died, and the law was satisfied. The law bore its spite against sin in flesh: Christ condemned sin in flesh: the law could not do it, Christ did it for the law; or rather he did it for the Lawgiver, even his Father, of whose holiness the law is the bearing and the pressure upon sinful flesh. As the sin of Adam did not need to be done over again in every person of Adam's kind, but by the principle of imputation death passed upon all men, and the law appeared in due time to shew the abundance of the transgression; so neither doth the work of righteousness, under the law, need to be done over again: but, being once done in Christ, is for ever done; and the law being satisfied with Christ, giveth itself up to Christ, and saith, Thou, O man, art worthy to have, to hold, to exercise me, thou great Lord of law!

And Christ having become sole proprietor of the law, doth say, in his own right, Stand aside, thou grace-eclipsing law: thou hast had thy time; and a better time awaiteth thee yet, when my throne of righteousness shall be established; but for the present, be thou content to take thyself out of the way, that the grace of my Father, through me, may shine forth unto the ends of the earth. And now, ye swift messengers, ye gentle ministers of grace, go forth and preach the good tidings of great joy unto all men; preach the gospel of salvation unto every creature under heaven. This message hath been proclaimed unto the earth since the resurrection; that men are no longer under the law, that God is gracious, that their sins are forgiven, and that God is love. This is the grace, this is the peace, which unto men, unto all men, is proclaimed; and the world is under the law no longer, but under grace. And thus, by one man the law hath been satisfied, and by one man the grace of God hath been revealed from behind the eclipse which the law had brought upon it. For it was but an eclipse, because the promise was before the law, and the law, which came four hundred and thirty years after, could not make the promise of none effect.

The Covenant with Abraham and the Law

The promise was of grace, and not of merit: of faith, and not of works. Abraham believed, and it was counted unto him for righteousness. Abraham lived under a dispensation under which sin was not imputed. "For," saith the apostle, "sin is not imputed, where there is no law" (Romans 5.13); and he quoteth, as applicable to that period, these words of the psalmist,—"Blessed is he whose transgression is forgiven, whose sin is covered: blessed is the man to whom the Lord imputeth not iniquity" (Psalm 32.1). If, then, Abraham and his seed until the law came were free from the imputation of sin, by virtue of the promise of Christ, surely much more are we free who live under the gospel of Christ. I say, much more, not in respect of the degree of freedom, but in respect of the clearness with which it is revealed. For, in respect to the substance of the thing, that we have the same with Abraham, he the same with us, is clear, not only from the general reasonings of Paul, in the Romans and in the Galatians, but by two express declarations of the New Testament to that effect. The first in the prophecy of Zacharias, at the circumcision of his son the Baptist, wherein, speaking of Jesus, he states, as the end of his mission, "to perform the mercy promised to our fathers, and to remember his holy covenant, the oath which he sware to our father Abraham" (Luke 1.72). Now that which is remembered hath had a previous existence; and that which is performed under a covenant hath been previously promised, in the giving of the covenant of promise.

The other passage is still more explicit:

> Christ hath redeemed us from the curse of the law, being made a curse for us; for it is written, Cursed is every one that hangeth on a tree; that the blessing of Abraham might come on the Gentiles through Jesus Christ, that we might receive the promise of the Spirit through faith. (Galatians 3.13)

And thus we conclude, that from Abraham until now, the dispensation of grace and imputed righteousness, the dispensation which hath no law, and imputeth no sin, hath been in the world; that when given unto Abraham, it was given unto him for all nations; according as it is written in the same Epistle to the Galatians: "The Scripture, foreseeing that God would justify the nations through faith, preached before the gospel unto Abraham, saying, In thee shall all nations be blessed" (Galatians 3.8).

The law did not annul that dispensation of grace, but was a safeguard unto it; to preserve the hope, and to define the object of it, and to drive men from self-righteousness into the arms of merciful grace: unto which end the law serveth still, as we have shewn above, or else it will drive men into destruction, and leave them under despair. In this sense, indeed, Christ hath the whips and scourges of the law, and shall use them too, against the day of judgment, which is the law's triumphal and eternal glory. But as to Moses, he is defunct; and let him rest in his grave. The Son of Man is Lord also of the law, which is with him in better keeping than ever it was with Moses; for he shall make it triumphant in the age to come, when Moses on the one hand, and Elias on the other, shall bear up the glory of the transfigured world. But, meanwhile, the law being lifted up from present time, and transported unto another age, we have now the gospel of the grace of God proclaimed by the church unto the wide world. The world is under grace, and is no longer under law. For, as old Luther hath bravely spoken it, "Wherefore if sin afflict thee, and death terrify thee, think that it is, as indeed it is, but an imagination, and a false illusion of the devil; for in very deed, there is now no sin, no curse, no death, no devil to hurt us any more, for Christ vanquished and abolished all these things."[12]

JESUS CHRIST AS REPRESENTATIVE AND EXAMPLE

I said above, that the law is fraught with so much wisdom and righteousness as to become an object of adoration to the good feeling of the natural man. But when it thus bristleth with threatenings and terrors against infirm humanity, and will not intermarry with grace or mercy, it doth alienate the affections of the natural man, and become to him the occasion of fear and dread. Being taken out of the way therefore as an offence, a deadly offence, to humanity's infirm condition, the question ariseth, And what now is there left for man to pay his reverence and worship unto? Taking away this fine ideal of everything righteous, good, and perfect, what have you to put in its stead? Man cannot be without a model according to which to shape himself, and in which to behold that excellence to which he would attain, and do homage. Brethren, this is a question into the resolution of which I shall enter a little; and, at one and the same time, spite those adorers of Moses, and confound those idle and wicked dreamers about Christ's immortal body, while I instruct you more perfectly in the method of this great salvation.

---

12. Irving appears to be quoting from Luther's commentary on Galatians. See M. Luther, *A Commentary on St Paul's Epistle to the Galatians: A Revised and Completed Translation Based on the 'Middleton' Edition of the English Version of 1573* (London: James Clarke, 1953), 3.13, 278–82.

The Fraternal Christ as Focus of Our Admiration

The object, then, which now standeth unto our admiration and homage, instead of the law, is the person of Christ; who, while he is holy as the law, is tender and pitiful as a brother, and endued with the almightiness of God; who is so far from irritating the weakness and overwhelming the remorse and compunction of sinful flesh, so far from threatening its every backsliding and transgression with death, that he hath himself become touched with the fellow-feeling of our infirmities, being in all points tempted like as we are, hath carried our diseases, and borne our sicknesses, and is the grace of that God of whom the law is the holiness. The person of Christ Jesus, therefore, by right taketh, as by nature he attracteth, the admiration, affection, and homage of sinful flesh. He taketh us by right of being the living law, holy as it is, perfect as it is, admirable as it is. He attracteth us by being a person, a living, moving, breathing person; bone of our bone, and flesh of our flesh. He hath purchased us, moreover, by redeeming us from the curse of the law, and pouring into the wounded conscience the oil of joy; and, finally, he demandeth us as very God, as the very grace of God, who in himself concentrateth all grace, and unto whom God giveth the singular and sole glory of his grace.

Compared with this person, thus accomplished, with God's grace and man's infirmity, thus recommended by the achievement of holiness, in union with most perfect grace and compassion, object of fearless love, object of doubtless trust; who that hath a heart to feel, or a mind to understand, will ever speak again in praise, will ever revert again in confidence, to that awful iron-hearted law, which neither knows pity for the fallen, nor shews compassion for the penitent? Yet true it is, and of verity, that, like the Galatians of old, we who have received the Spirit, by the hearing of faith, would go back to be perfected by the law. We would believe in Christ, we would possess the Spirit, and, so qualified, pay our homage to the law, which maketh void the work of Christ, and proveth that we have never known the Spirit. Perverseness this, debasement this, which the church would not have come to, had she, unto her faith of the Lord's atonement, added the lively faith of his true sympathising humanity, of his merciful and faithful high priesthood in the heavens: and from which base pandering to the law, and preferring of Moses above Christ, nothing will ever deliver the church, but the revival and frequent reiteration of that great truth, which Satan is attempting to bring into question,—that Christ was in very deed consubstantial with the fallen creature, and hath taken up with him into the heavens the ever-present consciousness and sympathy of the conditions and trials of his members upon the earth.

Exclusively Forensic Understanding of the Atonement Obscures Its Fraternal Aspect

The church hath been so spoiled in its tenderer and nobler parts, by the continual and exclusive doctrine of debt and payment, of barter and exchange; of suffering for suffering, of clearing the account and setting things straight with God; that she hath lost the relish for discourse of the brotherly covenant, of the spousal relation, of the consubstantial union betwixt her and the Lord Jesus. She hath lost relish for high discourse concerning the mystery of his person, as God-man; the beauty, the grace, the excellency of that constitution of being which he possessed. Strong as the strongest, even of almighty strength; weak as the weakest,—of all infirmities conscious; holy as the holiest, the only holy thing, yet consubstantial with the sinful creatures, sinful in his substance as they, tempted as they, liable to fall as they. The church likewise, by this profit-and-loss theology, by this divinity of the exchange, hath come to lose the relish of that most noble discourse, which treateth of the grandeur and the glory of the risen Christ wielding the scepter of the heavens, yet, from his peerless height of place, consenting to cast his eye perpetually upon the poorest, the meanest, the most deeply tried and overwhelmed of all his people.

And now that the Lord has stirred up my mind, and the minds of some others of his servants, to awaken and arouse the church to thoughts, to loves, to hopes of a higher mood, the servants of the wicked one would come in, and fix her for ever at the level of these low waters, by daring to assert that Jesus our Lord had no such sympathies with the fallen creatures, and that the church may not aspire to such close, spousal, sisterly thoughts of him. For if, as they dream, and dare to put forth, Christ was other than a fallen man, and never knew the fellowship of our temptations, from the flesh, from the world, from Satan, how can human nature, in its fallen state, go out with confidence and affection, and without fear, to repose herself upon his intercession and mediation?

You say, he hath borne her sin, and therefore made her unspeakably his debtor: you say, our sins were imputed to him, and he bore them; he pitied us so much as to bear them; and therefore we ought to have confidence in him. Nay, but, thou half reasoner, art thou so ignorant of human nature as not to know that the debt of obligation is not favourable to the growth of love? It is love which begetteth love, and love annihilates all distance by condescension, and love raiseth through all distance the poor one who hath thus been condescended to in love. Knowest thou not, O man, that a king, who keeps his state and distance as a king, yet by his almoner sendeth gifts to the most distressed and needy of his people, doth not expect that they should thereupon cast themselves into his bosom, or take liberties with his royal state? They are beholden to him, and they shew it in the reverent distance and lowly humility which they bear before him.

And if, as thou sayest, the Son of God, in doing us this bounty, did yet keep the distance and the dignity of an unfallen creature, avoiding by an inestimable distance our devil-haunted and sin-defiled religion, flitting amongst us like a shadow, but not inhabiting our tenement at all; amongst us, but not one of us; then I say, that his bounty conferred, the very magnitude, the very value of it, will only put another impediment and obstruction in the way of that brotherhood, of those espousals, of that fellow-feeling, trust, and confidence, which the soul ought to have towards him for whom she is called to give up her own high and noble thoughts concerning this fair proportioned and authoritative law of God. The soul, instead of coming into melting tenderness towards such a one, will be appalled far away from his inscrutable holiness, and will feel it to be her duty to worship him at a distance, and to acknowledge him with fear and trembling.

Ah, no: ye half reasoners, ye are not yet so wise as God, whose method of wooing a fallen creature is far more exquisite and far more effectual than yours. You come roughly on, loading her whose affections you would gain with gifts, but all the while keeping in her presence a state whereat she trembleth; more after the manner of an eastern prince purchasing a fair slave, than the manner by which the human soul is won. But God sent his Son to make acquaintance with human kind, upon the lowly level of their condition; as if that eastern prince should lay aside his crown and sceptre, and dress himself in humble guise, and be a servant to gain the humble maiden whose hand he desireth.

So God wisely purposed; and so Christ wisely, graciously, nobly, divinely performed; speaking of no benefit, though he had given us all; keeping no state, though he was the Lord of creation. In the lowly level of fallen humanity, he wooed his bride, and thus he won her love. By the very act, and in the very act of his humiliation unto her estate, he took away the fear of distance and the sense of obligation. But still the load would be too great for love to grow under, exalted as he is now, Potentate of potentates, were it not for the same faculty and power of condescension which abideth in him still. He is removed away from us, but not by being above the care of us. Only to lift his handmaiden unto the same dignity hath he gone to claim his birthright crown, that he may raise her to the fellowship of the same; and meanwhile the Spirit is his messenger, the Spirit is the comforter of his spouse, who cometh not, in the form of infinite Godhead, to overwhelm and consume the faculties of the creature whom he would possess; nor yet, in the form of perfect and unfallen manhood, to rebuke the fallen creature's

weak and sinful condition, but in the form of risen, redeemed manhood—
manhood that once was fallen, but now is risen and redeemed.

The Reception of the Spirit and the Continuation of the Work of Jesus Christ

It is the Spirit of Christ, of the risen Christ, which we receive. Not until he
ascended up on high, did Christ receive the Spirit to bestow it upon his
church. It is, therefore, the Spirit of the risen Christ, the triumphant Christ,
Christ the vanquisher of sin and death, which we receive;—a distinct person
of the blessed Trinity, condescending from the absoluteness of his divinity,
to carry on the communication between Christ and his people; a communication not made by words merely, but by regeneration and the quickening
of a new life, in all things consentaneous unto, and defined by, and identical
with, the life of Christ. As my natural life is instinct with all Adam's fallen
propensities, so is my renewed life instinct with all Christ's risen glories.
With the communication of life, therefore, kindred life, unto his own warm,
congenial life; with the inspiration of all divine, pure, and holy affection,
with a new heart, with a right mind; with power from on high, power which
sweetly and gently condescendeth to all our weaknesses and infirmities, in
order to strengthen them, and make us more than conquerors over all our
enemies; with gentle love, which whispereth peace unto our troubled souls,
and biddeth its waves to be still; with wisdom from above, which coun-
selleth our ignorance and our folly, and represseth all our wayward violence;
with good government and righteous lordship, which doth reprove, rebuke,
restrain, chastise, and restore us to the paths of righteousness;—with these,
the forms of redeemed manhood; with these, the tender respects unto our
frailty, and healing treatment of our diseases, and restoration of our health,
and renewal of our being after the image of God, in righteousness and true
holiness, doth the Holy Ghost, as the Spirit of Christ, come forth from the
bosom of the risen God-man, to cherish, to revive, to comfort, and to establish the peace, joy, and blessedness of his spouse upon the earth, and to
carry on that excellent work of gaining her love, that he may teach her to be
obedient and dutiful unto the will of his Father.

We say that Christ—first in fallen yet sinless manhood, and next, in
fallen manhood redeemed and risen—doth indeed accomplish a perfect
work of winning the heart, taking the admiration, possessing the confidence, and occupying all the soul, of those whom the Father hath given
to him for an inheritance; those whom he purchased unto himself for an
inheritance, those whom the Spirit cleanseth and clotheth, to be unto him

for a chaste and holy spouse. Sublime mystery of love! O love most excellent, love most glorious! Blessed indeed are the people who are thus beloved. My soul, rejoice in God thy Saviour. All that is within me bless his holy name, and forget not all his benefits, who forgiveth all thine iniquities, who healeth all thy diseases, who redeemeth thy life from destruction, who crowneth thee with loving kindness and tender mercies, who satisfieth thy mouth with good things, so that thy youth is renewed like the eagle's.[13]

THE CHRISTIAN'S FREEDOM FROM THE LAW

Now, brethren, this is the object, even this man Jesus Christ, which I have set before you, over and against that law which our natural man reverenceth so much. Is the law holy? Christ is also holy, who hath kept the law and made it honourable. Is the law venerable in its antiquity? more venerable is he who was in the beginning with God, who was God. Is the law good, discerning between the good and the evil, and judging righteously, defending the oppressed, upholding the weak? so good is Christ, who shall bring every hidden work of darkness unto light; who shall judge between the evil and the good, and discern between the just and the unjust, in that day, in that age, in which he will set judgment upon the earth, and establish righteousness among the nations. What is there in the law holy, and just, and good, which is not in Jesus, the Holy, the Just, and the Good? And for the curse of the law, you have the blessing of the promise in Christ; and for the certain condemnation of the law, you have the certain justification and salvation of Christ.

In the law there is righteousness, but there is no mercy: in Christ mercy and truth are met together, righteousness and peace have kissed each other. In the law there is no help: but in Christ there is the help of the Holy Ghost. In the law there is no life, but chill cold death: in Christ there is life, more abundant life, everlasting life. In the law, God's holiness in terrible thunderings, and lightnings, and darkness, and a fearful voice is set forth; and who can abide it? which, when the children of Israel heard, they prayed that it might not be spoken unto them any more: but in Christ you have righteousness presented in grace; the grace of God shining forth in the person of the Holy One and the Just. In the law you have manhood racked, tortured, and slain: in Christ you have the same fallen manhood sanctified, beautified, glorified, blessed for ever. And what more shall I say, than that the law is the direful expression of that everlasting contradiction which there is between God and a fallen creature, the impassable gulf which had never been passed,

13. Irving is referring to Psalm 103.1–5.

and seemed impassable until Christ came forth, made of a woman, made under the law, who is the expression of God's grace, God's pity, and God's compassion towards the fallen creature, of God's purpose to redeem it, and to set his glory and his strength in it, for ever and for ever.

Who, then, that understandeth these things, will prefer the iron-hearted law to the human-hearted Christ; will set up justification by works, in the stead of justification by faith; will prefer to live under the law, rather than to live under grace? But I say unto you, brethren, that if ye, having believed in Christ, and received the Spirit, will yet make the law your measure and your master, ye do dishonour unto these divine persons; ye do bring Christ back from the right hand of the glory, to travail in flesh again. And, instead of prospering in holiness by such an unworthy preposterous course, you will fall away into legality and formality, and live in fear and trembling. If Christ had intended his people to be under the law, as he was himself, then would he have bestowed upon them the Holy Spirit before he ascended up on high; the Holy Spirit would have proceeded from the body of his humiliation, and not from the body of his glory. But it is expressly said, that the Holy Ghost was not yet given, because that Jesus was not yet glorified. Besides, if we had to keep the law over again, there would be no vicariousness in the work of Christ. Imputation and atonement would be empty words, if so were that the law had a demand upon us still, and that we were either now to be under its authority, or hereafter judged by its statutes. Christ hath died in vain, if we be still under the law; or, as Paul saith, "If we be under the law, we are fallen from grace" (Galatians 5.4). Surely, if the first Adam begetteth in his likeness, the Second Adam begetteth in his likeness also: and what is that likeness? The likeness not now of sinful flesh, but of glorious flesh; the image of God, the image of the invisible God, which Christ was not in his veiled flesh, but which he is in his transcendent glory: and this is distinctly and unequivocally declared, in that passage of Scripture where it is written, that "we are renewed after the image of God, in righteousness and true holiness" (Ephesians 4.24).

When, therefore, any legalist will prove to me, that Christ the Father of the regeneration is under the law, I will believe that the children of the regeneration are under the law; but not till then: and I think it will puzzle them to prove that the Lord of all is not Lord of the Ten Commandments also. And yet I know that there are men so ignorant and foolish as to maintain this also, who go about to say, and to affirm, that the law of the Ten Commandments is the epitome, so to speak, of the divine will, and that God himself is under the obligations of law; or, as they are pleased to say, that a thing is not right because it is the will of God, but it is the will of God because it is right. Base theologians, and poor philosophers! would you dethrone God also from his sovereignty, and bring him under the fate, the *fatum*, of the ancients? Is the Word before God; or doth the Word proceed from God? Doth not the father generate the Word? Is not the Father alone self-originated? I cannot enough wonder that men should so exaggerate as to put the moral law into any connexion with God otherwise than as the Giver of it. The object of it is not God; the object of it is not even unfallen man; nor hath it anything to do with the regenerated man. The only object of it is the fallen man; and I say again, what I have often said, it is the perfection of the fallen manhood, and it is no more.

And if, as I believe in the age to come, men, flesh-and-blood men, shall be constituted under this law, and by the ejection of Satan out of flesh, and out of the world holding of flesh, and through the righteous government of Christ instead thereof, shall be enabled to keep the law;—if the law, as I believe, shall then become the statute law of the world, still it will only be a form of fallen humanity; the best from which it can attain unto, but yet not the redeemed, or rather the regenerated form. For still, men will be fallible, and this estate of humanity will end in an apostasy; so that, from the beginning unto the ending of it, the law of the two stone tables hath nothing to do with the work of the Spirit, hath no authority over the renewed man, who is wholly devoted unto Christ, and acknowledgeth none but he; and is renewed in the likeness of the risen Christ, or after the image of the risen God, in righteousness and true holiness.

Now, it may seem to many a very idle, and to others it may seem a very dangerous thing, thus to assert the believer's independence of any law;—the former saying, Why take away any safeguard from morality? The latter saying, You teach licentiousness;—to whom I answer, It is want of faith in you both. The subject which I handle is the most momentous, and lies at the root of all holiness. Doth it serve, O ye objectors, the interests of holiness, or doth it disserve them, to break the law, and to dishonour the law? And do ye not daily break it, in thought, word, and deed? And if ye be under it, is it not violated and dishonoured by you? and where, then, is the holiness of God? Can a man, who is familiar with the everyday breaking of the law, have either it or the Lawgiver long in reverence? And if Christ and the Holy Spirit are to come in and patch up the matter, what a system have we here, but grace fighting with debt, and mercy fighting with justice; or rather grace and mercy becoming the great indulgence of unholiness? I speak not of the dishonour of Christ and of the Holy Ghost in such a scheme,—I speak of the dishonour of the law itself. O ye gainsayers of the truth, ye dishonour the law, and the Lawgiver; but we honor the law, we magnify the law and make it honourable. We say it standeth the awful and unstained monument of God's holiness, condemning us, and condemning all. We live not by it; we die before it: we live only by grace; we live only by pardon, and from the time forth of receiving our pardon. We do not go and commit the same offences over again, which we must needs do, if we were under that law of subjection; but we receive the Spirit of adoption from the Father, and from the rank of his subjects we are admitted unto the honour of his family: from the rank of rebels we pass into the freedom of sons; and as sons we receive the Spirit of our Father, and through the Spirit do live unto the praise and the glory of him who hath redeemed, and recovered, and regenerated us. Now be ye judges, whether one possessed of the Spirit, and under the power of love, is more in a condition to sanctify the living God, than one who is under the law, and without the Spirit. But, moreover, if it be true that a man who will live under the law cannot have the Spirit, what a predicament it places you legalists in! And this now is what Paul expressly declares:

This only would I learn of you, Received ye by the Spirit by the works of the law, or by the hearing of faith? Are ye so foolish, having begun in the Spirit, are ye now made perfect by the flesh? Have ye suffered so many things in vain, if it be yet in vain? he therefore that ministereth to you the Spirit, and worketh miracles among you, doeth he it by the works of the law, or by the hearing of faith? (Galatians 3.2–5)

THE WORK OF THE SPIRIT IN THE OBEDIENCE OF JESUS CHRIST

The only escape which it is possible to make from the cogency of this argument, which we have held upon the removal of the law, is by this question: But if the law be removed, what model or example have we by which to walk? I answer, The model and example of Christ. But they reply, Was not Christ under the law; and how can he be a model to those that are not under the law? To this question I will reply by explaining a little further the work of the Spirit in the man Christ Jesus. And this will have the advantage of still further exposing the vile heresy of the immortal and incorruptible body of Christ. For if Christ's human nature were not in like wise constituted, as ours is, then, in addition to all the results above mentioned, there must come this also, that the work of the Holy Ghost should not be understood, and should become of secondary, instead of being of primary importance, in the belief of every Christian.

And I must confess, that the narrow apprehension of the atonement which prevaileth, and the reducing of the mystery to mere imputation, and I would say, moreover, the mean and meagre views of imputation itself, have brought to pass a very insufficient doctrine on the subject of the Holy Spirit. The work to be accomplished must always be the measure of the power necessary to accomplish it; and from believing that the work to be accomplished by Christ is merely the bearing of so much inflicted wrath, vengeance, and punishment, it cometh naturally to pass that the need of the Holy Ghost towards the accomplishment of his work is not perceived. The union of the divine and human nature in itself sufficeth;—the human nature to suffer the mighty load, the divine nature to sustain the Sufferer. And besides these, what need of a third principle, and that a person, and a divine person also? Accordingly, the Holy Spirit in the work of Christ is almost or altogether avoided; which, however, is in several parts of the Acts, and in the 9th chapter of the Hebrews, expressly declared to have been the power in which he performed his mighty works, and offered his blameless sacrifice.

This, now, is made much worse by those who suppose he had not such a human nature in all respects as we fallen men have. For to the difficulty, just mentioned, is added this other: how suffering could in any wise reach him. If so be he was not fallen, or in any middle condition between the fallen and the unfallen, what meaning, or purpose, or use could there be for the Holy Ghost unto the person composed of the eternal Son and a faultless creature, I cannot for a moment imagine. And the fact is positive and undeniable, that the work of the Spirit in the person of Christ, though formerly a commonplace in divinity, and standing topic of discourse, is no longer either the one or the other; and being so, I will prophesy that the work of the Holy Ghost must in such a case become a very confused and idle theory; for whatever is not seen realized in the person of Christ, ceaseth from being a theological reality, and hasteneth to become a confused hypothesis. And I have some hope that this argument which I have been long waging may haply be profitable to enlighten the mind of the church upon the work of the Spirit also.

CHRIST'S RECEPTION OF THE SPIRIT AS PROTOTYPE FOR CHRISTIANS

But to come to the question of our model and example: The work of the Holy Ghost in the human nature of Christ, from his conception unto his baptism, was to fulfil all the righteousness of the law; and I think that word which he spake at his baptism, "Thus it becometh us to fulfil all righteousness" (Matthew 3.15), is the amen with which he concluded that great accomplishment. The baptism of John was the isthmus which connected the fulfillment of the law upon the one hand, with the opening of the spiritual and evangelical holiness upon the other: to which our Lord alludes, in these words: "The kingdom of heaven suffereth violence from the baptism of John until now, and the violent take it by force" (Matthew 11.12); giving them to understand that the baptism of John had initiated into the kingdom, as the baptism of Moses in the cloud, and in the sea, initiated into the law.

From the anointing with the Dove, I believe that our Lord entered upon a higher and holier walk than mere law-fulfilling, giving to us the example of that spiritual holiness which knoweth no law but the law of liberty; that is, the will inclined unto the will of God. Therefore it was that our Lord broke the Sabbath without offence; and touched lepers, and otherwise offended the law; and therefore, also, he went up to the feasts, or went not up, according to his mind. And many things besides he did, which are all expressed in these two similitudes, of which, when challenged for this neglect, he made use: "no man putteth new wine into old bottles; no man putteth a piece of new cloth into an old garment" (Mark 2.22); signifying that the spirit of his discipleship, of which he was then performing the novitiate, would not piece on to, much less be contained within, the old worn-out commandments of Moses.

Besides, the works which he did by the Spirit were the self-same works which the Spirit in the apostles did: and it is continually written, he set us an example that we should follow his steps. Now, it is my conviction, from these and many other grounds which I cannot now enter upon, that our Lord enjoyed, during his public ministry, that measure of the Spirit which his church was to be endowed with after the resurrection, to the end that his life might be the model of every Christian's life who is regenerated with the Holy Ghost. He walked in liberty, he rejoiced in power, he triumphed in victory from the time he received the Spirit after his baptism, until the time he fell, as it were, plumb down from that elevation into the agony of the garden and the abandonment of the cross. Before entering upon which, he was strengthened with that voice out of the heavens, "I have both glorified my name, and I will glorify it again" (John 12.28). Then came on that hour and power of darkness of which he said himself, "Now is my soul troubled, and what shall I say? Father, save me from this hour? but for this cause came I to this hour: Father, glorify thy name. Then came there a voice from heaven, saying, I have both glorified it, and will glorify it again" (John 12.28). This, I think, brought on the great crisis, and put him upon his probation to the very uttermost. And now openeth that scene of agony, that ocean of sorrow, concerning which it is not our present purpose to discourse, save to mark it as a grand epoch in the Redeemer's life. It is my conviction that our Lord's life between these two points of time, the descending of the Dove, and the bringing of the Greeks unto him, when that fearful hour began, is truly the great realisation and prototype of the Spirit's work in every re-generate man, in order that his life might not only fulfil the law of Moses, but give the prototype and the example of all spiritual righteousness. The Father, when his Son had accomplished and fulfilled the law, did bestow upon him a measure of that resurrection-life in the Spirit which he himself should afterwards be honoured and privileged to bestow upon the church. The Father baptized him with the Holy Ghost, who was afterwards to bap-tize all the elect children; and so he became an example unto us, and must have tasted a great enjoyment of his Father's countenance, far above and beyond what he enjoyed before, and in the removal of which I deem the misery of that agony and death to have chiefly consisted. He had the Spirit lifting him into a high communion with his Father, to the end of shewing him the regenerate church, and what should be the measure of their enjoy-ment; and this being accomplished, I say again, he was let plumb down into the former measure of the Spirit, to swim in the tempestuous ocean, which all the elements of moral disorder could raise around him. Fearful chaos! awful valley of the shadow of death! season of the hour and power of dark-ness!—Thus have we two measures of the Spirit: the first for law-keeping, to be in lieu of the obedience of those elect ones before, who had believed on him under the law, or, as it is written, "for the transgressions that were under the first covenant" (Hebrews 9.15); the second measure of the Spirit being for an example unto us of that baptism of the Dove with which we should be baptized. And there is a third measure of the Spirit, which quickened him in the tomb, with which also our bodies shall be anointed when we shall be quickened in the tomb.

And thus have we the whole mystery of the Holy Ghost realised in the life of Christ. First, the mystery of law-keeping, done for the sake of those that were under the law, but not for us; secondly, the mystery of the Holy Ghost, which the church now enjoyeth; and thirdly, the mystery of the Holy Ghost, which shall constitute the New Jerusalem of the risen saints in the millennial kingdom. And thus the work of the Holy Ghost is substantiated and realised in the person of Christ; is a fact, is a thing upon which faith may be rested by every poor creature of whose substance Christ hath taken a part. And thus is answered the only question which remained against the removal of the law: What model remaineth to us in its stead? Christ's life from his baptism to his agony is our model of the liberty and power of the Holy Ghost. And let this suffice for the subject of the removal of the law.

Part 4: Conclusions

It may be asked, after this discourse concerning the method of the incarnation, And what serveth it that Christ should thus have reconciled all flesh unto God, and taken away the middle wall of partition which was between Jew and Gentile, and preached peace unto them which were near, and to them which were afar off, seeing that it is only to a chosen and elect portion of the fallen creatures that salvation and blessedness, and glory, do eventually come? Is there not in this method something which is inconsistent with itself, which either makes Christ over-generous to cast away his bounty, or the Father over-stinted to restrain his Spirit? Hath not some part of the work of Christ been wrought to no effect? or hath not a promise and hope been held out unto men, larger than the Father purposed to fulfil?—Not so, by any means. The purpose of the Father is the purpose of the Godhead: the work of Christ is the will of the Father, shewing forth that purpose of the Godhead; and so also is the work of the Spirit. Though wrought in different persons, it is by the same one absolute will, by the same one substance of God wrought. To explain this matter, I shall now address myself in a few words.

THE END OF CREATION IS THE GLORY OF GOD

The purpose of God in creating man, was the manifestation and communication of his own glory unto the creatures which he had made, or which he was about to make; and to bring the creature wholly to depend upon him, and to worship him. As he was to make it out of nothing, he would have it remember its nothingness in itself, and to acknowledge the will, the absolute will, from which it derived its form and blessedness; to this single end of bringing the creature to apprehend the nothingness of its substance, and the absoluteness of its dependence upon the divine will, which is the very truth. This, I say, is the great object which God hath in view, and the great consummation unto which he will attain, by his dealings with the creatures.

To this end, a fall was ordained, that the creatures might know their own insufficiency, their own emptiness. Then came the law, which as a schoolmaster did instruct the creature in its sinfulness, did bring into vision, and openly shew how far it came short of its own perfection. The law added no iniquity to the creature; but it brought all its iniquity clearly to view. As there be certain chemical solutions, with which, if you anoint the skins of ancient parchments whereon no letter now appeareth, straightway the letters, and words, and sentences come up again from the erasure of time, and the oblivion of ages; even so the law, operating upon the fleshly being of man, did bring to view volumes of sins which were not known to be there, and did load the conscience with a weight of dead works, and shew in the heart an ever-open fountain of wickedness from which men needed to be purged by the blood of Christ, ere ever they could be in fit trim to serve the living God.

By the law, therefore, human nature was shewn to be exceeding sinful. The hatefulness of the creature in the sight of a holy God was established: the obstinacy of sin, its remediless poison in the flesh, the creature's total helplessness in itself, the creature's total alienation from God, were excellently displayed; but the law was only an unfulfilled prophecy, a despised statute, an abortive thing, producing no life, but death, until Christ came. It was a definition of what man in the fallen state should be, and would be, yet which none of the myriads that had been was, until Christ came and perfectly fulfilled it. Christ therefore is the rebuke of men; Christ is the measure of human delinquency; Christ the Holy One and the Just, sheweth the unholiness and unrighteousness of all besides himself—Now behold extremes meet. In him, in whom mercy and truth have met together, righteousness and peace have kissed each other, the Godhead, taking experience of the fallen manhood by junction and personal union therewith, doth, after seeing, feeling, having its infirmities, freely, fully, for ever discharge them, cancel its sins, and bear away its transgressions. The law, therefore, ends in the removal of law. The imputation of sins ends in the forgiveness of sins; and unto the creature grace is preached, peace is preached, glad tidings of great joy are proclaimed, which I do now again proclaim unto every one who hears me, saying, Your sins are remitted, your peace is made: believe, be ye saved. Go home, and tell it to your children; gather your kinsfolk, and tell it unto them: tell it in your villages and towns: pass the seas, and tell it unto the nations. Let the wide world know it, and the races of men believe it, that their sins are forgiven, their peace made, God gracious, abundant in mercy and truth.

This is the gospel which hath now for eighteen hundred years, yea, from the beginning, been proclaimed unto the earth. The creature hath known the grace of God to it, whose power and severity it knew heretofore in the law. And yet, behold, how fruitless and unefficacious it hath been! Who hath believed the report? Their sound hath gone into all the earth, and their words unto the world's end; but unto whom have they been welcome, and by whom have they been prized? All the Lord required of those that believe in the glad tidings was, that they should be baptized; and this not for the end of binding them over to be his serfs, or bondsmen, but to bring them to be his sons. All he besought was, that they might receive his

Son, laden with unspeakable gifts; and by their baptism signify the same, to the end they might receive power from the Holy Ghost to become the sons of God. No bloody circumcision, no pains and penalties of the law, no burden of ceremonies, no national peculiarities, no local restrictions; liberty, love, peace, joy, hope, holiness, and whatever else most excellent the soul desireth, whatever else most noble the soul aspireth to, this were they entreated, sued to receive by baptism. This single act, acknowledging God for the good gift of Christ, and hoping for the higher gift of the life of Christ by the Holy Ghost, men being entreated unto by the ministers of the gospel, by the labours of the church, have obstinately rejected for these eighteen hundred years. They have slain the bearers of the good tidings; they have persecuted the believers in the good tidings; they have rejected the grace of God; they have crucified the Son of God afresh, and put him to an open shame; they have trampled under foot the blood of the covenant with which they should have been sanctified, and counted it an unholy thing.

Tell me now, brethren, if hereby the sinfulness of the fallen creature hath not been awfully illustrated, beyond measure augmented, magnified, until it is become almost unpardonable. What a thing, what an unheard-of thing, that the great God should thus condescend unto his creatures in love immense, and his creatures reject his unspeakable gift! The world is drenched in guilt; the red waters of its guilt flow up unto the very lip, and in a few, few instants shall overwhelm its life. In blood, in a deluge of blood, its height of hope shall be drowned, its star of hope quenched: the day is far spent, the night is at hand. The night cometh, and likewise the morning. If the law did bring out the letters of guilt which had sunk beneath the surface, and escaped the knowledge of mankind, then the gospel hath made these letters to burn like fire, which shall consume to the lowest hell; to flame like the bale-light which, flaming from afar, betokens woe and misery to the land. Oh the guilt, oh the misery of the nations which have rejected the gospel! Truly, very truly, is it written, "This is the condemnation, that light is come into the world, but men loved darkness rather than light, their deeds being evil" (John 3.19). Ay, ay, this indeed is the condemnation, that we sin against the Father and the Son; the gracious Father, the crucified and risen Son. This is the world's doom, that she hath refused, rejected, and sinned against the Holy Ghost, testifying in Jesus, and in the church. It is not a vain thing, therefore, that Christ hath tasted death for every man; it is a part of God's great scheme, consistent therewith, yea, the crowning thereof, to shew forth the sinfulness of the creature in all possible advantages in which it could be placed,—to prove that when it was created good, it would not obey the slightest command; that when it fell, it would not receive the completest redemption, the largest grace. Inveterate purpose of sinning! Not a habit, but a law; not an accident, but an essence; the very being, the very essence, the unalterable law of the creature, proving that as it came out of nothing, it hath nothing, it can do nothing, it is void and empty; and therefore if it should ever be brought to something, it must be brought thither and maintained there by the eternal and all-sufficient power of God. And thus is the great truth in the way of being proved, that the creature came out of absolute nothingness; is absolutely nothing in itself, and hath its being, hath its something, whatever it be, only from the all-sustaining and absolute will of God. But this is not all: there is yet a deeper view of the question which we now go to inquire into.

THE CHURCH, THE SPIRIT, AND APOSTASY

Besides this object, which the Creator had in his mind, of making the insufficiency and inability of the creature to appear, there is another, which is, to make his own power to appear; his own power and goodness in delivering the creature from its own nothingness and sinfulness, into the estate of regeneration, power, and glory, where it may know, fell, and possess some portion of his own blessedness. And to this part of the purpose the former is but subservient. Historically, monumentally, and eternally to establish the nothingness and vileness of the creature, by its successive plunges out of light into darkness, until it reach the very base of being in the second death, is only to the end of shewing, by the negative, more effectually this affirmative, That the power, and efficiency, and glory, and blessedness unto which he should bring the creature, are not due unto itself but due only unto him the Creator.

Therefore parallel and alongside with, yea, and in the very midst of this great historical demonstration of the creature's sinfulness and weakness, we have continually proceeding a demonstration of the Creator's power, to transcend all these base propensities, and to surmount all these difficulties, insuperable save to himself, and to make, out of such emptiness, fulness to come forth; out of such wickedness, holiness; out of such enmity, love; out of such frailty, infallible strength. This is the demonstration of electing love, and constitutes election as indispensable a part of the great mystery of God as is the sinfulness of the creature. These elect persons, in whom God prevaileth against the natural man's obstinate aversions, constitute the church; and their souls are now gathering unto Christ, in the New Jerusalem, which is above. These being upon the earth, are a distinct and separate people from the rest; having in them, and upon them, a purpose of God, which the others have neither in them nor upon them. They are written in the Lamb's book of life before the foundation of the world. They were the Father's witnesses unto a coming Christ, until he came: and now they are the Father's witnesses of a living Christ, of a risen Christ, of a reigning Christ, of a Christ yet about to come. Demonstrations are they of the Trinity, of the Father's will above the creature's will, of the Son's revival and resurrection of the creature by personal union thereunto; of the Holy Ghost's ability to do this work of revival and regeneration in other creatures besides Christ. Thus are they not mere word-of-mouth witnesses, but witnesses in life, living witnesses, witnesses by their being, of that great truth that God is three persons in one substance.

The Historical Continuity of the Elect People of God

Now, that this election might be known unto men, as a great original principle of the purpose of God, it is not merely written in a book, as our word-idolaters teach; but it is embodied in a living, moving, continued chain of persons, who, beginning from the fall, shall preserve onward the continuity of the election, until they stand in immutable and infallible glory, to be used by the Creator in the effecting of his still unaccomplished purpose, whatever it may be. This co-fraternity of elected ones, this communion of saints, took an outward symbol, received an outward symbol and definition, in the person of Abraham, the friend of God; from which time until this present, they have continued defined and separated by an outward symbol, first of circumcision, and then of baptism, unto this day. Unto this end therefore, I say, the church is embodied, even unto the end of enjoying all the blessedness of God's electing love, and testifying, in the midst of the world, unto that goodness and power of God which riseth strong and sublime above all let and hindrance, and accomplisheth God-like purposes and God-like acts, by means of the empty nothingness of creature-substance, by means of the violent aversions, and ungodly propensities, and Antichristian determinations of creature-substance.

Now, as God's purpose is essentially one and indivisible, like himself, though for the convenience of discourse we must handle it under several parts, this power of election is given, not here and there, but everywhere, in the midst and in the duration of the creature's being: and, in like manner, the down-drawing powers of the creature are proved not here and there, but everywhere in the midst and in the duration of the creature. Therefore it is necessary to the unity of the divine purpose, and to the demonstration of its pervading omnipresence, that the election should be gathered out of all kindreds, and nations, and tongues, and peoples; and moreover, it is in like manner necessary, that in the election itself there should be an invisibility, an impenetrable secrecy, a hiddenness, beyond the research, and utterly defying the discovery, of man, to the end it may not be possible to describe a bound or limit, whether physical or metaphysical, within which the election is contained. For if that bound could be described, then most clear and manifest it is, that the rest would be excluded; and so God's upholding and sustaining power would only be proved over a part of his handiwork, and not over the whole. But, by means of the invisibility, that which is only a part hath yet given to it the faculty of proving, for the whole, the mighty power of God to sustain and uphold the creature, so that no creature, defined by any conditions whatever, should be able to say, "God cannot uphold me: I am beyond the province of electing power. My wickedness, my infirmity, is greater than God can overcome."

To prevent such a fell conclusion, it is that the election or true church is essentially invisible, and must continue so until the time be arrived for some great manifestation and demonstration of the divine power, after another kind and manner than that of election. Now, if the election must be invisible, God, when he gives to it a symbol, such as circumcision and baptism, must necessarily admit within the pale thereof, reprobate as well as elect ones; for if only elect ones were admitted within the pale, then they would at once become visible, have a definite place, a definite number, a definite form; and so exclude all beyond that place, number, and form, from the action of God's power and love. It is to this intermingling of the election and reprobation in the church, I would call your attention, as being the second great method by which God unfolds the exceeding sinfulness of sin, and which makes the sin of the church of a deeper dye than the sin of the outward world; for I do believe that to this end the church was made visible, and all the evils of a visible church permitted, in order that men might be proved capable of sinning against the Holy Ghost, as well as of sinning against the Son.

The Church as the Fulness of the Holy Spirit

The church, by which I mean the glorified Head and the members, invisible as well as visible,—the church is the fulness of the Holy Ghost: the church is a greater mystery of God's power than the incarnation. The incarnation shewed the power of God in flesh, when personally united unto the Son. The church sheweth the power of God in flesh, not personally united unto his Son, but only mystically united with him. The flesh in Christ never sinned, though ever passive and pervious unto temptation of all kinds; but our flesh ever sinneth, and is burdened with an incredible amount of sinfulness, of actual sinfulness; habits innumerable, hardness impenetrable, enmity insurmountable is there in every man, at the time at which electing love begins to exhibit an irresistible almighty power against all these enormities and excesses of the sinful creature. Wherefore, I say again, the work of the Spirit in the church is a mightier work than in the incarnation of Christ. The former is the forthshewing of God's good pleasure in his Son; the latter was the forthshewing of his anger against his Son. The former is the putting forth of the power of the Son in his immortal body; the latter was the putting forth of his power in a mortal body. The former is that mighty working of the Spirit which he wrought in Christ when he raised him from the dead; the latter was the working of the same Spirit, when he created a holy thing out of an unholy, and supported a holy thing against unholy conditions. In one word, the church is the demonstration of the Father's electing love, of Christ's mighty power to do God's will, God's work, God's pleasure by the vile impotent creature. The incarnation is only God's power to destroy the enmity between himself and the creature, and put the creature upon the footing of grace, favour, forgiveness of sin; to cast Satan out of it; to withhold sin from mastering it; and to reveal Christ the Lord of it, the Redeemer of it, the Defender of it: and to place it through Christ, in the equipoise of its own inclination; and so to shew forth the native abhorrence and disinclination which it hath to God, even when he is manifested as a Father, as a forgiving, gracious Father. But the church riseth much higher than this equipoise, and hath the counterpoise of God's almighty power and efficacy to do in it, and for it, the mighty works of his good pleasure.

Being so, therefore, that the church is this fuller vessel of God's power, even the fulness of him that filleth all in all; the fruit of the Father's love, the power of the Son's endless life, the work of the Holy Ghost: whoso sinneth against the church doth sin a greater sin than doth he that sinneth against the preached gospel only. This is a point which many of my dear brethren cannot understand; but which, by the blessing of God, I hope this discourse may convince them of. I mean those beloved brethren who see the freeness of the gospel, and the guilt incurred by rejecting it: but who see not the fulness of the church, and the guilt of sinning against its holy ordinances. Such brethren are fit for missionaries; but they have to learn the higher profession of a minister of the church, of the established ministers of a Christian state, and a baptized people. They preach not up to the measure of the people's privileges as an election; they preach not down to the depths of the people's sinfulness, as sinning against the peculiar life, love, and holiness of the election. They see the sin against the Son of Man, but the sin against the Holy Ghost they see not, they weigh not, they reprove not: yet is it this, and nothing else, which the apostle alludeth to in the 6th and the 10th chapters of the Hebrews, and which Peter alludeth to in the 2d chapter of his Second Epistle.

But why refer to passages in Scripture, when all Scripture and all providence beareth out the greater guilt and heavier judgements of a people in covenant? This is what makes the sin of Babylon so much more awful than the sin of the world; so that the beast and the false prophet feel the anguish of the burning lake, one thousand years before the rest of the world,—yea, one thousand years before the devil himself. The Jews sinned not this sin against the Holy Ghost, because the Holy Ghost was not yet given, and therefore by stripes can their sin be remitted. The unbaptized world, that rejected Christ, shall in a deluge of blood be drenched, and come out from her fearful baptism more beautiful than ever; but the church, the adulterous Popery, and the gainsaying infidel Protestantism, all who have rebelled against the baptized church, and refused the Spirit-filled ordinances, go down quick into the pit, and welter in the lake of fire which shall never be quenched, during the season that Satan abideth in the bottomless pit, during the season that the nations which are saved walk in the light, and the kings of the earth bring their glory and honour into the gates of the resurrection city. But, woe is me! who perceiveth this the greater wickedness of the church? who warneth her of this her heavier doom? Are we ministers then? No, the servant of a house understandeth the laws of that house, and in his service observeth them and setteth them forth; but the ministers of the church know not the difference between the world and the church; and how then can they set it forth? This is what I mean, when I preach so much of baptism; when I preach so much of the apostasy; and I give God thanks that you, at least, have attained unto the understanding thereof; and I pray you to be diligent in the meditation of this our greater responsibility, and to entreat the church, and by all means set ourselves, to contend against the ignorance of this our heavier account, which pertaineth to us as a church.

Now, by permitting this reprobation in the midst of the election, sin is shewn to be of a deeper dye than by any other means it could have been proved to be. The sin against the Holy Ghost is established, the sin, not only against the incarnate, but against the risen Christ; the sin against the Father's love, and the Father's strength; that sin passing forgiveness, that sin passing remission; whose deepest, blackest, vilest spot the blood of Christ cannot cleanse; whose weight and misery of eternal woe the goodness of God will not through eternity remove. What an awful thought! so awful is the sin, the hideous, enormous sin, under which Christendom now groans; with the wrath of which the heaven is now frowning, for the beginning of the judgment of which the dark portentous clouds are gathering, whose presence I feel in the obstinacy and infidelity of the times; and oh, let me speak the truth,—whose influences I feel every day in my own wicked heart! God deliver me, God deliver my people, whom he hath instructed me to warn. God bring out an election from the midst of us, and in us shew the pillar and foundation, which nothing can shake, and which nothing can remove. With this prayer, with this earnest prayer for you all, I dismiss this second head of conclusions—namely, the greater sinfulness which is shewn forth by a constituted church, over and above that which is shewn forth by an evangelised but unbaptized world.

UNIVERSAL REDEMPTION AND LIMITED ELECTION

But I cannot conclude such a weighty discourse without a word of opening into every soul, touching the freeness of their door of entrance into the election. That the gift is to be communicated to a part only of the human race is evident, as well from the fact as from the language of Scripture, and the continual doctrine of the church; universalism having always been regarded as a most damnable heresy. Now, this limitation doth not stand in the thing itself which Christ did: Christ's work is as capable of being applied to the whole as to a part: and in fact, so far as title of Lordship is concerned, it doth apply unto the whole. In Christ all shall be made alive; by Christ all shall be judged, and this because he is the Son of Man; but in Christ all shall not be saved, but only a chosen portion.

Now, the thing which men search into is, What is the cause, and what gives the limitation unto the saved portion? And the answer is in Christ's own words frequently repeated: "All that the Father giveth me, shall come to me; and him that cometh to me, I will in no wise cast out," (John 6. 37). And again: "This is the Father's will which hath sent me, that of all which he hath given me, I should lose nothing, but should raise it up again at the last day" (John 6.34). And again: "No man can come to me, except the Father which hath sent me draw him, and I will raise him up at the last day" (John 6.44). And again: "Every man therefore, that hath heard and hath learned of the Father, cometh unto me" (John 6.45). It is a thing, therefore, at no rate to be doubted, but unto the death to be maintained, that the Father hath reserved in his own personal propriety, the measure and extent unto which he will make that redemption to go, which Christ hath wrought out equally and alike for the whole created substance; whereby Christ's work is put under subjection to the Father's will, which may extend the benefits of it to whom he pleaseth, to all, if so he had pleased. The election of the Father, therefore, taketh place in Jesus Christ; that is to say, not one could have been elected, but in virtue of the redemption of Christ for sin, both appointed, and, as we say, contracted for by covenant.

Yet at the same time, while the Father doth thus preserve and glorify his own holiness, and shew forth all righteousness as in his Son contained, and from his Son proceeding, and so constitutes him the Head of the church, and the Lord of all; he doth reserve unto his own unrevealed will the extension of that righteousness which in Christ is stored up, unto as many as he pleaseth, unto no one if he pleaseth. The glory of his creative and redemptive power would have been shewn forth in the act of redeeming that portion of the created substance which Christ had assumed into his own personality; but the glory of his grace would not thus have been manifested, if, without applying the benefit unto another creature, he had merely lifted up Christ, and in him reigned and ruled over all. To shew forth his grace, therefore, in great magnificence, he, according to the good pleasure of his will, according to the riches of his grace, according to his good pleasure which he hath purposed in himself, did graciously resolve to apply the benefits of Christ's death unto a chosen portion of the human race. But reserving, in the mystery of his own unrevealed and incomprehensible essence, the number and the individual persons of the elect, he instituted the ministry of reconciliation which we fill, and commanded it to be preached unto every creature: "That God is in Christ reconciling the world unto himself, not imputing their trespasses unto them. And now we are ambassadors for Christ, as though God did beseech you by us; we pray you in Christ's stead, be ye reconciled to God" (2 Corinthians 5.19).

But while we preach reconciliation accomplished between God and a wicked world, and shew forth the wonders of God's love and mercy in the humiliation of his Son; we preach this, not as the complete message of God, which is able to perfect the salvation of a sinner, because we declare, at the same time, that no one can come unto Christ, except the Father which hath sent Christ draw him. We preach the reconciliation in Christ, as mankind's free passage and safe conduct unto the Father. We preach Christ's reconciliation as the removal of all lets and hindrances which stood between God and man, in consequence of sin. And so we bring the guilty conscience to be disburdened of its guilt, and the countenance of God to be cleared from its clouds and wrathful frowns. To the sinner Christ bringeth peace; God he presenteth as full of grace; and so, my brethren, the reconciliation being preached, as done for the behoof of mankind in general, mankind in general are visited with the glad tidings, and left without excuse, if they draw not near to a reconciled God.

APPEAL TO READER

This, our ministry being accomplished, and you believing the same, it remaineth then for you, through Christ's mediation, to transact with God; and, when your spirit invisible doth with the invisible God transact, through the mediation of Christ, we are taught to declare unto you, that God will manifest himself in your souls in a way which no tongue can tell of. Then beginneth the true work of effectual calling, regeneration, sanctification, and the new life, when the soul, believing to have found redemption in Christ, doth cast itself upon God, and doth receive unto itself the manifestations of his love. But this is an invisible being, a spiritual work. It is a life hid with Christ in God: it is foolishness unto the world, enthusiasm, empiricism, fanaticism, whereof some of the outward manifestations are to be seen in the subjection of the flesh, and the cessation of its works; but whereof the glorious fulness is known only to the soul, which is conscious thereof. This is that which flows from the Father's fountain-will, directly into the soul of a believer in Christ the Redeemer, and a believing observer of the ordinances of Christ, the great Head and High Priest of the church. Unto the edge of this surpassing blessedness and immortal glory Christ bringeth you all; and saith unto you by our mouth, Pass over, pass over into the enjoyment of God, the Invisible and Incomprehensible. Commit yourself to him—commit yourself to him in faith, and fearlessly. See what he hath done for you by me: let that be your warrant to trust him for the rest. Pass onward, pass forward into the absolute and unrevealed will of God. And thus all the virtue of Christ's work, and all the virtue of the preaching of it, amounteth unto this, of shewing the intelligent creation what grace there is in God, and counteracting all murmurings which might have come from the inheritance of a fallen nature; yea, not only counteracting, but through the fall presenting the universal grace of God in his Son, and there leaving us suspended upon that gracious will, that absolute will of God in Christ, revealed to be gracious. The end of the revealed Godhead is to draw us to worship, and to have intercourse with, the unrevealed Godhead. The revealed Godhead standing in the person of the Son, being, verily, no more than God's appeal unto the comprehension of his creatures, unto that part of his creature man which holdeth of the visible, in order that the spiritual part, which holdeth not of the visible, may have to do with the unrevealed Godhead standing hidden in the person of the Father. And redemption endeth where election beginneth. Redemption is no more than the porch which introduceth unto the temple of election. It appertaineth, therefore, unto the Father, and to him alone, to seal a soul which Christ hath redeemed.

Having made known unto you these two great truths, how Christ's reconciliation between your sinful substance and the Godhead hath been produced; and that this the Father hath done in order to bring you unto the acknowledgement of his right and sovereignty in you; I leave you there to transact for yourselves with the Father. It is vain to ask how the election of the Father proceedeth. If I could tell how, if it depended on any conditions which man can apprehend, then the very end of it would be destroyed: it would come under the visible, the comprehensible, the revealed; under which, if all were brought that concerneth us, then I ask, what would remain to bind us to the invisible? The redemption is comprehensible and visible, and applicable in common, to the very end that the election may be invisible, incomprehensible, and revealed only to the person of the individual. With the same diligence with which we preach the redemption to be the common privilege of mankind, we preach the election to be the special communication of the Father unto individual souls: and this is religion, this is godliness, even such communication and intercourse between the spirit and the Father of spirits. Revelation is not religion, but revelation is unto religion. The church is not salvation, but the church is unto salvation.

To the end, therefore, of hanging and suspending the whole creation from his will, through the mediation of Christ, the Father hath limited the salvation unto a portion of mankind, while he hath made the reconciliation common to them all. If he had made the salvation likewise universal, then there would have been nothing left with himself: the creature would have ascribed its salvation unto the revealed Godhead alone, and would never have known nor acknowledged an unrevealed Godhead, which is the beginning and the end of all worship. But, as it now is, we know God in Christ, and knowing what is revealed in him, we commit ourselves to him in faith; and through faith we receive from the trusted Father the seal of the Holy Ghost. Redemption, therefore, by Christ,—I say it again, redemption by Christ is only the stepping-stone unto faith in the electing Father; and through that faith in one unknown, at least in that part of his will which is unknown, through such honour of the invisible Godhead we receive the seal of the Holy Ghost, or the impartation and communication of the gift which the Father hath kept in his own power.

THE TRINITARIAN STRUCTURE OF REDEMPTION

The gift of the Holy Ghost is the communication to the individual of the electing love of God, unto his soul in particular, as the work of Christ in flesh is the gift of reconciliation unto the world in general. The work of the

Spirit is not the mere reconciliation; but it is that which God thereto addeth of his special and electing grace; the fruit of pure faith in the unrevealed will of God. The work of Christ holdeth as much of knowledge as it doth of faith: I mean the work which he wrought in the flesh, and which is recorded in the word of God. This must be known before it can be revealed. It is faith resting upon knowledge. But the faith which is followed by the gift of the Holy Ghost is a faith wholly upon the invisible. It is the faith of a promise, and, to all human appearance, an impossibility that God can create in us a new nature, diverse from and opposite to the old. This is the work which gives individuality and personality to a man. This is the work which exalts and dignifies a man—a work unto which no other man can help him—and I may say, not the whole church, nor the written word, nor Christ the cruci-fied, but the Father only.

And in this way, all Christ's work in the flesh doth but honour the invisible Father the more, bringing all the benefits of his passion and death to weigh and poise the world back into its places of dependency from the visible throne. Christ in the flesh is the great example of faith upon the in-visible Father, as he is likewise the great example of faith rewarded with the fulness of the Holy Ghost. He lived by faith, even as we do live by faith. Now, because Christ did thus glorify the Father, and, wherever his gospel is proclaimed, doth glorify the Father: therefore the Father glorifieth Christ, the risen Christ, the ruling Christ, by giving unto him power to communi-cate of his victory over the devil, the world, and the flesh, unto as many as the Father pleaseth, unto all those who, receiving the reconciliation at the hands of the Peace-maker, having the faith of the promise, cast themselves upon the gracious Father. "To them that received him, gave he power to become the sons of God, even to them that believe on his name; which are born not of blood, nor of the will of the flesh, nor of the will of man, but of God" (John 1.12).

The invisible Father, I say, doth glorify his risen Son, doth glorify the manhood of his risen Son, by appointing and ordaining that the regenera-tion, sanctification, and salvation of his elect ones should proceed through the risen man Jesus Christ, unto and upon all who believe in the reconcilia-tion wrought in Jesus Christ while tabernacling in flesh, and wrestling with its infirmities. Therefore is Christ the Head of the church by power com-municated to him at his resurrection, as he is Head of the creation by virtue of his holy life, meritorious death, and incorrupt resurrection. All that the Father hath given unto him he feedeth with a rod of love, and bringeth with a rod of power out of the prison-house of the grave. And how, then, doth Christ communicate of this power which he hath received? Doth he do over again in our flesh what he did in his own? No verily. His own flesh he sanctified, ours he doth never sanctify until the resurrection. Sin never dwelt in his flesh so as to prevail over the holiness which was in him. But this cannot be said of men; no, not of the greatest saints; in whom there is an original and an actual sin, for which they shall see corruption.

What is it, then, which Christ bestoweth? As Adam did not communicate unto Cain his unfallen, but his fallen likeness, so doth Christ not communicate unto his children the likeness of his humility, but the likeness of his power. He regenerateth not be power antecedent, but posterior, to his resurrection. The new man, therefore, is after the likeness of the risen Christ, inheritor of his joy, of his power, and of his glory. And thus the regenerate have a double image: in the flesh, bearing the image of the earthly; in the spirit, bearing the Spirit of the heavenly Adam;—as to the former, holding of the curse; as to the latter, holding of the blessing; —as to the former, holding of the cross; as to the latter, holding of the resurrection. But because Christ is greater than all, and because he is ruling in the church for the Father, we know that the child of Christ, which is born by regeneration of the Holy Ghost in us, is stronger and mightier, and able to subdue and subject the child of Adam, which we have by generation, though upholden by the devil, the world, and the flesh. Christ's life in the flesh was a life of law-keeping; and because he kept the law, he arose into a life which knoweth no law, but is of all things the living law; and of this life it is that he doth communicate unto us.

The Holy Spirit, taking possession of us, and making his habitation in us, doth reveal unto us power from on high; whereby we are able to put to death the rebel flesh, and so be done with the condemning law: for when the flesh is dead, the law hath no more to say. The executioner is satisfied, when the traitor is lying dead at his feet. And thus the Spirit of Christ doth satisfy the law, and make it honourable, by quelling and killing the guilty body of sin and death. This is the way that Christ makes the law honourable in us now, by putting down and suppressing that rebel flesh which ever riseth in mutiny against the law: and there the law standeth in its iron-crested pride, satisfied the meanwhile to have made clean work with the rebels, but awaiting still the higher satisfaction of serving God as the rule of flesh and blood, the guide, the blessing thereof; no longer its oppressor, its imprisoner, and its murderer.

This was not the condition of Christ's flesh, which the Spirit enabled to keep the law, and to fulfil all righteousness: so that, though obnoxious to sin, it never sinned; and though obnoxious to death, like other flesh, it did not see corruption, which is the work of death. As sin tried him always, but could prevail over him never, the Spirit ever enabling his soul to reject it; so death took him, but could not prevail over him that he should see corruption, the Spirit interposing and raising him to see glory. But we both sin with our flesh, and our flesh, so long as it liveth, cannot cease from sin; and when we die, our flesh shall see corruption, because it hath sinned. The only possibility of righteousness, therefore, in this fallen, sinful creature, is by a premature death, so to speak; and this is what the Spirit accomplisheth, enabling us, as it were, with our own hand to slay, not our child, but our very self; and in slaying ourself to slay our children also, so that they shall be born holy, and baptized as it were in our baptism. Mystery most profound, mystery most fruitful, which hath been to me the consolation of many unknown and unutterable wringings of the heart!

This power which Christ hath to change the very being of the living man, and as it were to strike a mighty power to the extremities of the living flesh, is shewn unto us by the triumphant debate which he made with the powers camped in his flesh, and waging war therein; paralysing them, defeating them, destroying them; and, being so, what remaineth that he cannot do? Is he not able, is he not much more able, being glorified, to beat back, and astonish, and freeze into death, those powers of the devil, the world, and the flesh, that are camped in you and me? Verily, verily, as he hath suffered in the flesh himself, he can arm us with the same mind, that we, suffering in the flesh, may cease from sin. So can he bring us into death, as he brought himself into death; and so are we crucified with him. And we are buried with him; and so our bodies, which could not be united with him in this life, are united with him by death, and rest in this grave until the resurrection.

But this mortification of the old man, this putting off of his corruptions and lusts, is not the whole of the Spirit's work, proceeding from the risen Christ. Yea, I may say, it is only the preparation for his work, only the death and burial unto a resurrection; for we rise with Christ to newness of life, we are planted in the likeness of his death, only that we may be in the likeness of his resurrection. The body, every member of the body, is not only separated from being the members of the harlot flesh, but is betrothed and wedded unto the risen body of Christ. Therefore the Spirit killeth only to make alive. If he sendeth the chill touch of death throughout the bounds of flesh and blood, it is but that he may send the touch of life through the bounds of flesh and blood. He begetteth a life from the dead in every regenerate man; and where his work is, there is not only the agonies of dying flesh, and the shudder of death, but there is the thrill of life, of immortal life, and the power of an irresistible holiness, and the security of an inviolable peace, and the brightness of an indestructible joy.

This change in the spirit of our mind, this prevalency of the risen powers of creation in Christ's hand, wielded over the powers of the fallen creation, resting still in Satan's withered hand, is the manifestation of the Father's electing love, in the heart of every chosen one. And can the man, who this possesseth, be ignorant that he possesseth it? and must he go and try its measure by the Ten Commandments? Out upon such an idle tale! The man who hath received this baptism of the Holy Ghost, is a man invested with the holiness of a priest, and with the power of a king, and with the knowledge of a prophet. Light is the habitation of his soul; he dwelleth in light; he is in the light. He is holy, as saith the apostle, and cannot sin because he is born of God. The flesh, by reason of unbelief and traffic with the law, may awake and sin, yea, and attain unto such a prurient lustfulness, as that it may be necessary for the church to give such a one to Satan, for the destruction of the flesh, that his spirit may be saved in the day of the Lord: and such a one may be brought into deep waters; and great straits, and doubts, and perplexities may beset him round; but whence are these doubts? from the devil. And why hath the devil power against him? Because he believeth not that Christ hath bruised his head. How shall such a one be delivered? By doing for him what I have now been attempting; even by shewing him the common reconciliation, and so leading him onwards into the knowledge, or rather the mystery, of God's election, and of the Spirit's procession through Christ to work in him the death unto sin, and the resurrection unto holiness.

Introduction to "The Preparation For, and Act of, the Incarnation"

Only a small portion of this sermon has been reproduced here. The first section of this sermon, which has been omitted, is devoted to showing how the incarnation and the redemptive sufferings of Jesus Christ is the continuation of God's action in the world in relation to the people of Israel. It is not an alternative solution, but part of the same unfolding of the pre-temporal divine will to redeem. The sacrificial system, the Levitical priesthood, the prophetic vocation are all identified as forerunners of Jesus Christ, who is sacrifice, high priest, and prophet.

The main part of the sermon concerns the self-limitation of the Son to assume human nature into union with himself. In his discussion of the true humanity of Jesus Christ, which has been reproduced here, Irving characteristically prioritizes the role of the Spirit in empowering Christ to overcome the flesh and the devil. Irving treats the assumption of fallen human nature under the category of "humiliation." This has two important connections in Irving's thought. First, he identifies this willingness to undergo such limitation as godliness itself. The incarnation as the willing act of God's self-limitation is presented as the highest act of divinity, consonant with divine being. Second, he broadens the scope of the saving work of Christ beyond the passive obedience on the cross to the whole course of his God the Son's incarnate existence. Irving conceives of redemption as an arc of humiliation and glorification: God the Son's coming out from the Father, assuming human nature into union with himself, bearing the abuse of his creation, resisting the temptation of the devil, suffering death and hell before being raised up in the resurrection and ascension.

Irving identifies three modes of this self-limitation, of which just one is included in this abridgement. The first, which has been omitted here, describes the Son's condescension to enter into a struggle with Satan. Irving considers Christ's life to have been characterized by a continuous, but ultimately victorious, battle against the power of Satan. Irving certainly does not downplay the power of Satan, seeing it as second only to divine power, and even appearing greater than the power of God from the perspective of the earth. However, it is this power that God the Son met and overcame as a human. The second, which is included here, describes the Son's willing humiliation to enter into a struggle with sin in the flesh. The power of sin as that disorientation of the human will away from the ground of existence, Irving argues, had its seat in the flesh (in the Pauline sense, not in a dualistic sense) assumed by Christ just as it does for the rest of humanity. The third, which is omitted here, describes the Son's humiliation to suffer the contradiction and vitriol of his creation. Engaging with the Passion narrative and Psalm 22, Irving describes the hatred poured out on the incarnate Son by the people he loved. This is indicative, Irving suggests, of the greatness of divine love and the restraining of his wrath.

The final section of this sermon addresses the Son's alienation from the Father and the Son's faith in the face of that terrible isolation. Irving considers this theme through two sayings on the cross: "my God, my God why have you forsaken me" and "Father, into your hands I commit my spirit." In this, the Son assumed our condition under the law and the judgement of God and from that position actualized a new obedience and a new act of faith, meeting us at our lowest point and dragging us to the Father.

Irving concludes his sermon with pastoral comments regarding Christian life. First, Christ's presence among sinful humanity means that Christians cannot retreat into holy communities, but remain connected to the world around them, suffering its hatred as and when it comes. Second, Christ's victory over Satan, the flesh and death give the Christian courage to continue the struggle in their own life, confident in the assurance that Christ has already overcome and we are included in his victory. As ever, Irving concludes by encouraging his listeners to not look to themselves and their own circumstances, but to look to Christ as the author and perfector of our faith.

AJDI

4

The Preparation For, and Act of, the Incarnation

And the Word was made flesh

JOHN 1.14[1]

THE POWER OF THE SPIRIT AT WORK IN CHRIST

Into the mystery [. . .] of the union between the divine and human nature, it is hard to enter; and those who have dared it too far have most frequently lost themselves in error. It is revealed that his body was created by the power of the Holy Ghost in the womb of the Virgin Mary, that he might be the woman's seed, according to the promise. He grew in wisdom as he grew in years, like any other child; though he was from the womb the very Word of God, which had created the heavens and the earth, and spoken by the mouth of all the prophets: who was conscious of the eternity of his being, and of the blessedness thereof, before the world was. And he was obedient to the law, in its letter and in its spirit; and he made the Word of God his

---

1. Omitted material can be found in Irving, *CW* 5, 258–267.

meditation, as we do; and he lived by faith upon it, as do all his people. He prayed and was strengthened by prayer, as we are: he was afflicted with all our afflictions, and tried with all our trials, and was sustained by the power of the Holy Ghost, even as we are.

For we are not to suppose, with the early heretics, that his body was only an appearance or an illusion, but a real manifestation of the second person of the blessed Trinity as man. He was not the Only-begotten in the bosom of the Father, at the same time that he was the Messiah on earth; but he was the Only-begotten come out of the bosom of the Father, in order to become the Messiah upon earth. The Word had been revealed in the universal creation once, but now he is to be revealed in the individual man. In the former work the individual was seen in the universal; in the latter the universal is to be revealed in the individual, and gathered into him. It was a high honour put upon human nature; but it was for a very high object; which we know only in part, and which will doubtless illustrate the being and glory of the Godhead more than the creation of the heavens and the earth. No wonder that the Word of God, foreseeing this great act of his incarnation should speak of it by the mouth of all his prophets: for it is a singular act, whose extraordinary wonderfulness shall reach through all eternity. No wonder that the rumour of it came before, nor that sacrifice should be instituted to signify it, and the tabernacle to witness it, and the temple to confirm it, and the whole Jewish state to be, as it were, the womb of this great conception; in the foresight of which the prophet bursteth forth so sublimely: "For unto us a child is born, unto us a Son is given; and the government shall be upon his shoulder; and his name shall be called Wonderful, Counsellor, The mighty God, The everlasting Father, The Prince of Peace" (Isaiah 9.6).

He was anointed to his holy office by the Spirit in the form of a dove; and declared to be the Son of God whom the people were to hear. And it was by the Spirit that he was led into temptation; and it was by the Spirit that the man Jesus Christ prevailed. Whatever power he might possess otherwise, it is certain he prevailed against Satan by that word and Spirit by which we are to prevail he was travelling in the valley of humility; and it was no pretence of doing so, but it was so. He was emptied: he did not seem to be emptied, but he was so. And he preached by the Holy Spirit, which was upon him, and with which he had been anointed. And in the power of the Holy Spirit he went about doing good, and healing them that were possessed "with the devil." And the Chief Shepherd of the sheep offered himself by the eternal Spirit. And he was justified in the Spirit, by the resurrection from the dead. So that in very deed, and in very truth, he was the Christ Jesus, the Son of Man, the Second Adam; who hath now joined the human nature to the divine, and is become a quickening Spirit; baptizing with the Holy Spirit all who believe in his name and receive him as the Prophet of God; bestowing the regeneration of the Holy Ghost, the fellowship of his priesthood, and the inheritance of his glorious kingdom.

Without, therefore, adventuring into that subtle speculation in which so many of the early heretics lost themselves, I would rather proceed humbly, with the Holy Scriptures in my hand, to set forth in order the work of the humiliation and ministry of Christ Jesus in the flesh: which I conceive to be of the last importance in this argument of the incarnation; being, in truth, both the meritorious and prevailing cause of our justification before God, and the great example to every child of the Holy Spirit—that is, to every member of his church. From the day of his baptism until the day of his death, I conceive that he sustained the very trials, and achieved the very victories, into the fellowship of which we are called from the day of our baptism to the day of our death, and into the actual fellowship of which we enter from the day of our regeneration by the Holy Spirit, under which we, who have the first-fruits of the Spirit, do groan.

And yet I approach this subject with a certain awe, which nothing can overcome, save the necessity, to the establishment of the church, that you should be well acquainted with your great Prototype, the Author and the Finisher of your faith: for the mystery of it is very great. I confess that it has been a relief to me to look at it under the veil of the Levitical dispensation; and I tremble to approach the confines of the naked sufferings of the Lord. For he condescended to dwell in concern and communion with the flesh; to look up through fleshly eyes; by fleshly senses to converse with the great wickedness of the earth; and, through the faculties of the human soul, to commune with every impious, ungodly, and blasphemous chamber of the fallen intellect and feeling of men. Whereof, brethren, the condescension overcometh me: I cannot attain unto the understanding of it. For the divine and Almighty Creator to empty himself of himself, to take the limitation of a creature, and bind himself under the appointed law of the action and suffering thereof, is very wonderful; but for the Holy Creator, the Thrice-Holy One, by dwelling therein, to bring himself into actual communication with, real sense of, and sympathy in, all the wickedness of this world, passeth all humiliation which can be conceived.

THE MYSTERY OF GODLINESS

That his divine nature should suffer such contradiction of sinners as he endured, and bear such limitations of power; should endure such a pressure of iniquity as his human nature, his sin-bearing body, brought him into the sense, feeling, bondage, and suffering of; is the depth of the mystery of godliness. And herein consisteth the greatness of his love in enduring, the greatness of his Father's love in giving him up to endure, our nature. It is not in the *kind* of life or *kind* of death; it is in *the* life and *the* death of the Man-God that we are to find the great merit of the love. The *humiliation* was the sacrifice; the *becoming* man, the *being made flesh*. For the rest, it is only, as it were, the wise adaptation of the act to something past and to something future: the *act* itself is that in which the marvel lies.

The Gospels of his human life are of great value, as containing the ratification and fulfilment of the former covenant, as laying out the platform and scheme of the new covenant or spiritual dispensation, and presenting us with the pattern of the perfect man before the Lord; but it is the fourth Gospel, that of St John, as commented upon and broadly illustrated in St Paul's Epistles, which makes us familiar with the fulness of the Godhead manifested in him bodily. And here I must declare, that I love not the carnal estate of Christ's visible sufferings as a man, and of his death as a man, save only as they give heart to his disciples passing through the same scenes of trial, and shew us the reality of his passive manhood. But as the measure of what all his elect would have had to suffer through all eternity and a set-off against this, in the way of barter or exchange, I must confess it appears to me to be a poor, petty, dishonourable, insufficient view of the matter, which the thinnest-witted Socinian would blow to atoms by a breath.

The whole act of the incarnation is a mystery to the fleshly man and ought not to be debased down to his fleshly sympathies. It is the basest part of Popery to have done so, with their crosses and relics, and their true blood, true tears and true sweat. The spiritual have nothing to do with such matters. Let it abide a mystery of love for the heart and mind, as they are enlightened and purified of the Holy Spirit, to enter into, further, and further, and still further, until they be separated from this spirit-clouding flesh and carnal mind: for it is only to be apprehended according as we have Christ formed within us by the Holy Spirit; when not by the nature mind, nor the natural heart, but by the spiritual mind and heart, we do enter into the great mystery of the sufferings of the Son of God while incarnate in a fleshly body;—as we now proceed to shew in this discourse, praying the Holy Spirit to be our guide through the deep valley, while we descend into those lowly abasements of being into which the Son of God descended for our sakes.[2]

---

2. Omitted material can be found in Irving, *CW*, 271–74

SELF-LIMITATION TO CONTEST
WITH SIN IN THE FLESH

The second great head of our Lord's humiliation was his contest with sin in the flesh; which brings us properly into the regions of humanity: and to understand which, it is necessary to have a sufficient and worthy idea of the divine law; for "the strength of the sin is the law" (1 Corinthians 15.56). Which holy and just and venerable law is become very terrible to a fallen creature, meeting him on every side, and engirdling him with a thousand deaths. Every commandment saith, "Do this or die;" and nature replies, "But I cannot do it." "Die, then," saith the inexorable law. "Dost thou love the Lord thy God with all the heart and soul and strength and mind?" "No." "Then die thou must. Dost thou love thy neighbour as thyself?" "No." "Then thou must die." "What? For one sin death?" "Yea, death for the least transgression." And, moreover, if thou keep the whole law, and offend but in one point, thou art guilty of all: "the law revived and I died" (Romans 7.9).

Oh, fearful condition, into which the fall hath brought mankind! An estate truly of sin and misery! Now, brethren, this law, this inexorable law, stood around the Son of Man with its fiery points of death, as it standeth around every one of us. For he had come into humanity's accursed region; and his flesh, his human nature, was as assailable on every side as is ours: otherwise it had not been human nature.

> Forasmuch as the children were partakers of flesh and blood, he himself also took part of the same. [. . .] In all things it behooved him to be made like unto his brethren. [. . .] In that he himself hath suffered, being tempted, he is able to succour them that are tempted. [. . .]. For we have not an high priest that cannot be touched with the feeling of our infirmities, but was in all points tempted like as we are (Hebrews 2.14, 17, 18; 4.15)

Wherefore I believe that the Son of Man was assailable on the side of his flesh, or human nature, with every temptation, with every infirmity, to which I or any one now hearing me is obnoxious.

Did not Satan address the sense by its strongest, sternest, craving, when he tempted the hungered Son of man to turn the stones of the wilderness into bread? Did he not tempt the lust of the eye, when he shewed him all the kingdoms of the earth, for the guerdon[3] of which to worship him? And with what craftiness and mystery of arch-angelic deceit wrought he upon the faith of the Son of Man, when he quoted Scripture, and dared him to put it to the proof! Did I but say that I believed the Son of Man was proved and tried with all the proofs and trials which my human nature, and the human nature of every one hearing me, is or hath been tried withal? I should have said, that he was tried with every trial with which it is *possible* for human nature to be tried by the putting forth of all the subtlety and power of Satan. For how were he able to succour all them that have been, that are, or that shall be tempted, if he had not undergone the sum and substance of all possible temptation? Therefore is it most true that he bore our sicknesses and carried our sins; that "He was a man of sorrows and acquainted with grief" (Isaiah 53.3).

Behold, then, the Son of Man compressing within the short period of his prophetic office the sum-total of all mankind's liability to be tempted unto sin: conceive every variety of human passion, every variety of human affection, every variety of human error, every variety of human wickedness, which hath ever been realised, or is possible to be realised, inherent in the humanity and combined against the holiness of him who was not only a man, but the Son of Man, the heir of all the infirmities which man entaileth upon his children, which he took freely and fully upon him, all to bear; and bearing all, to annihilate all; and to bring in a righteousness, universal as the fall and the temptation was universal: and then shall you have an idea of the Son of Man's oppression and load; against whom, thus on every side best behind and before, stood up the law, as widely comprehensive as the temptation and said to him, Thou art man, very man, though thou be very God: as very man receive thou these continual assaults and yield to one of them, and thou also shalt die. The Son of God die? The Life die? Brethren, I know it could not be, I know it hath not been; but I am shewing you the proof to which the Son of God was put, the hideous and enormous proof to which he was put: for otherwise you shall neither have an adequate idea of the truth—the comfortable, the all-comforting truth—of his manhood; nor an adequate idea of the almighty power and infinite love of his Godhead.

Sin had its fullest range against the Son of God by virtue of his being the Son of Man. The law laid its full curse upon him. His divinity screened him not a jot. It bore him through it, but it saved him not a jot. We had not known the power of the Divinity to contend with sin, otherwise than by the incarnation. Sin would have seemed omnipotent, and death inevitable, and

3. A reward or recompense.

Satan invincible; having an indefeasible right, an unanswerable claim, and a power never to be gainsaid nor to be case out, where once they had got a footing. It is thus that God is glorified by the Godhead contending against sin in flesh, overcoming it, and proving it to be weaker than God in its own region, not capable of resisting God, not capable of holding those whom he would redeem.[4]

---

4. The rest of this sermon has been omitted. See Irving, *CW* 5, 277–311.

5

Synopsis of "The Fruits of the Incarnation"

In this sermon on Ephesians 1:2—omitted from this collection—Edward Irving addresses the benefits of the incarnation that belong to believers. This is a vast topic, but Irving limits himself to the fruits that are accrued by believers in this life rather than the next. In order to unfold the fruits that belong to believers Irving divides his sermon into three parts. In part one, he identifies two fruit: the grace of God and the peace which belongs to believers. In part two, he addresses the manner in which God's grace and peace ought to be declared to sinners. In the final part, he covers the application and appropriation of these fruit in the life of the believer.

Irving identifies the first fruit of the incarnation—grace—as an attribute of God. Grace, he explains, is more than mere goodness, "it is forgiveness and favour to those who have deserved our displeasure." This leads him to claim that sin is a pre-requisite to grace; without a fall there is no grace. God's grace does more than just repair the fallen state of humans; however, it elevates fallen humanity above their original state. Irving's treatment of grace is characteristically Trinitarian. He explains that the Father's grace is manifested in his willingness to "suffer his Son to go forth from his bosom, and take sinful flesh, and come under cursed conditions." The Son's grace is especially apparent in his willingness to become incarnate, restraining his divine power, might, and glory. As such the Son acts out of humanity

161

empowered by the Spirit. This makes all of Christ's works meritorious and allows him to set an example for believers to imitate. Finally, the Spirit's grace is shown in how he sustains Christ's humanity and empowers him to endure the Father's wrath and sin's sting.

The second fruit of the incarnation that belongs to believers is peace. The incarnation itself is a display of peace, for in the incarnation we "behold the nature of sinful, fallen, suffering man entering into sweet and harmonious union with the sinless nature of God." This peace displayed in the hypostatic union, however, is not Irving's primary focus in this sermon. Rather, Irving focuses on the type of peace expounded upon by Paul in his letter to the Ephesians. Peace consists of the breaking down of the wall of separation between Jew and Gentile, our reconciliation to God through the paschal work of Christ, and the love and fellowship we experience through the bond of the Holy Spirit.

Having identified grace and peace as fruit of the incarnation Irving turns his attention to explaining how these fruits ought to be proclaimed. As can be expected given Irving's emphasis on Christ as our exemplar he argues that we ought to take Jesus's example of proclamation as normative. In his proclamation of the good news to Nicodemus (John 3:1–21) Jesus brings up three points which Irving believes ought to be included in every gospel proclamation. Once again, these three aspects of gospel proclamation are Trinitarian in form. First, any gospel proclamation ought to state that Christ gave himself for the salvation of the world. Second, it ought to make clear the impossibility of salvation apart from the new birth by the Holy Spirit. Finally, it ought to stress that the preceding aspects are grounded in the loving and gracious will of the Father. Gospel proclamation ought to be fully trinitarian, otherwise, says Irving, a gospel proclamation does not actually contain the gospel. The second half of this part of the sermon is devoted to addressing the errors that follow when Christians ignore the persons of the Trinity in their gospel proclamation. Those who err in regards to the Father, Irving says, can be identified either as Antinomians or Arminians. Those who err in regards to the Son are those who are called "Bible-Christians" and intellectuals. Finally, those who err in regards to the Spirit are called "mystics." To avoid these errors one ought to have a properly Trinitarian theology. Moreover, to avoid other common theological errors, one ought to focus on the persons of the Trinity themselves rather than the gifts the persons grant to believers.

The final part of the sermon Irving discusses the application of grace and peace in the life of individuals. God's grace brings salvation, is offered to all persons (the elect and the reprobate), leads to godliness and righteousness, and creates an expectation for Christ's return. This grace is applied to individuals by the operation of the Holy Spirit. It is appropriated by faith. It results in humility, joy, and hope.

Several themes which characterize Irving's theology are present throughout this sermon. Through the sermon Irving stresses the importance of trinitarian theology. Grace is explicated in trinitarian terms as is the form of gospel proclamation. Likewise, various theological errors are explained as being rooted in subpar Trinitarian theology. A second theme that appears in this sermon is Irving's fallen human nature Christology. If Christ did not assume our fallen humanity then fallen human beings could not be the recipients of grace. If Christ did not assume a humanity like our own, relying on the Holy Spirit, Irving reasons, then Christ would not be imitable. Irving's Christology, therefore, forms the basis for the reception of grace and the application of grace in the life of believers. His Christology even sets the terms for a philosophy of ministry. Thus, "The Fruits of the Incarnation," serves as an example of Irving's practical theology.

CGW

6

Conclusions Concerning Divine Being and Created Being[1]

No man hath seen God at any time; the only-begotten Son, which is in the bosom of the Father, he hath declared him.

JOHN 1:18

While meditating the above sermons on the incarnation, various thoughts connected with this great subject have stirred my mind, touching its relations unto other great subjects; and I have been led to perceive distinctly, how the incarnation of the Son of God is the ground and basis of all real knowledge with respect to the Godhead, is the ground and basis of all worship of the Godhead by the creature, and of the creature's own eternal being and blessedness. I perceive, moreover, through the light cast upon these subjects by the incarnation, how a creation out of God, and yet worshipping God, is not possible without the knowledge of God in three persons subsisting, which, if it can be speculatively attained by the reason, is a truth

1. The full title of this sermon is "Conclusions Concerning the Subsistence of God, and the Subsistence of the Creature, Derived from Reflecting on the Incarnation." This is the sixth sermon in the series. Sermon 5 has been omitted in its entirety and is summarised in the introduction to this sermon.

realised only by the incarnation. Now, it is my desire to point out some of these high relations of the subject, which God hath enabled me to perceive; in doing which, the great difficulty is to observe order and method,—for the thoughts are high, and the range of them is very far. Yet, by the grace of God, I shall endeavour to comprehend them under these three heads:—

First, the coming of the Godhead into action to create, and to manifest itself unto the creatures whom it hath made, and to receive their worship and homage. This will open insight into the manner of the divine existence in three personalities.

Secondly, we would endeavour to shew how the creature shall subsist in an infallible and indestructible state, distinct from the godhead, with, and by means of Christ a form of existence between the two, which is of both, and, being of both, distinct from each. This will open insight into the three great distinctions, between the incomprehensible Godhead, the Christhead, and the infallible creature, inhabited by the Holy Ghost; which three things may never be mingled together, so as to be confused with one another.

Thirdly, we shall endeavour to open the connexions and communions, not the less subsisting amongst these three existences, the incomprehensible Godhead, the Godmanhood, and the Spirit-inhabited creature, in such wise as secureth worship unto the first, lordship unto the second, and infallibility unto the third.

And if we shall be able to open these three great heads of doctrine, we shall have comprehended and resolved the great problem of creation, and seen clean through unto the ultimate end of God, which is to manifest and communicate himself unto the creatures; for I consider creation to be no more than the indelible, indestructible expression of that truth, God of one substance in three persons subsisting.

CREATION AND REVELATION MANIFESTS THE TRIUNITY OF GOD

First, then, in the work of the creation we have maintained these heads of doctrine concerning the Trinity.

The Invisible God Assumes Finite Form to Act toward Creation

That the infinite God, who is also invisible and incomprehensible, cannot communicate himself, or the knowledge of himself, unto his creatures, without assuming himself a finite form. In order to be visible and comprehensible, nay, we may go a step higher, and say, that in order to fashion finite creatures, in order to do a finite action, it is necessary that the actor should assume a finite form. But, without doing more than to mention this great principle of divine operations, we observe, that if the end of God in creation be, to manifest himself unto the creatures, which is indeed the only end that he hath declared; and if his method of doing this be by bringing in his own Son, and setting him up for ever, in the form of the Lamb slain and risen from the dead, or in the form of risen God-man, and in that form to shew himself for ever and ever unto the creatures which he proposed to create; then is it never to be doubted, that he who worketh all things to the praise of his own glory, and who leaveth no loose or open parts in his purpose, but maketh it to be altogether harmonious, and consenting unto the great end, would from the beginning of creation bring himself into action under that form, which he was afterwards to assume: that is to say, everything would have an eye and aim to the risen God-man, everything would tell and fortell of him, everything would have its origin in that idea or purpose, and have the definition of its being thereby determined.

And this is what I understand, by all things being made for Christ, as well as by Christ. The Christ form of being, God and man in one person, was only an idea and purpose until the incarnation, when it became a fact. The person of the eternal Son, I mean, did not become the Christ in very deed, until he took human substance of the virgin. Therefore, the only meaning that can be assigned to such expressions as that all things were made by him and for him is, that the person of the Son—not in his absolute infinity, which I have said I even believe to be impossible, but in the finite creature from which he was in the fulness of time to assume and to retain for ever and ever—did create all things visible and invisible, whether they be thrones, or principalities, or dominions, or powers; wherefore, also, he is called first-begotten from the dead, first-born of every creature.

This, then, is the only ground of revelation anterior to Christ, that God might testify unto him that is to come; and creation till he come, is but that same testimony, from the strongest archangel down to the worm that crawleth on the ground. I believe there is no sportiveness, playfulness, idleness, extravagance, or waste of creation power, but one concatenated[2] systematic testimony unto the Christ; into whom, as all the disjected members are to be gathered up again into the head, so believe I, that in their present disjected state, the only end and purpose of their being is, to testify to him of whom man is the only image, and Adam before his fall the only perfect type.

2. Items joined together in a series

Now, the counterpart of revelation is faith; and if the end of creation is to reveal Christ, then the object of all faith must be Christ. And all knowledge in the creature subsisting, whether of itself, or of other creatures, or of God, is no true knowledge, until it hath turned to a testimony, is either incomplete or is false, until it hath revealed something concerning Christ, who is the end of all created things; and therefore faith comes in where knowledge endeth; or, I should say, knowledge is but as the needle that pointeth unto Christ, in whom I must believe: and the rivers of knowledge pour themselves into the ocean of faith; for the end of knowledge is not itself, but something which is to be. And the Word, being the communication of knowledge, doth, therefore, no more than set out Christ that I may believe upon him; and the preaching of the Word is the testimony of Jesus. But we have not yet arrived at the root of the matter, which is deeper still.

The end of all things created by the Godhead being, as hath been said, the bringing of the Christ, and that not at the beginning, but onward a good way in the procession of the purpose, the preceding period must necessarily be the season of faith, during which the creatures can live only by faith. For the thing visible is not the real thing that is to be for ever; but is to be changed into its eternal form, whenever the Christ in his eternal form shall be revealed. Seeing, then, that faith is the condition of all the creatures until Christ come, they must be constituted fit subjects for faith: they must be constituted, also, fit subjects of hope, and altogether imperfect without hope: and these two principles of faith and hope must be wrought into the very vitals of their constitution.

Now this is truly the condition of man; who is born to believe, having no knowledge until he receive it from another; and is born to hope, having nothing in possession to begin with, but nakedness, helplessness, hunger, and want of every kind. To a creature thus constituted, faith and hope become the elements of his being; and therefore, in his very nature, man proveth himself a witness for something that is to come. And such a creature is proper to become the subject of a divine revelation; and through such creatures that divine revelation must be communicated to other creatures, who are not in like manner constituted; even as the apostle expressly declareth, in the Epistle to the Ephesians, That it is by the church the manifold wisdom of God is made known unto the heavenly hosts: and through the intelligence and power which man possesseth over the lower creatures, God expecteth of his piety, and of his diligence, that he would make the speak the praises of God their Creator, which is Christ, and make them prophesy concerning him which is to come: so that, as God destined man to be the form which he should assume, he hath made man also to be the great witness unto his coming in that form.

If all things then were created by the Son, in the assumed form of the Christ, or the risen God-man, then all things spoken by God unto man must be spoken by the Son in that same character. But it may be asked here, What need to speak at all? I answer, Because when the creature had fallen into sin and death, it necessarily became overspread with darkness, and ignorance, and error. And this was one reason of the fall, even to negate that light of revelation which the creature possessed in itself; to shew that the creature was not the true light, but only a witness of the true light; and that the witness might not be mistaken for the person witnessed of, it came to pass that darkness was permitted to cover the earth, and gross darkness the people. Yet, under this the cloud of darkness, the mystery lay shrouded; but so shrouded as that the creature, in himself, should not be able to discover it. And thus, during the fall-season of the creature, it is connected with the Creator by its very imperfectness; having in itself the ground of the truth of the promise of God, but yet, not being able of itself to read the lesson thereof; having a will, but in bondage; having an understanding, but in darkness; having a body, but under the law of sin and death; having a world for a possession, but a world ever rising in arms against its Master; having a being craving for faith, but ever falling into superstition; having a being formed for hope, but ever falling into delusion. A miserable estate indeed, had it been cut off and separated from divine teaching! But, being connected with divine teaching, [was] the only state of being in which it was good for the creature to be during the preparatory and preliminary season before the coming of Christ. For, by these very defects, by these very unsatisfied cravings, it was taught its need of a higher Teacher; which lesson, without such imperfections, the creature could never have learned.

And thus the fall becomes the ground of a revelation, such as we now possess; that is, a revelation of words superinduced upon the marred revelation of creation. The fall made the knot which no fallen being could loose; which every one, by his own nature, should be craving to have loosed; but could not otherwise have loosed, that from some one higher than himself. The fall made the riddle, which no fallen intellect could resolve, and which might create a craving for superhuman intelligence; and thus it is, that the fallen world, without a revelation, were indeed a solecism in the idea: but a fallen world with a revelation is a better state of the creation than its first or unfallen estate, because in this there existed nothing to distinguish it from God, and to teach it that it was not God in itself; not incompleteness, no mystery, no suffering, no evil, no apparent contradiction to be reconciled. But in the other state, the creature by its very want, from clothes of skin to clothing of righteousness, from succession of seasons to give him bread unto the preparation of the times and seasons for giving him bread from heaven, all from new-born babyhood unto the birth of the resurrection morn, is man in the fallen state of his being dependent upon the word of the revelation of God. Oh, what a mystery of goodness, as well as of wisdom, there is to be seen in the fall of man, which made way for the revelation of word and of ordinance, and enabled a church to be preserved upon the earth, exclusive of none which should maintain the testimony, until he that is to come should come!

Thus was the creature linked to the Creator, by the very act of its falling away from him, and hung in total dependence upon his gracious word, by the very act of disobeying his word: just as the infant, which with anguish is rent from its parent, becomes, in that very act of its birth, the object of its parent's tenderest care. It was no longer a creation out of God, but a creation that had been out of him, brought into him, and standing in him by his gracious and faithful word. And not only did the fall of the creature thus make way for the revelation of the grace of God, but it did also, in a manner, render that revelation absolutely necessary, in order to maintain the completeness and accomplish the ends of the divine purpose. Because now the creation being made subject unto vanity, and possessed with the spirit of a lie, wanting its high Prophet to interpret its ever misinterpreted mystery; man himself having become subject to the deceiver, and being no more able to understand or prophesy the truth; either the creation must fail from its high design of being and speaking and acting for Christ, or God himself must interfere with a divine commentary and interpretation thereof. And forasmuch as we cannot believe that God is ever to be thwarted, or the testimony of Christ ever defeated, it doth necessarily remain, that a revelation shall be superinduced upon a fall; and that God shall first appear a Prophet, to gainsay the gainsayers, and to deliver truth from the jaws of the lion, before he becometh a High Priest to purify and sanctify the whole lump, and a King of kings to rule over it in righteousness. In which character of the Prophet he shall separate the truth from the lie, and preserve the testimony of the truth against the many witnesses of the lie.

The Trinitarian Structure of Revelation

And, secondly, we have maintained that this word of revelation is to be made consistently with the acting of God in a Trinity of persons. All things being made for the Christ, and by the Christ, all things must be spoken for him and by him. Wherefore also he hath his name of the Word, which was with God in the beginning, and which was God; to signify that his character of Revealer by word is as indefeasible a prerogative of his person in the blessed Trinity, as is his character of Creator of all things, or his character of the Lamb slain from the beginning of the world, or his character of only-begotten and first-begotten from the dead. It proves, moreover, that a revelation by word is older than the fountain-head of time, even old as the purpose of the Ancient of Days.

And it moreover proveth, that the covenant between the Father and the Son, before the world was, is a true idea; and that all word external, and uttered, is but the extension of that deed which was done and sealed with the blood of the Lamb before the world was. Wherefore, also, the Holy Scriptures are called the two testaments or covenants. If Christ, then, be the Word of God, the Light that lighteth every man who by God is sent into the world, the true and faithful Witness, who, having dwelt in the bosom of the Father, is the only one able to reveal him, because he only hath seen him, he only hath known him; then through him must this work proceed, and he must speak it in that form of the creature in which he is for ever to reveal the Godhead, that is, in the form of risen God-man. So that when he says, "Let us make man in our own image" (Genesis 1.26), it is not the image of the infinite Godhead, but the image of that risen God-manhood in which the Godhead is to manifest itself. The word is not uttered by the invisible Father, who speaketh nothing but by the Son; nor is it spoken by the Holy Ghost, who speaketh nothing which he hath not first heard of the Son; but it is spoken by the Son, who speaketh nothing of himself, but what he heareth from the Father. Neither by the Son is it spoken in his infinite Godhead, but in his predestinated creature form; or, as we would say, in character, and in keeping with that manifestation of God which is to be for ever, are all manifestations of God which have been from the beginning, to the end that Christ's working in the whole, and the working of the whole for Christ, may be made manifest.

This matter will bear yet a little more consideration, for it is a deep and a most important matter. Christ did not assume the form of risen God-manhood, without the Holy Ghost; who created his body, who informed it against the fallen tendencies of the creature, who raised it from the grave, and doth now inform all its members, proceeding form the Head, and by the presence of the Holy Ghost, in the actings of Christ, is the presence of the Father manifested. The Son, in his proper divinity, is infinite, as the Father is infinite, and as the Holy Ghost is infinite; and yet these are not three infinites, but one infinite. Now, before the infinite Godhead in the Son could act in the finite form, whether before taking that form or after, he must act not of himself only, but with the consent and concurrence of the other persons of the Trinity. And this is not a small matter, but is in fact that which determineth all the rest. This is the fountain head of divine goodness, that the Godhead should once act in a finite form, to the accomplishment of a finite end: and this involveth in it all which follows of creation, of the fall, of revelation, of redemption, of resurrection, and eternal glory: it is all shut up in that one word, that it is the good pleasure of the infinite Godhead to do finite things. The choice of the form in which it was to be done, whether of angel, or of archangel, or of man, are inferior questions to this, that it should be done at all.

Now, how is this assent, and concurrence of the three persons of the blessed Trinity secured, to this great undertaking of Godhead? Here comes in the doctrine of the orthodox fathers concerning the Holy Ghost, as the *viniculum Trinitatis*, the circle of communication between the Father and the Son, through whom the will of the Father expresseth itself to the Son, and the obedience of the Son expresseth itself back again to the Father. The action to be done is, that, in the person of the Son, Deity should go forth in finite works of creation. The will of the Father is communicated to the Son, and the obedience of the Son returned, through the Holy Ghost: and thus, as it is in the origination, so it is in the details of the accomplishment. In everything done in creation, in everything spoken in revelation, in everything acted in the incarnation, in everything suffered in the church, and in everything to be executed in the kingdom; Christ is the doer, the Father is the willer, and the Holy Ghost the suggester of the will. And thus the Divinity follows out still its eternal and necessary law of being in the secret recesses of its own harmonious purpose, with which no creature intermeddleth, and of which no creature is competent to discourse, further than to say, Thus it is, because it is revealed that there is a Trinity of persons in the Godhead.

And thus the Son, in coming into action in the finite form, doth already possess the consenting goodness, the harmonious mind of the three infinite personalities of the Godhead. And thus, he is not a manifestation of the Son, in action upon finite things, but he is a manifestation of the Godhed, acting by the Son, in finite things; and this he is, from the first beginning to create, until eternal and eternal ages, during which he shall in finite form reveal the Godhead unto every creature. And observe further, that thus he can refer back to the Godhead, as greater than he, because he can only be known by limitations: and yet he can say, that in him dwelleth all the fulness of the Godhead. And forasmuch as the Son thus taketh in hand the manifestation to rule over it, the Father must keep in hand the unmanifested of the unmanifestable Godhead, to represent it, and to call it by his name.

Likewise, the Holy Spirit, who thus bringeth unto Christ's ear the voice of the Father, doth receive from Christ the signification of the voice of his obedience, and doth carry into effect the limited form of acting which the

Son hath condescended unto: and according to the word of the voice of the Father, which the Son hath heard, and bowed himself submissively to, the Holy Ghost goeth forth to do the thing: and from the creature thus informed by the word of the Son, and inspired with the Holy Ghost, the Holy Ghost doth carry up unto the Father the glory of the creature's obedience, and the gladness of the creature's joy, and the gratitude of the creature's blessedness.

But yet not unto the Father direct, but through the Head, which is Christ, who hath received the dignity of Mediator, and Intercessor, and Priest, and King, wholly to intercept and to convey the communication of the Godhead with the creatures, God informed; because it was through his voluntary obedience and humiliation that the creatures were created, were spoken to when they had fallen, were redeemed from their fallen state. This is the superadded prerogative of the Son, and likewise the constitution of the creature, after the divine purpose, that the Father should give unto the Son the honour of being its Sovereign and conservative Head, together with the honour of conveying upwards unto the Father all its homage and service: so that creation, the fall, and redemption amount simply to this, that it is a purpose of the Father to give outward glory unto the Son, because of that humiliation of himself which he underwent, in order to manifest forth the glory of the Father. In both which acts, reciprocal from the Father to the Son, and from the Son to the Father, the Holy Ghost is the great agent and operator.

The Incarnate Son Is the Only Basis of the Knowledge of God

Thirdly, we have maintained and made good that through Christ, and Christ only, who is the Godhead in a body, could the Godhead out of a body, the infinite and invisible Godhead, ever have been known. The attributes of infinitude are not cognoscible by a finite creature, and I hold that all those *a priori* speculations concerning the attributes of God, are nothing more than descriptions of the pure intellect of man;—they are the categories of the pure reason of man, and no knowledge of God whatever. God is known by his acts: the invisible things of God from the creation of the world are clearly seen, being understood by the things that are made, even his eternal power and glory. Creation is for the knowledge of God; and the end of creation is to be seen summed up in the creature-part of Christ.

The being of man reflects the being of Christ; the being of Christ reflecteth the being of God. It is not the tale which Christ telleth concerning the invisible world, as your Socinians talk; it is not as a tale hearer at all, but it is as he is seen, as he is (not excluding what he spake certainly, but including that also), that he sheweth God. A prophet told of God; but Christ is God, the brightness of his glory, and the express image of his person, made visible to the creatures, that the creatures might see and know him. Seeing and knowing are used synonymously in Scripture, as, for example, "No man hath seen god at any time; the only-begotten Son, which is in the bosom of the Father, he hath revealed him" (John 1.18). And again, "This is life eternal that they might know thee, the only true God, and Jesus Christ whom he hath sent" (John 17.3).

An act, not a thought, nor a word, is the work of God. The Father's it is to will; the Son's to work what the Father hath willed; and the Spirit's it is to bring it into existence, as a thing separate and outward from the Creator. In the first form, it is a purpose; in the second, it is a covenant; in the third, it is a work of God accomplished. Here, then, is Christ: look upon him, and know God; look away from him, and be lost in darkness: hear him, and believe that what he saith is in the purpose, and shall be in the manifestation. And what saith He? He saith that the Father is another person from himself, whom he worshipeth, whom he serveth; and yet that the invisible Father is only to be known, by knowing the visible Son. No man knoweth the Father, but the Son, and he to whom the Son shall reveal him: therefore, believe that the Father is another person from the Son, seeing he speaketh of them as twain: "I and my Father will come unto you, and we will take up our abode with you" (John 14.23): and through twain, in respect of personality, yet one in substance; for the Son doeth nothing of himself, but what he seeth the Father do: "The words which I speak, I speak not of myself, and the Father which dwelleth in me, he doeth the works: I and my Father are one. He that hath seen me, Philip, hath seen the Father; and how then sayest thou, Shew us the Father?" (John 14.9).

Thus come we by the knowledge of the invisible Godhead of the Father, through the visible Godhead of the Son; and in like manner come we by the knowledge of the personality and Godhead of the Holy Ghost; for Christ speaketh of him as one that is to be sent to supply his room when he is gone away. He is called another Comforter. He is the Spirit of Truth, which abideth always; not the Son of God who must depart for a season: and as Christ heareth the Father, so this other divine person heareth Christ: "What he shall hear, that he shall speak, and he will shew you things to come" (John 16.13). There is between them a distinctity which admits of the personal pronouns, *his* and *mine*: "He shall take of the things of mine, and shall shew them unto you" (John 16.11). Yet not the less is he one with Christ: in act he is what Christ is in word. Christ breathes on them, and they receive the Holy Ghost. The Holy Ghost must beget them before they can see the kingdom. This is the power which Christ giveth to them that believe;

to become the sons of God as he was the Son of God, through the inhabitation of his human nature; by that Holy Spirit,—and every act of Christ is an
act done by the Holy Spirit;—his life, the Holy Spirit's life; his Holiness, the
holiness of the Holy Spirit; his power, the power of the Holy Ghost; and thus,
from the visible Christ, cometh the knowledge of the three subsistencies in
the Godhead, and of their common substance, what its purpose is, what its
word is, and what its act is; and knowledge is obtained of the invisible and
unchangeable God, by the manifestation of Christ. And this I regard as a
great end which was served by the bringing of the Christ into the world.

Jesus Christ as the Object and Subject of Worship

Still further, as concerneth worship, or continual acknowledgement and
service of the Creator, as the great first cause, and deep abysmal will, which
is separate from the creature, yet the life of the creature, and the basis of
its being; this is a mystery which cannot be otherwise understood, than by
perusing the Christ, who, though God, did not worship himself, but did
evermore worship the invisible Father, and yet he was God. But being God,
united to the creature, and seen only through the actings of the creature, it
is most needful that nothing terminate in him, but pass through him into
the region of the invisible: therefore, whenever the people were disposed
to rest in him, he did not always refer them back unto the Father, saying,
"Ye cannot come unto me, except the Father which hath sent me to draw
you" (John 6.55).

Now, I know well, that the ignorance of this time, upon the subject
of the Trinity, passeth all ignorance of any former time; and therefore I do
deem it of the more importance to draw your attention particularly to this
part of the subject which concerneth worship. Christ's human nature, inhabited by the Holy Ghost, and from which the Holy Ghost never was and
never shall be separated, was not an object of worship, and never shall be
an object of worship; and if Christ received worship upon earth, from those
who were ignorant of his divinity, he did receive it, not as man, but as God.
This I hold to be a most important point of doctrine, and most necessary to
preserve men from creature-worship, and, above all, from saint-worship; for
I believe that Christ's human nature is not distinct from, but most closely
united to, and indeed the very support, yea, and substance, of the renewed
nature of every believer. Whosoever by faith eats his body and drinks his
blood, is one with him, as he is one with the Father; and that is one substance in diverse personalities. As by nature I am of the substance of Adam,
and coequal with him in all pains and penalties of this fallen being, so by

faith I am coequal in honour, and to be coequal in glory, with the human nature of Christ; one with him, I say again, as he is one with the Father. Such unity it is as all visible unity only resembleth, but doth never equal. Such unity giveth faith, as that it can be said, we are of his flesh and of his bones; and is of the essence and substance of faith, and he who hath not this hath no life abiding in him. His human nature is inhabited by the Holy Ghost; and our human nature is by the Holy Ghost likewise inhabited. If, therefore, inhabitation by the Holy Ghost maketh any creature-substance as the body of Christ to be worshipped, then must it also make his members, which are of the same substance, and the by the same Spirit inhabited, to be in like manner worshipped; and so have you saint-worship introduced at once; as, indeed, it was introduced into the Papal church, and must ever be introduced, where the body of Christ is worshipped; and it doth destroy the whole end of redemption, which is to get the creature separated from the Creator, and delivered from the worship of itself.

But as the creature, in its redeemed state, is inhabited by the Holy Ghost, this would constitute it an object to be worshipped, if Christ's body, which is inhabited by the Holy Ghost, might be worshipped. Wherein then consisteth that pre-eminent dignity of Christ above all redeemed creatures, which placeth him at distance infinite above them, though in substance most closely united with them? It consisteth in his divine nature, with which his human nature mingleth not, though to it in one person united. This constituteth him Head over all, though Brother of all the redeemed; Brother by the community of the human substance, and the inhabitation of the Holy Ghost; Head by the solitary pre-eminence, by the divine dignity of being the eternal and only-begotten Son of God. Nevertheless, though in his divine personality he be a proper object of worship, like as is the Holy Ghost in his divine personality; yet, as the Holy Ghost inhabiting the creature doth cease from worship contemplated therein, so the Son, taking the redeemed creature into union with his own person, and shewing the Godhead in the manhood, doth cease from being the object of worship, being therein the great Leader of the chorus, the great Head of the worshippers.

And who, then, is the proper object of worship? I answer, the Father, the Son, and the Holy Ghost, one God;—not as inhabiting the creature, for then the creature would worship a deity within itself;—not as sustaining the redeemed creature, for then the creature would worship its visible Head, and still the object of its worship would be in and of itself: but the object of its worship is God the Father, Son, and Holy Ghost, their invisible, incommunicable, indivisible being, represented in the person of the Father. Let no one start at this, as if it denied worship to the Son and the Holy Ghost. The Son and the Holy Ghost are one with the Father, who are worshipped when he is worshipped. The divine person of the Son is not contained in his manhood: the ocean, the round immense of space, were better said to be contained within a household dish, than that the divine nature of the Son should be contained in manhood. And to guard against this error, is the very reason why divines rest so much upon the distinctness of the Godhead from the manhood.

But, save through the manhood of Christ, God shall never be known to any creature, nor communicated to any creature; and for this reason, that the fulness of the Godhead cannot thus, or in any way, be to the creatures communicated, most necessary it is, in order to the existence of true worship, that the Godhead, not in its manifested likeness and limited proportions, nor in its felt influences and operative powers, but in its invisible, ineffable, incomprehensible fulness and essential separateness, from the creature, that is, in the person of the Father, representing the substance of Father, Son, and Holy Ghost, should be worshipped. And this, verily, is the end of the whole mystery, that God should inhabit the creature in the person of the Holy Ghost, and yet not be worshipped there: that God should sustain the creature, in the person of the Son, united unto man, and yet not be worshipped there, but be worshipped in the absolute invisible person of the Father: so that God supporteth all, inhabiteth all the redeemed creatures, and, for the security and blessedness thereof, receiveth their homage out of and beside them all. Such is the true account of divine worship, and such is the way in which it is attained.

While, however, I argue, that the Godhead, in the person of the invisible Father, approaches unto by the manifest Christ, through the indwelling Spirit, is the only ultimate object of worship from whom all petitions are to be sought, and all favours understood to proceed, I do not the less preserve unto the Godhead, manifest in the person of the Son, a superlative dignity above every visible creature;—the King of all power; the Priest of all holiness; the Heir of all possession; the Revealer of the Godhead; the Light coming forth from the mystery of light, in which the Father dwelleth inaccessible; the life, also, felt in all redeemed creatures, and the visible object of all their homage, reverence, and obedience; and so bound to, and submitted to, and in that sense worshipped by, all the angels of God: as it is written, "When he bringeth his Son the second time into the world, he saith, And let all the angels of God worship him" (Hebrews 1.6): and not the angels only, but every creature; as it is written, "That at the name of Jesus every knee might bow" (Philippians 2.10). But still, while this supremacy and lordship of God-manifest may never be doubted, I argue not the less that Christ will suffer no worship to terminate in himself, as an ultimate object, but will lead it up to the invisible and infinite Godhead of the Father, Son, and Holy Ghost; where again no worship is received, nor petition answered, which doth not come through the manifest Godhead as its way, and from the indwelling Spirit as its source: so that the end of the whole matter is, that the creature is taken into the circle of the intercommunion of the blessed Trinity, and therein consisteth its blessedness and its stability.

Now I may say, that any difficulties which may appear on this subject vanish at once, to any one who will but look on Christ, who, though he was very God and very man, did not the less direct his worship unto the Father, and pray unto him continually. And when he gave that form of prayer commonly called the Lord's Prayer, it was addressed unto the Father. This was not for example's sake, nor did it arise out of his humiliation, but is the example of what he shall ever be, as the Head of redeemed creation; evermore directing his homage unto the invisible God. Let no one think that this is derogate from the divinity of the Son, or of the Holy Ghost; any more than it is to derogate from the divinity of the Father, to say that he dwelleth in us, by the indwelling of the Holy Ghost, and shall never otherwise be felt; any more than it derogates from the divinity of the Father, to say that he is manifest in the Son. It is not the Holy Ghost inhabiting merely, but it is the substance of the Godhead, in the person of the Holy Ghost; and it is not the Son merely, sustaining and redeeming all things, but it is the Godhead in the person of the Son; and it is not the Father merely that it is worshipped, but it is the Godhead in the person of the Father, and the Son is worshipped equally with the Father; and so, also, the Holy Ghost: and the Father is manifested equally with the Son; and so, also, is the Holy Ghost: and the Father inhabiteth equally with the Holy Ghost; and so, also, doth the Son.

The same substance is present in the threefold personalities; the personalities most distinct, the substance most entirely one. And herein is the mystery of the Trinity most excellent and most glorious; and herein are all Sabellian schemes of the Trinity, which do not hold the distinctness of the personalities, devoutly to be abhorred; for, if you keep not the personalities distinct, observe what follows. Confound the personality of the Son with the personality of the Holy Ghost, or deny the latter, which is virtually, yea, and avowedly too, a most wide-spread heresy; and it immediately follows, that every member of Christ, inhabited by the Holy Ghost, is upon an equal footing with Christ;—that every one of us is an Immanuel, or God with us, as certain blasphemously affirm;—and straightway there follows upon this a total loss of Christ's great act of love and of atonement.

Again, confound the personality of the Father with the personality of the Son, which is to all intents and purposes done by worshipping the Son as the ultimate object of worship, instead of regarding him as High Priest and Intercessor, and you mingle at once God and the creature; and will come to worship him, not as a personal God, separate from the creature, but as a widely-diffused power and omnipresent influence. So that, without the doctrine of the Trinity of persons in a unity of substance, the whole scheme of redemption and revelation, of a creation, of a fall, and of a regeneration, is an ineffectual and vain display of power and suffering, which accomplisheth nothing.

THE DOCTRINE OF THE TRINITY AS THE GROUND OF TRANSCENDENCE AND IMMANENCE

So much have I to say with respect to the light which this discourse of the incarnation casteth upon the actings of the one Godhead in a Trinity of persons to the end of creation, revelation, and worship: and I now proceed to see what light it sheddeth upon the reconstituted creation under Christ the Head thereof. In creation there are three things to be kept distinct by an impassable gulf. The first is, the redeemed creature; the second is, the Head of the redeemed creature; the third, the invisible God. If the creature jostle or mingle with its Head, then the procuring cause of its redemption, and the abiding cause of its stability, atonement, intercession, manifestation of God, and everything else, which since the fall hath been transacted, becometh a dead and unmeaning thing. Therefore, I say, the Head of the redeemed creation and the redeemed creation must be distinct and separate by a gulf impassable. This is the first distinctness; and these two existences so distinct must yet be united more closely than any visible union: for every visible union is disunited, as the body from the soul, and the members of the body from each other; but by an indissoluble union must the redeemed creature be united with its Head, in order that it may know and feel that it standeth only in Christ, and though Christ only can worship the Father.

Now this union, beyond all unions close, yet in distinctness and separation impassable, is compassed by the union of the two natures in the person of Christ. Christ the Head, being God and redeemed manhood in one person, which redeemed manhood maketh the redeemed creature of one substance with him; so that in that manhood every elect creature standeth, and yet no elect creature tasteth of his Godhead; and thus is the Christ personal separated from, yet united to, the Christ mystical, with all that dependeth thence. To constitute the union, the Holy Ghost laboureth; to preserve the distinctness, the distinct personality of the Son from that of the Holy Ghost laboureth; to preserve the distinctness, the distinct personality of the Son from that of the Holy Ghost prevaileth: and finally, to prevent the creature thus redeemed by the Holy Ghost, and headed up in Christ, from aspiring to, or mixing with, the invisible Godhead; to throw in another impassable gulf between the creature redeemed by the Son, inhabited by the Spirit, and the invisible, infinite, incommunicable, incomprehensible Godhead, the distinct personality of the Father prevaileth. So that to accomplish this threefold distinctness, (and unless this be accomplished, all, all is vain), nothing prevaileth, but the distinct separate personalities of the Godhead, never to be confounded, in one substance never to be disunited.

The doctrine of the Trinity is the only view of God which will give him separateness from the creature, and yet communicate to the creature of his indefectibility and blessedness: and the great end served by the coming of the Son of God in the flesh is the making known of the great truth of the Godhead as one substance in three persons as subsisting, whose distinctness from one another is the ground and basis of all distinction between the redeemed creature inhabited and possessed by the Holy Ghost, and its Head, which is the Lord Jesus Christ; and between these two, considered as the whole visible existence, and the invisible Godhead. This necessity of perfect distinctness between these three subsistences—to wit, the redeemed creature, the Head of the redeemed creature, and the invisible Godhead,—is the reason, and ground, and fruit of the doctrine of the three persons in the Godhead.

Now, this is a subject of such great importance in itself, and in its consequences so unbounded, and withal a subject so little understood, or treated as a speculation,—whereas, it is the only defence against Spinozism, and Sabellianism, and that philosophy of the West and religion of the East, which makes God the souls of the creatures, or the creatures an emanation from God,—that I deem it food to open it at some length, and to shew how it is the essence and the substance of all sound doctrine whatsoever concerning the creatures, and concerning God the object of the creature's worship.

The End of Creation Is to Give Share in the Divine Life

The end of God, in giving existence beside himself, is to communicate life in such a way as shall consist with his own being and glory. Accordingly, the creation was complete in a living soul; but Adam, thus formed, was not the perfect or complete creature, but only the likeness or type of him that is to be. And therefore Adam could not have eternal or immortal life to give; which required that the life should be manifested, which was done in the person of Christ, who brought life and immortality to light. In him was life, and to him only it belongeth to convey life, who could say, "I am the life.

I am the resurrection and the life: he that believeth in me shall never die: he that believeth in me hath everlasting life" (John 11.25). Adam was not the life, nor was he able to communicate eternal life; as it is written, "The first man Adam was a living soul, the Second Adam a life-giving Spirit" (1 Corinthians 15.45).

Adam therefore, the head of creation's unfallen state, was only to prepare the way for Christ. The Son of God was to come in flesh, or in human nature; and, therefore, there must be flesh, or human nature in which he might come. If Adam had possessed life in himself, then no one should have been able to take it from him, and God's gifts are without repentance. Seeing, then, that death did lay hold upon him, it is proof sufficient that God had not invested him with eternal life, over which death hath not any power. Creation, therefore, in its unfallen state, was only to make way for creation in the fallen state; and this, though last in accomplishment, was, as consisteth with the very idea of a purpose, first in the design.

So far, therefore, is it from being derogatory unto God for one to say, that creation was only the imperfect rudiments of his work, that it is the only way of preserving the honour and glory of God. For if herein he put forth all his strength, and gave Adam immortal life, then is the fall a failure, and redemption is an after-thought, and expedient to remedy and repair a failure, and God hath no purpose not foresight of things at all; and there is a chance and possibility that the redemption also may be, by some unforeseen hap and hazard, likewise subverted and overthrown; and there is neither ground for faith, nor yet for hope, nor for promise, nor for fulfilment, nor for covenant, nor for faithfulness of an Almighty God at all.

We may, therefore, without offence unto, but in a high justification of, God, inquire a little into the necessity of a fall, for the accomplishment of God's purpose. The creature unfallen was very good, but it knew not evil as yet; and, not knowing evil, it could not know its own inferiority to, and distinctness from, God: for God is also very good, and the creature is very good; how shall the creature distinguish between itself and God? Moreover, God is invisible, and the creature is visible, and by so much the creature is in advantage over God. In that state, therefore, the creature could not fulfil the great end of God, that it should pay its homage, and place its dependence upon God; which is any one deny, then I appeal unto the fact, that the first time the creature was tried with a temptation, though the weakest imaginable, he, or rather she, preferred the inanimate creature unto God; and he preferred the love of woman unto the obedience of God;—proof positive, experiment decisive, and so arranged of God, for the ending of all strife upon this subject, and for proving beyond a question, that the creation state was not the state in which a creature could stand and worship God.

If any one cut me short here with an interruption, and ask, Why then put the creature forth in the creation state at all? Why not bring in the Second Adam at the beginning, and present him in the glorious humanity at once, as he was being risen from the dead? This indeed, I answer, would have prevented the necessity of the fall; but it would have been as far as ever from accomplishing the end of God, which is not merely eternal life in the creature, but along with this consciousness of a being separate from God, as the indispensable preliminary unto the worship of God only, and not of itself also. For if Christ had come in the unfallen state, God and man, putting forth the power of the Godhead and the wisdom of Godhead in the creature form, it would have made things worse instead of better, with the creature, unto which he propagated, or communicated, the same glorious and eternal life; for there would have been no act demonstrative of the creature's separateness from the Godhead of the Son. From the first of its existence, upon this hypothesis, it standeth supported by the power, and shewing forth the glory of God; and so it is to continue without a change of its condition, with no knowledge of its infirmity, with every experience of its power and sufficiency; and how such a creature should know of a Godhead beyond and beside itself, how it should know itself not to be the all-sufficient God, is what I cannot for a moment imagine. For, as I said in the former head of discourse, these are things not to be told by words, but to be embodied in the being of things. A word must have a correspondency, in the being of him who is spoken to, or it amounteth to nothing; and especially such a word as this, that there is a God beside the creature, whom to know, to worship, and to enjoy, is the very end of the creature, must not be left to an airy carriage, but must be infixed in the heart of the being itself; for which, upon this idea, that Christ in the form of risen God-man is brought into the world first of all, there is no provision in the being of the creatures propagated by him, but, on the other hand, everything to confuse, to bewilder, and to contradict the knowledge of an invisible God, above and beside themselves, who is to be worshipped.

In order, therefore, to preserve distinctness between the invisible and absolute God and the visible limited creature, it was necessary that the creature should fall; and, by falling, should know the end and inferiority that is in itself; and that the goodness which it had originally, is a goodness derived from another source than itself, seeing there hath not been, in itself, the power of retaining it. And to the end the creature might know evil by feeling evil, it is necessary that it should also know good by feeling good. There must exist in the creature, after it hath fallen, something to be unto it for a continual memorial of its state above the fall; that is, there must be a conscience of good struggling against the oppression of evil. If the creature were all evil, without a conscience of good, then there would be no memorial, no remembrance of its unfallen state; which would stand only as a page of the book, instead of being written on the heart of man. Mistake me not, as if I held the Pelagian, and what is now called Arminian, though it is baser still than Arminian heresy, that man can do any good thing in himself; for it is one thing not to be at all, and another thing to be in bondage; it is one thing to be a devil, and another thing to be under the oppression of the devil.

I believe with St Paul, that God leaveth not the wickedest heathen without a witness; that there is a law written in the heart, and that there are thoughts which accuse or else excuse one another. The state above the fall was a state of goodness; the state below the fall is a state of the knowledge of good and evil;—not the knowledge of evil only, but the knowledge of good also; and yet in this consisteth the wickedness of it, that there should be the knowledge of evil at all, and the obedience of it at all. It is this warfare in itself, it is this incompleteness in itself (which is, I may say, the great fact of human existence, denied by none except a few Stoics, who form the small exception that confirms the rule);—it is this incompleteness, whether you look to the body or to the mind; pain and death, in the former; error, prejudice, ignorance, and dark uncertainty beyond the grave, in the latter;—this knowledge of good and evil, and prevalence of the evil over the good, which is felt by sage and by savage, by prince and by peasant alike; for all suffer, and all die, and all by nature are in trouble, and dark uncertainty;—this is the very condition of conscious existence unto which the creature must be brought, in order that the creature may know itself not to be God.

For set the greatest atheist before me, and I will pose him with a single question: Whence hadst thou thy manifold thoughts, purposes, sufferings, and enjoyments? Is it not from life? Yea, from life, he must answer; for the dead have them not. Shew whence hast thou life? Not from thyself, else thou coudst keep it; but keep it thou canst not. Not from other men, for they are in the like plight. Then thou hast it from one unseen, who can only be known by this, that he hath life in himself; that he can lay it down, and take it up again, and give it even eternally unto whom it pleaseth him; and thus death is the great demonstration unto the creature of a God, besides and over the creature: and resurrection from death, and power to overcome death, and to communicate a life which is eternal, is the great demonstration unto the creature of a God, besides and over the creature: and resurrection from death, and power to overcome death, and to communicate a life which is eternal, is the great demonstration that he who doth it is not a creature, but is God.

The creatures, therefore, were brought into the condition of death, that they might be negatived, might know themselves not to be God; might know that he, who should be above and over this condition of death, is the very God. So that I may take a step here in advance, and say, that in no other way than by coming under the power of death, and overcoming death, when under its power, could the eternal Son of God, when he came, have been known to be the very God. And this I believe to be the reason why Christ and the resurrection were preached together: Christ, to shew that he was the Messiah, or the Seed of the woman, so long promised; the resurrection, to shew that he was God. Wherefore also Paul maketh express declaration, "That he was determined to be the Son of God with power, according to the Spirit of holiness, by the resurrection from the dead" (Romans 1:4). Wherefore also Peter declareth, that God by the resurrection hath proved him to be "both Lord and Christ" (Acts 2.36).

Fallen Humanity Empowered by the Spirit

The end, therefore, of the fall of creation under death, being no other than to separate and distinguish the creature from the Creator, and to put a negative upon every creature's pretension to be God, that the solitary creature who should overcome death might be known to be God, we may well conceive how important an end in the great scheme and purpose of God it is to keep the distinction for ever clear. And let us now follow onward to the redemption, and see how it is provided for in this third stage of the creature. This brings us to consider the Son of God, the great Head of redemption, who appeared as a man in all respects; a man indeed anointed with the Holy Ghost above measure, but still a very man, and a fallen man also in all the attributes of a fallen man, except that he never sinned; who also was cut off by death, thereby proving himself to have taken the form of the fallen creature; but before going into death, continually declaring, that he would rise again, and overcome death, and never see corruption; which accordingly having accomplished, he proveth himself to be not a creature, but the Creator of the creatures, who, though in human form, was not subject unto humanity's laws: and at the same time he proveth, that the creature substance which he has taken is not of the Godhead apart, but with the Godhead united, and thence deriving everlasting life.

Be it moreover observed, that in the like manner he dealeth with all the redeemed, propagating in them their eternal life, before they die, according to his own word, "He that believeth on me hath everlasting life" (John 5.24). Every believer hath now, and doth not wait for, everlasting life. But to the end that he may know that this eternal life is not inherent in the creature itself, or in any powers which it possesseth, it is so ordered, that it should exist in the creature, while in a dying state, and not prevent the creature from dying, but permit the dissolution of body and soul, which is death; to the end, that every creature who is redeemed might know of a surety, that not from itself, but from a power without itself, it hath this present regeneration unto eternal life, and is to have the future resurrection to the same.

Now, at this point of the subject it is, that a new distinction is revealed to us, which is the distinction between the father of this new life, or the Second Adam, and the children. To shew out this distinctness between Christ, the Head of the redemption, and the redeemed ones, is a first and primary object of the redemption which now cometh into view, and which is procured by that very thing, that while we are dead in trespasses and sins, Christ reneweth us unto God, and sustaineth us in this renewed estate, not only without the help, but in despite of all the powers of sin and death weighing down the creature. If this second distinction be lost, an evil is sustained of hardly less amount than by the loss of the distinctness between the creature and the Creator. For the whole power, and strength, and love, and grace of God in Christ is lost, and Christ's own divine nature is lost, and the divine nature of the Holy Ghost also, if we do not preserve Christ as head of power and fountain of holiness. And of truth, the merit of Christ departs, the value of his life and death, as an atonement, is lost, everything escapes the vision and hold of the mind, if the man Jesus Christ, as a Father of redeemed ones, be not in some conspicuous way distinguished from the redeemed ones who he begetteth. Which great distinction is secured, by his doing the thing for every one of us while we underlie the curse of sin and death. His life and death brought him to our level, his resurrection, and his regenerating of us while under the curse of sin and death, proveth him to be the procuring cause, the instrumental cause, the final cause; and, in one word, the all in all of our redemption. And this is likewise the demonstration of his divinity. Every act of communicating life unto a creature fallen, and held to death by God's appointment, is an act as demonstrative of Godhead as is the resurrection itself. And hence, I may observe in passing, it cometh to pass, that even under the kingdom, men will be subject unto death, because otherwise they could not know and experience the headship of Christ. And, therefore, the last enemy that is to be destroyed is death; and so it cometh to pass, that death is God's great means of giving dignity and demonstration of divinity unto the Prince of Life.

The redemption, therefore, doth introduce us to a new distinction, the distinction between the fallen creature redeemed, and its divine redemption-head; which distinction forms the basis of all our obligations unto Christ, and constitutes the inferiority and dependence of the redeemed creation upon Christ its Head. So that, while he is a creature, he is yet above the creatures; while he is Head unto the church, he is yet above the church; linking the whole creation unto himself in firmest bond by his human nature, and by his divine connecting it with the Godhead,—truly Mediator between the invisible Godhead and the visible creature, the way unto the Father, and the Father's way unto us! Now, to give this distinctness is another great end of the fall of the creatures. For being by their fall taught their wickedness and their weakness, they were thereby prepared to receive and acknowledge righteousness and strength in him who should recover and restore them. But for the fall, the eternal Son of God could not have been known by the creatures, in any of his offices, as Prophet, Priest, and King; in any of his names, as Jesus Christ, and Lord. So that the fall is as essential for giving the God-man his dignity over and above the creatures, as it is for teaching the creature its distinctness from the invisible and incomprehensible Godhead.

Against Universalism

Thus then have we establishes two great distinctions, and three great distinct substances. First, the invisible, infinite, absolute Godhead; secondly, the manifest Godhead in the Son of Man; and, thirdly, the redeemed creatures. And now I have to add a fourth, which is, the unredeemed creation, or the reprobate part of the creatures. The whole creation hath fallen, excepting only a part of the angelic form of being who are elect in Christ, and intended, in the divine purpose, to shew the mighty power of the Christ-head of creation, which should stretch its arms of salvation both ways, and sustain the infirmity of the creature in all its forms. The elect angels, no doubt, looked forward to him that was to come, and stood in that hope; they were his witnesses in the spiritual region of creation; they are his trophy, won from that domain wherein sin was first conceived, because that domain was first in being. Besides these, the rest of creation hath all fallen; and out of that fall, God hath from the beginning been signifying his purpose to take, by redemption, a part, and only a part.

Therefore he separated the clean and the unclean of animals, and required the clean to be presented in sacrifice, in order to signify that the elected part should be made a sacrifice of, as was first shewn in Christ, and now is shewing in the church. Then, from amongst the families of the earth, he chose one to bless above the rest, with his covenant; and now, from all the Gentiles, he is taking whom it pleaseth him to take. The end of this mystery of electing only a part, is to shew forth God's sovereignty, and God's right over the creatures; to establish the immutable distinction between God and the creature still more effectually, and above all to mark out, for ever, the nature of guilt, the nature of sin. If the scheme of God had ended in the redemption of all the creatures, then it would have seemed but a great scheme for manifesting his own power and being, as the Three-One God; for distinguishing himself from the creature, and securing to himself the worship of the creature, and unto the creature its own blessedness: but God being a holy God, the nature of holiness itself, the nature of sin, and the nature of atonement and satisfaction, the nature of priesthood, which is an essential part of Christ, as the Head of the creatures, would have been forever lost; for if sin, after any curve of aberration, or cycle of change, is able to arrive at the same point with holiness, then, at that point, the difference between sin and holiness ceaseth for ever. It turns out that there is no essential and eternal difference between the obedience and the disobedience of God, but only a temporary and expedient one; and it further follows, that the creatures have only been in the hand of God like the men upon a chessboard, to perform a certain great exploit of purpose and forecast.

I have no hesitation in saying, moreover, that this scheme of saving all at the last, doth destroy the very existence of a will altogether; and a will is the substance of a spirit, of an intelligent being: reason, without a will, is like a visible world without a sensible creature to possess it. The will is before reason, as the sense is before the sensible world. Now, if the fallen will should not manifest for ever its un-changeableness in itself, the demonstration would be wanting of what a will is, which would seem to be nothing else than a material substance which changed and changed again for ever. All this, and much more, I can see would flow from the universal redemption of all the fallen creatures. Reprobation, eternal reprobation of part, is the very ground upon which the nature of sin resteth, without which sin is but a change, ordained of God, whereof the creature must be patient; a circumstance of creation, which we must be content for a while to stand under, but which will soon betake itself away. The very possibility of understanding the true difference between obedience and disobedience, throughout eternity, would be destroyed; government under Christ would be, what government under Christ's lieutenants on the earth hath at length become, on principles of expediency alone administered; a frightful materialism would invert all things; and God would be the world, and the world would be God.

Besides this, it were to lose the whole end of God's scheme in bringing his purpose to pass, by a creation, and a fall, and a redemption, instead of bringing it to pass by one single act, were a part of the creature not left for ever in an unredeemed state. For, as hath been so often said, the great end of the scheme is to separate between the creature and the Creator, and in bringing it up again from its fall, so to bring it up as that, while it stood infallibly, by standing in Christ, the Head, it should yet know itself not to be God, by knowing itself not to be its head, and by knowing even its Head not to be the infinite and invisible God, but only such manifestation of him as the creatures are competent to apprehend. If now, as the universalists falsely assert, there should be no reprobation of the creatures, there would be no evidence of what creation is when standing out of God. Redemption would have no glory above creation, because creation hath no apparent inferiority beneath redemption. And as I believe that redemption and its glories, above creation and its infirmities, is the very principle with which God will go forth to people the spheres innumerable with which we are surrounded, I do hold it to be a most essential point, that the glories of redemption should be seen reflected from the dark background of a reprobate creation, existing under the conditions of the second death. For, if there be one principle which, from the beginning of the world until now, hath been declared at sundry times, and in divers manners, this is the principle, that the chosen and elected part is chosen of free grace, chiefly for the end of shewing forth the wickedness of the part not elected. In one word, without reprobation of the fallen creatures, helpless and irremediable, free grace is no better than an empty name. Grace is favour where no right remained, where no far-distant possibility of reparation existed, where no law nor scheme of God comprehended restoration, and where restoration could not otherwise than by grace come to pass.

Seeing, therefore, it is essential for every good and holy purpose of the Creator, that a part of the creation should be left in its fallen state, or rather brought up again by a resurrection, and be constituted in the estate of the second death which is not annihilation, and which is not life, but the second death, in which the worm dieth not, and the fire is not quenched, the question next occurs, by what means, and by what mighty workmanship, is the redemption of the part to be redeemed accomplished? This is taught us in the redemption of the body of Christ, concerning which we have already discoursed. The fallen woman's substance was, by the Holy Ghost, sanctified, and preserved holy, against all the powers of hell and death. The human will of Christ was, by the power of the Holy Ghost, preserved perfectly concentric with the divine and absolute will of the Godhead, so that the latter found the former always a vehicle for expressing itself intelligibly to the creatures: yet did the human will of Christ know temptation of the flesh, as we see by his temptation, when he said, "No my will, but thine be done;" that is to say, the flesh which beareth our will to a side, away from its centre, and maketh it sinful, which is a will in bondage, was not able to carry Christ's will away, though nature shook, and shrunk, and quivered again, under the mighty power which held it in unswerving from its rectitude.

Ah that word, "My will," toucheth me to the heart, shewing me that Christ called human nature by the name I!—and that his human nature would have swerved him from his centre, but for the Holy Ghost, which abode in him. Now, one who will receive this,—and they are not many, for the time is come when they shall not receive sound doctrine;—one who will receive this, I say, can understand how the distinction is made, whereof I now discourse, between the redeemed and the unredeemed creature. The ground of that distinction is not in the creature, but in the Creator: it is the will of God to save whom it pleaseth him to save. This act of the divine will being absolute, and not revealed, is properly reserved with the Father, who representeth and retaineth the absolute attributes of the Godhead; and thus without the doctrine of election, you have, I may say, no absolute God, but only a revealed and manifested God, and you can, therefore, have no worship of the invisible Godhead. I mention this, however, only by the way, because it doth not properly belong to the head of distinctions, but to the head of unions, which will come hereafter to be discoursed of. The ground, therefore, of the distinction between the redeemed and unredeemed of creation is in the absolute will of God; and the origin of it in the manifestation, is the eternal Son taking unto himself a body,—which body is the beginning and the ending, the first and the last of the redeemed creation.

Therefore, all redemption, which in the purpose dependeth from the goodness of the Father, doth in the manifestation depend from the humiliation of Christ. It was an act of his own self-existent personality to contract that infinite circle of his being, in the bosom of his Father, and to make all its acting pass through that concentric and limited circle of the human being which he assumed. And for this act never to be unacted; for what God doth, he doeth for ever; the Father bestowed upon his human nature the power of the Holy Ghost, or, I should say, the Holy Ghost, in his independent personality, did condescend to inform that human nature, and never to act towards the creatures save in it and through it; so that the great operative cause in the redemption of the creature is the Holy Spirit taking the possession of it, and sanctifying or separating it from the wicked mass. Now, with respect to the manner in which this is effected, it is by taking it out from the waste, digging it out from the miry clay, drawing it up from the fearful pit of this our fallen nature; and by might of divine influence, resisting the force of corrupt nature upon the will or spirit of man, which hath made it move contrary to the will of God, unto which will the Holy Spirit constraineth it to return back and be agreeable.

It is not that there are two wills, or spirits, in the renewed man; but that his will is, upon the one hand, acted on by the powers of a fallen creation, and on the other by a power of the Holy Spirit acting under the risen

God-man. And the effect of the Holy Spirit is, to unite the fallen creature unto, and make it one with, the body of Christ: so that the end of redemption is the gathering out for salvation of the fixed quantity of the creation's substance, and joining it to Christ's body; and when this is completed, the dispensation of election is completed, and the Son of God, who heretofore appeared one substance in one person, shall hereafter shew his glorious human substance in many persons; that is, in all the elect church, which shall come with him in the power and glory of his kingdom.

But for himself, he alone partaking of the divine nature, shall stand alone and eminent above them all, the manifest Godhead for ever. From which era, of the accomplishment of the elect, and the bringing in of the kingdom, shall begin the work of government, wherein the manhood shall manifest itself victorious over that with which it warred against; this is, flesh and blood, and sin, and Satan, and death;—not now in the Christ personal and individual merely, but in the Christ plural; that is, in the whole redeemed church. But further into this we may not enter at present. And for the creatures which are left unredeemed; all these, being raised up at the end of the kingdom in that form which is proper to endure the second death, and with them the fallen angels, shall—in punishment of that resistance which they made unto the truth, and of that preference which they gave to sin over righteousness; and for their denial of the law of God, written on their hearts by Christ their Creator; and for the distinguishing of holiness from goodness, and of sin from weakness; and in general for the eternal distinctions of obedience and disobedience, of truth and falsehood, of right and wrong, and in order to lay the basis of government for ever—be case into the lake that burneth, which is the second death. And thus we have these four distinct things in existence: First, the invisible Godhead, which is never changed; secondly, the manifest Godhead, in the creature form of the God-man; thirdly, the redeemed creatures, standing in the human nature of Christ, and parts of that one substance; fourthly, the unredeemed forms of the wicked creation in the state called the lake that burneth, or the second death.

The Ultimate Ground of Distinction: The Divine Persons

Now, the distinctness of these four existences must be kept for ever and for ever. The invisible essence of the Godhead must be kept distinct, that the Creator may not be confounded with the visible creature, but receive its homage, and worship, and service for ever. Secondly, the great Head of creation, which is the Christ, must be kept distinct from the redeemed creatures, in order that he may be the representative, the brightness of the glory, and the express image of the invisible God, and, in this dignity, maintain for ever the order and subordination of the redeemed creatures, ever looking up to him as the face of God, and ever listening to him as the Word of God, and ever honouring him and revering him as the way for God to come unto the creature. Thirdly, the redeemed creation, or body of Christ inhabited by the Spirit, must ever be kept distinct from the reprobate creatures lying in the penalty of the second death, in order that the eternal distinction between holiness and unholiness, between blessedness and misery, between God and sin, may be for ever established in the sight and knowledge of all creatures, which are yet to be created of God during the ages of eternity.

Now, eternal distinctions, which enter into the purpose of God, must have an eternal basis to rest upon. These three eternal and unchangeable distinctions must have an eternal ground in the being of God himself; and this ground is, the personalities of the Godhead. If God is one personality, then there never can be a creation out of God. God and the creature will be for ever confounded and worshipped, and service of the Godhead is forever lost. This is unitarianism.

Again, if there be but two personalities in the Godhead, then creation might, indeed, be separated from God under the Son; but it would be as a procession of emanation from God, and having in it of the essential being of God, which is the philosophy and religion of the Persian sophists, the Brahmins, and others of the East. But by three personalities in the essence existing, we can, as hath been set forth above, bring out the grand problem of a creation standing under God, worshipping God, and serving God, separate and distinct from itself; which I take to be the great end of the purpose of God, and the great problem which was to be resolved; and this is the reason why the doctrine of the Trinity out ever to be held as the great fountainhead of all doctrine whatever, which flows from it like the crystalline streams from the secret recesses of the pure mountain snow.

And however much men, and orthodox men, may cavil with us, who would thus seek the stream of life in its fountainhead,—which I confess is a perilous and dangerous undertaking, not by every head to be attempted, yet when Satan hath found his way thither, and poisoned the streams of all the valleys,—it is most needful, and cannot be dispensed with, that some of those who dwell in the fertilised, but now poisoned, valleys, should straightway, for the sake of all the families, their flocks and their hers, venture forth, though it were alone, in order to clear out the poisoned fountainheads. Or, to make my figure more exact, if a company of wicked, diabolical people should take post there, for the very end of diffusing poison by the necessary ailment of life, it is most necessary that the dales-men and the inhabitants of the plan should keep a host of valiant men, strong of body and true of heart, ever encamped in the cold and rocky upland, to dislodge these murderers and destroyers from their evil haunts and wicked purposes. For, to drop all figure, I do maintain that all doctrine whatsoever, concerning intercession, atonement, and mediation; concerning the creation, the fall, and regeneration; us truly, and verily, an indefensible doctrine, save by the presupposition of the doctrine of the Trinity, which, in all systems of sound faith, is advances into the first and highest place.

Now, the doctrine of the Trinity hath its practical form, only in the maintenance of these three great distinctions, whereof I have discoursed above: (1) the essence existing in the Godhead standing under the Father; (2) the Head Christ, being the Godhead manifested in the person of the Son; (3) the redeemed creatures, being the subsistence of the Holy Ghost proceeding through the humanity of the Son; and these three subsistencies are preserved distinct, no otherwise than by the distinctness of the personalities of the Godhead, while, by the unity of the substance of the Godhead, they are united in relations manifold, which I shall open in the next head: and the whole redeemed creature, thus recapitulated into Christ, and standing in everlasting blessedness, being only a part, and not the whole of the creature created, doth stand distinguished from mere creature, which remaineth in the condition of the second death, concerning which condition I can say no more; and I think no more is revealed than this, that it is also eternal and unchangeable.

And here I conclude these heads and hints of deep discourse; to the all-important doctrine of which I have nothing to add, except to open, in another head, the unions in three distinctions; and I pray you looks upon the incarnation as chiefly valuable, or I should rather say invaluable, not for the sake of atonement, which is a mere part of its infinite fruitfulness, but for the sake of manifesting the existence of the Godhead, as outward from the creature, and never to be mingled with it, and the subsistence of the Godhead in three persons, under whose separate personality the great distinctions necessary to worship, to redemption, and to subjection, together with the union in those distinctions, might be clearly and for ever fixed. I have opened to you a great mystery: see ye receive it, and enter into it, and be no more children tossed about by every wind of doctrine, and cunning slight of men, which lie in wait to deceive, but, being rooted in truth and in love, may grow up into him which is the Head, God over all, blessed for ever. Amen.

UNIONS AND CONNECTIONS

We have shewn out under the two preceding heads, the three personalities in the Godhead, and the three great distinctions preserved thereby, for ever and ever in creation; namely, first, the distinction between the invisible Creator and the visible creature; secondly, between the redeemed and the unredeemed parts of the creatures; and thirdly, between the redeemed creature and Christ its Head. We have shewn, also, that these distinctions come to pass and are maintained through the three separate personalities in the Godhead; the invisible and infinite Godhead, standing under the personality of the Father; the visible and manifest Godhead standing under the person of the Son: the redeemed creatures consisting in, and standing under, the person of the Holy Ghost, which three ever distinct and never to be confounded personalities, of Father, Son, and Holy Ghost, keeping distinctness between these three existencies, doth leave a fourth, or the creature in its fallen state, or rather in the state of the second death, remaining as the great monument of what the creature is, when separated from the Godhead, and not standing under the personalities thereof.

And we come now to open another head of conclusions, without which the mystery is not explained; namely, the essential unions which coexist with these distinctions: for the end of creation is not attained, merely by separating the creature from the Creator, but by the securing of its worship and service, in that estate of separateness; and we are now to shew how this constitution in Christ doth attain this the ultimate end of creation, by securing the most certain and complete obedience and worship from the creature towards the Creator; together with the continual descent of blessing and goodness from the Creator unto the creature. And here we shall begin at the fountainhead of being, which is the invisible Godhead, and down again to the Godhead inhabiting the redeemed creature, till we arrive at the waste ocean of the unredeemed creatures.

The Union of God and Creation in the Mediator, Jesus Christ

Concerning the Godhead and its unrevealed in incomprehensible being, we can only speak from the knowledge which we have from the Godhead manifested in Christ. Christ always referreth back to the invisible Father, and presents the great end an object of his coming to the world, as being to manifest the Father, whom no one at any time hath seen, or can see. Whenever the people were disposed to rest in Christ as the ultimate end of power and divinity, he always referred them to a higher source than himself, saying, "Ye cannot come unto me, except the Father which hath sent me draw you. My Father is greater than I" (John 6.65 and 14:28); and what he did by words, when needs was,—which, alas! occurred too seldom, because they were little disposed to rest in his manifest Godhead,—he did also continually by his acts, praying unto the Father for his help; And even when, as in the case of Lazarus, he was sure of that help, doing so that the people might observe it.

Christ's whole life is an act of obedience and of worship, offered unto the invisible Godhead, and yet was Christ the fullness of the Godhead in a bodily form. To the same end of carrying up the creatures beyond himself, into the invisible an incomprehensible Godhead, Christ continually declared, that he did not his own will, but the will of the Father which sent him; that he spoke not of himself the words which he spake, and that his Father did the works which he did. Was it then, that the incomprehensible Godhead of the Father was dwelling in the body of Jesus Christ, who said, he that hath seen me, hath seen the Father? No: the Holy Ghost dwelt in the body of Jesus Christ; And, in so much as the Holy Ghost proceedeth from the Father, and is one substance with the Father, and speaketh and acteth only as he heareth the Father speak and seeth him act, insomuch doth the Father dwell in the man Christ Jesus.

But this is not the mystery of the Father's Godhead, to which Christ maketh such continual reference. The mystery of the Father's Godhead, which Christ came forth to manifest, is this: that in the Father, who is the fountain of the Godhead, generating the Son, and through and with him the Holy Ghost, is hid and contained that incommunicable an inexhaustible fulness which no creature can receive or apprehend; but which every creature must worship and adore. The Father, of whom Christ speaketh so constantly, is not any manifestation of God, but God unmanifested; and therefore, he is so often styled God. The Godhead, purposing to communicate unto the creatures so much of the goodness and glory of his being as the creatures could receive, did accomplish this gracious end by the incarnation of the Son, and the inhabitation of the Holy Ghost, whose necessary limitation of being, for this end, made it necessary that the infinite Godhead should stand presented under the unrevealed person of the Father. It could not stand under the person of the Son, who, in becoming manifest, becomes limited and comprehensible, and therefore not fit to represent the unlimited an incomprehensible. Neither could the infinite Godhead stand under the person of the Holy Ghost, for the same reason; and, consequently, to the end there might be an Infinite and Incomprehensible to be worshipped through the finite and comprehensible, it standeth under the person of the Father, in whom the infinite Godhead of the Son and the infinite Godhead of the Holy

Ghost is worshipped, as well as the infinite Godhead of the Father; But all standing under the person of the Father, because of the offices in the visible, which the Son and Holy Ghost had undertaken, for bringing into effect the Christ constitution, or eternal purpose of God.

Now, the question is, how the communication of the visible creature, with the invisible, ineffable, incomprehensible Creator, shall be carried on: how the interchange of grace and goodness, yea, of life and being, on the one hand; And on the other, thanksgiving, and praise, and service, and worship, shall surely take place? This is accomplished by the procession of the Son from the bosom of the Father, to take a creature form, through which to speak and act the purposes of God. To do which the Son is the proper person, not only as being of one substance with the Father, which the Holy Ghost also is; But likewise, as being the inhabiter of the Father's bosom, from all eternity, his only begotten Son, the brightness of the Father's glory, and the express image of his person.

The ground of his propriety to be head of the creatures is, that he is nearest unto the Father, in the necessary order of the divine nature, being by necessary generation, from all eternity, the expression of the Father's fullness; And therefore it is said of the Son, what is not said of the Holy Ghost, "No one knoweth the Father but the Son, and he to whom the Son shall reveal him" (Matthew 11.27). But of the Holy Ghost it is said, "He shall take of the things of mine, and will shew them unto you" (John 16.15). The things of the Holy Ghost are first things of the Son. The Father, therefore, who in the necessary act of generation hath poured his fullness into the Son, doth, by a natural consequence, when the time cometh to create all things, performed this act of the Godhead by the Son, in to whom all fullness of the Godhead is poured; And when the time comes, to manifest unto the creatures whatever of the Godhead the creatures shall or can behold, the same congruity, or may I say necessity, requireth it to be done through the person of the Son; And thus creation, in the perfected form of redemption, cometh to be a simple opening of the mystery of the Father and of the Son, so far as the creatures are able to receive it.

And by what assurance, necessary and inviolable, the Son is observant of, affectionate to, one with the Father, by that same assurance doth the redeemed creatures, standing in the Son, become loving, reverent, and obedient, unto the invisible Godhead; So that I may say, that most perfect relation, most loving, most indissoluble, which from eternity, and through eternity, subsisteth between the Father and the Son, is propagated unto the creatures through their standing in the Son. They become not a part of the Godhead; But yet are one with Christ, and with one another, as Christ is one with the Father; And there can never fail of worship, there can never fail of love, there can never fail of obedience, there can never fail of blessing in the redeemed creatures towards God, unless these were to fail in the Son towards the Father. And in this way it is that the creature, under Christ, is ever preserved in its fealty, allegiance, and subserviency unto the invisible Godhead, through its being headed up in, and bound unto Christ. And so much have I to say with respect to the connexion in distinction subsisting between the creature and the Creator through the constitution in Christ; which will appear still more distinctly when we come to consider, in the next place, the way in which the connexion between the Son and the redeemed creatures is maintained.

The Union of Divine Nature and Human Nature in the One Person, Jesus Christ

This ariseth out of the union of the two natures in Christ, which is not the union of two persons, as husband and wife, which by God are regarded as one; Nor as parent and child, which by God, in baptism, are likewise regarded as one, but it is the union of the two natures in one person, and that the person, the self-existing person, of the eternal and only begotten Son of God. The personality of the second person of the Godhead is an eternal and necessary, not in apparent and temporary truth. The Son is a person because God *is;* And the same also say I of the personality of the Holy Ghost. This personality of Christ acted in creation, as well as in redemption; But in creation it was not united unto the creature as it became united in redemption: and yet, even in creation, the Son, though invisible, and acting outside of the creature, did nevertheless act under the conditions of the finite, and not under the absoluteness of the infinite; that is to say, he presupposed unto himself a form, though not [yet][3] created but only purpose, in the Creator's council; and [this][4] form, under which the world was created, was the form of the risen God-man, of the Lamb slain an living still, of the first begotten from the dead.

Under the condition of this creature form, though not yet in the reality of it, did the infinite Godhead, in the person of the Son, contract and bound itself for the purposes of creation. He created, as Christ, all things visible and invisible, as is set forth in the first chapter of the Colossians. But withal his own body was not yet created; Created indeed in substance it was in the first act of creation but in living form not yet quickened till the Holy Ghost came upon the virgin, and the power of the Highest did overshadow

3. Imperfection in original text obscures this word.
4. See above.

her. But when the fullness of the time for this great act of the Father, by the Holy Ghost, [was][5] come, the time was come for the Son, or the Godhead in the person of the Son, to appear in that form which from eternity had been resolved upon, and from creation had been assumed, but till now was not effected, though shadowed forth from the beginning and the person of Adam, who is on this account, and on no other, said to have been created in the image of God.

Now, by assuming into himself the human nature, and becoming the Christ of God, the personality of the Son is still the same: it is the eternal, only-begotten Son of God, who speaketh, who heareth, who acteth, who suffereth, and yet the divine nature is ever distinct, and never to be confounded with the human nature. So that it shall not be possible to say that the divine nature suffereth any change, which is a great mystery, no doubt, but yet a great truth, both necessary to be known and to be believed. Nor do I think that it is safe to remain in ignorance of such a truth and therefore I represented unto you thus: that the words, and acts, and sufferings of Christ, are not to be called of the divine nature only, nor of the human nature only, but of the person of Christ, God-man; one person, though two natures.

And here I must, though reluctantly, disagree with the method in which many of the orthodox Fathers, and reformers, and doctors, and ministers, are wont to speak, as if some actions of Christ were actions done in the Godhead only, and some others were actions done in the manhood only. And right glad am I that this, though current in the schools, and in sermons, hath not found its way into any of the standards of the church; For if this way of speaking were correct, it would lead necessarily to the making of two persons in Christ, or else of two ascendancies which in succession overrule his person, like the ascendancies of the flesh and the spirit in the person of a man,—which cannot be predicated of a divine person, who overruleth, and hath the ascendant, and is not overruled or acted upon by an ascendancy. It is, moreover, a false idea concerning the divine nature, to speak as if it could do a finite action, let that be ever so stupendous, even as creation itself, without assuming a finite form. It is, moreover, to subvert the whole purpose of the Creator, and confidence of the creature, to say that the personality of the Son may ever go into action separate from, or by suspension of, the human nature. If the human nature of Christ were thus ever, though only once, put *sub silentio*, it might be again and again, and forever, and so the whole mystery of a manifest Godhead is defeated.

I know from what this mode of speaking hath arisen, even from a desire to find in Christ's life that evident manifestation of Godhead which Christ

5. See above.

himself declareth that it contained not, when he said unto Peter, "Flesh and blood hath not revealed it unto thee, but my Father which is in heaven" (Matthew 16.17). It is also a well-meant attempt to preserve the Godhead of Christ impassive, by giving to it the acts of power, and to the manhood the acts of suffering. But really, though well-meant in this respect, it doth but save the flimsiest appearance: for in deed, and in truth, it is to the Godhead as disproportionate and unfit to suffer the pity and compassion of the mind which moveth to the healing of the sick, or the casting out of devils, as it is to suffer and abide the scourgings and buffetings of men; both being proper only to manhood, and not predicable of Godhead, except under a figure.

This mode of speaking, concerning the life of Christ, as being part all Godhead and part all manhood, is not only attended with these evil effects, but hath this moreover to answer for, that, first of all, it doth defeat the manifestation of the Holy Ghost in his manhood, which I affirm hath been almost forgotten to be a work of the Holy Ghost at all; and from this is chiefly derived that aimlessness, fancifulness, idleness, and unprofitableness with which men speak of the Holy Ghost altogether. And besides this, it hath destroyed Christ's life from being the great type, both as respecteth suffering, and as respecteth power, of what every Christian's life, under the influence of the Holy Ghost, ought to be: for I believe, that we cast not devils out, and heal not the sick, and do not the other parts of Christ's life, simply and truly because we have not faith, and are responsible unto Christ's challenge and rebuke, with which he chid his disciples when they fell short of their privilege to cast devils out, saying unto them, "O ye faithless generation, how long shall I bear with you?" (Mark 9.19). All these evils, I say, come of this false way of representing the activity of the two natures of Christ; And therefore it is not, as it were, a matter of ingenious speculation, but grave reformation of error, when I undertake a little to lay open the distinctness of the nature of Christ in the unity of person, and that in every word, action, and suffering of the same.

As I said, the person acting and suffering is the eternal and unchangeable second person of the Godhead. He is the *aye* who was in the bosom of the Father from all eternity; And in every action he is conscious God. When he sayeth, "I will," it is the Godhead that willeth. From the infinite Godhead, therefore, is the origin of every volition and action of Christ. The fountain is there, in the infinite. And how proceedeth it into the finite? It proceedeth into the finite by an act of self-humiliation and self-restriction, which is the peculiar, proper, and boundless condescension of the Son in his own self-existent personality. But no eye beholdeth it, no finite mind comprehend if it, no word can utter it; The greatness of this grace of self-humiliation on the part of the Son is known unto the Father only, whose bosom alone contained that fullness which is contracted into manhood's narrow limits. This divine act of self-contraction is the Godhead part of every act of Christ. It is the continuance, it is the abiding and eternal perpetuity of that one resolve which is written in the book, "Lo! I come; A body hast thou prepared for me" (Hebrews 10.5). This is the nature of God; What he doth, to do forever; he doth not exist in time. Time measureth him not, as space comprehendeth him not. That purpose of the Son, to humble himself into manhood, did not cast his Godhead away. He did not become, in person, a mere man. He continued to be in person the same Son of God, after as before he made this dedication of himself unto his Father's glory, and unto the creature's good. He is God still, but God thus self-determined to act and suffer the man. He cannot cease to be Son of God, nor can he cease from his own willingness to become Son of man; and thus he is always to be by these words defined, Son of God willing to become Son of man.

The divine nature, therefore, ever acts, and it ever finishes with acting, when the Son of Man begins to act. It is the Son of Man, whose action is seen, felt, reported, discoursed of, imitated, and delighted in by the creatures. The Son of Man only suffers, and the Son of Man only acts with power. His actions, and his words, are like his countenance, such as man's are; Such as every man's, who is full of the Holy Ghost, ought to be; And such, I believe, as mankind's will be, in the days of the kingdom. But, while thus I speak, I put no man into the level of Christ; For that action of his self-contracting power, which belongeth to him as a divine and self-existent person, which is the action, and the only action, of the Godhead, and yet is present in all his actings, and yet not mingled with the human parts man appurtenances of them, is that to which no man may aspire. Because the sage hath, by his self-contracting power, brought himself to speak and act with the children of the nursery, the sage is not therefore to be equaled with the child, nor is the child to presume himself a sage. Yet is the sage, though apparently but a child, a sage still; And by far the noblest part of his action is hidden in that previous self-contraction of his powers where of the children have no consciousness at all.

When thus explained in the way in which alone I believe it is capable of being explained, how small a matter doth that seem upon which so much stress is laid by the ignorant, who will allow Christ readily enough to descend to the unfallen but not to the fallen state of the creature; For the merit and the greatness of the act consisteth not so much in the nature of that finite form which he assumed, but in the assumption of a finite form; whether that finite form should be of the angel, or of the archangel, or of the man, hath little to do, or rather nothing to do, with the stupendous magnitude of the love, and condescension, and humiliation. It is not the bounds of the finite being, but it is the becoming finite in which the merit consisteth; And it betrayeth a degree of ignorance unpardonable in the Christian, to make a hesitation, after consenting to his becoming man, that he should become man in the fallen state. If, indeed, it brought him into sin, then the whole face of the question were altered. But if it bring him only into the controversy with sin, that he may overcome sin; And with the devil, that he may bruise the devil's head; with fallen man, that he may redeem him; then, while it is everything to us that it should be so, indeed it is an exceedingly small addition, I may say nothing at all, to him that, after taking the infinite descent of being a creature, he should step a hairs breadth further and take up the creature in its fallen state.

I make this remark, not to go back upon a thing which I have proved, nor yet to doubt the validity of the proof, but only to shew how little those who stumble here apprehend of the infinite grace which there is in the eternal Son of God taking up into the same personality with himself the nature of the creature, and consenting, through the finite powers of the same, to shew forth unto the creatures what the creatures can comprehend, on all sides, of the infinite being and perfections of the invisible Godhead.

The Union of the Head and the Body

Another of the internal distinctions which we laid down in our former head of discourse, is the distinction between the redeemed creatures inhabited by the Holy Ghost, and their head standing in the person of the Son. And I now proceed to shew how the union is maintained in this distinction; for union in distinctness is the key of the whole mystery. The redeemed creatures are only members of the body of Christ. They live, not by holding of Adam, by which tenure they inherit death; But they live by holding of Christ, in whom the life was manifested, and from whom the life proceedeth. The Holy Ghost is the eternal indwelling life of the creature; and no creature hath eternal life but through the indwelling of the Holy Ghost. Now it is Christ's to baptize with the Holy Ghost: "he shall baptize you with the Holy Ghost and with fire" (Luke 3.16): and to shew us that it is from the body of Christ, even his human nature, that this baptism with eternal life proceedeth, we have his body presented unto us as our only nourishment, in the Holy Supper;—just as, in natural life, the child sucketh milk from the breast of her that bear him, and liveth upon her body.

Seeing, then, that all life, eternal and immortal, proceedeth from, and feed us on, the body of Christ, we speak nothing but the truth when we say that all the redeemed creatures are but parts of his human substance, consubstantial with him as pertaineth to his manhood, as he is consubstantial with the Father as pertaineth to his Godhead. Now, no union is so close as this between the manhood of Christ and the redeemed creature. Husband and wife, who heretofore were one, and now become twain, separated ofttimes by every interest, and every passion, though by the church, and by the law, and before the Lord, as one regarded. The members of the body also are not so placed in union with each other, but that it is in the power of every disease and of every accident to part them asunder. Nor is the soul so fast confederate with the body, but that death can separate them more widely than imagination can conceive.

But this union, which Christ to the believer holdeth, hath in that strength and faithfulness which neither time, nor eternity, nor sin, nor death, nor angels, nor principalities, nor powers, can part asunder. And though I speak of this as union with his human nature only, it is not less union to the person of the eternal Son, which now includeth death and embraceth the human nature, with the same assurance in possession with which it embraceth the nature divine. But, while thus I speak, I would not be understood to mean that Christ's person, because it embraceth the human nature, doth also embrace his people. This were to make the union to swallow up and destroy the distinction: and it were, moreover, to confuse the personality of the Holy Ghost with the personality of the Son. Christ, in his person, as much transcendeth the person of any of his members, as God transcendeth man; And each of his members, by how much they feel the closeness of their union unto Christ, by his humanity, with the inseparable security derived thence, do by so much also honour that condescension of his, that love of his, that undertaking of his, whereby he did purchase them, and redeemed them from their bondage and misery, from their state of being sold under sin, into the glorious and blessed standing of grace which they now enjoy. All their delight, all their power, goes to his account, from whom it flowed a free grace unto them, and thus, between the redeemed creatures, and Christ their head, there is established a relation of union, which by its union produceth all love, joy, and blessedness; while there is preserved a relation of distinctness, which bringeth unto him all royal and priestly dignity, all divine majesty an monarchical power, all right of possession, all right of command, and worketh in us all deference, respect, dependence, security, protection, and every other feeling which is proper in a creature towards its Creator, who, for love of it, hath condescended to live and move, and have his being in a creature form.

While I thus draw out the union in distinction, which is established between the redeemed creatures and their divine Head, it is necessary to divide this from the worship of the invisible Godhead, which it is the very end of Christ's manifestation to promote. Christ, or the Son manifesting the Godhead in creature form, hath all that love, hath all that reverence and homeage, whereof I have discoursed; While at the same time the invisible Godhead, standing in the person of the Father, as the visible doth in the person of the Son, hath from the creatures that which is truly and really called worship. I do not mean that the Father only is worshiped; but that the Godhead in the invisible and unrevealed essence of it, and not the Godhead in the visible and creature form, is the proper object of what is truly called worship.

The Union between the Members of Christ and the Human Nature of Christ

The third union in distinction is the union of the members of Christ with the human nature of Christ, and with one another through the Holy Ghost; whereof the perfectness cannot be expressed by any similitude. That employed in Scripture is, being one with Christ, and with one another, as Christ is one with the Father;—union this which nothing can part; "neither life nor death, nor things present, nor things to come, nor principalities, nor powers, nor height, nor depth, nor any other creature" (Romans 8.38). All other unions can be separated. The union between the vine and its branches can be separated by the knife of the husbandman; the union between the members and the body can be separated by diseases and accidents manifold, and by death is utterly dissolved; the union between husband and wife, wickedness doth dissolve; And death dissolveth the union between the soul and the body; but the union which we have with Christ, through the Holy Ghost, is eternal life which nothing can ever dissolve, "Because he lives, we live also"[6] because he hath overcome all the powers of dissolution, we shall overcome them also.

And not only doth Christ's life in glory, and his divine gift of quickening immortal life, secure to us this continual and uninterrupted fellowship with himself; but it bringeth into one those who had been parted upon the earth by time and place, gathering them into one church, into one body, into one spouse, into one city, out of all kindreds and nations and tongues, against the day of his appearing, recalling the body from its dust-dissolved state, and joining it in its immortal glory unto the soul, in a union never again to be divided, joining also the saints unto the inheritance and possession from which they had been separated by the interposition of Satan;—all broken families of the faithful reuniting, all interrupted loves and

6. Irving appears to be alluding to John 14.9.

friendships of the faithful harmoniously reconciling, and bringing to pass such fellowship and unity of love as eye hath not seen, nor ear heard, nor the heart of man conceived.

And how is all this procured? It is procured by the Holy Spirit, which is one, and which, preceding from the body of Christ, doth gather into one all the election of God; Who, thenceforth, grow into the same image with Christ from glory to glory, by the Spirit of God. But how should the Holy Spirit be able to quicken in us, who are dead in trespasses and sins, that same life of godliness and image of perfection which was in Jesus Christ? Because, I answer, this is the very end of his proceeding from Christ, unto whom all power is given, in order to beget sons unto God; And not only to beget sons unto God, but likewise sons of God, according as it is written, "Behold! What manner of love the Father hath bestowed upon us, that we should be called the sons of God; [. . .] and when he who is our life shall appear, we also shall appear with him in glory" (1 John 3.1–2). The Holy Ghost cometh not with some indescribable influence to work some formless effect; but he doth come unto us for that same and for which he came unto the Virgin, in order to beget sons of God with in and out of our fallen substance.

And in the resurrection we shall be manifested sons of God, with what glory Christ also was manifested, and we shall reign with what glory he reigneth. Like peers of a royal court, we shall ever have liberty of access unto our King. The Holy Spirit cometh to quicken, in the living soul of every elect one, a spirit whose power of confirmation as to reveal in us Christ the hope of glory; to constrain and to overcome the old man, with his corruptions and lusts; To renew us after the image of God in righteousness and true holiness; And to give us, as we have shewed above, a new subsistence, which is not the subsistence of Adamhood, but the subsistence of Christhood: for I say that the renewed man is another and a higher form of creature than the created man, in as much as he possesseth in him, not the type, but the very child of Christ. For more truly therefore, brethren, then we are one in Adam, are we one in Christ: for the unity and Adam, stamped as it is on every feature of the body and of the mind, is ever contended against by the murderous power of Satan; But the union unto Christ, and the oneness of his people, is ever contended for by the Almighty Spirit of God.

And according as Christ live within us, according as, by faith, we do incorporate the body of Christ with ourselves, according as we assimilate the divine food of the Lord's Supper unto that life which we have in baptism, we do verily increase in the stature, in the wisdom, in the power of Christ; And we do increase in love, union, and fellowship with one another, through the Holy Ghost. That food which we receive from heaven, that immortal food which we have in the Supper of the Lord, though it be flesh and blood, is not flesh and blood subsisting through the power of the living soul; natural life cannot quicken it; natural life cannot assimilate it. It is the flesh and blood of the spiritual life which the Holy Spirit did sustain in Christ, pure and spotless, and which the Holy Ghost in us doth assimilate for the nourishment of his life. For the Holy Spirit, though he hath life in himself, hath laid aside the manifestation thereof; and have consented to be manifested, as having life derived from Christ: even as Christ sayeth that the Father had given unto him to have life in himself.

Therefore, brethren, words cannot express nor similitudes shadow forth, the true union which there is between a believer and Christ his head; between believers and one another. We live not up to our privileges, else we would know this. If we possessed that faith which feedeth on Christ, we would never be weak, we would never be weary, we would never be overcome, we would never be hidden from his presence. He would dwell in us, and his Father would dwell in us, and they together would make their abode with us. And whatever we should ask the Father in his name, believing, we should receive; and he would prove himself a faithful High Priest, who could be touched with the feeling of our infirmities.

And if we realized that faith which maketh one with Christ, we would be blessed with the communion of saints, whereby our burdens would be borne, our sorrows shared, our strength imparted to the weak, and our weakness supplied from the strong; our poverty made up out of their plenty, and a divine circulation of the living spirit of life would be felt unseen; in a degree it would also be seen, but far beyond the range of sight it would be felt amongst the members of Christ: to express whose love, neighbourhood availeth not, nor family availeth; For we must hate father and mother and brother and sister, to be his disciple. No form of communion or fellowship in this world, lying in the wicked one, availeth to represent the communion of the saints and the unity of the holy catholic church.

The loaf which was presented at the table this morning, one lump, and not without form, to be broken into parts, representeth the oneness of the substance of Christ's body, where of all the redeemed are parts: the identity of these fragments of the loaf which we took into our hands and eat with our mouths, the perfect identity of every crumb with the whole loaf, is our identity and oneness with the Lord Jesus Christ, and with one another. Into which, as ye grow by the bonds of holy charity, ye shall rejoice and increase, and live more abundantly to his praise, who is overall God blessed forever. Amen.

The Fallen Humanity of Christ and the Work of the Spirit in the Thought of Edward Irving

Daniel Jordan Cameron

When thus explained in the way in which alone I believe it is capable of being explained, how small a matter doth that seem upon which so much stress is laid by the ignorant, who will allow Christ readily enough to descend to the unfallen but not to the fallen state of the creature.

EDWARD IRVING[1]

INTRODUCTION

In the last several years a debate has been stewing in the background of theological conversation. This debate has to do with a question of the "how" of the incarnation. There are those, like Irving, who argue that in order for Jesus to save fallen humanity he had to assume a fallen human nature in the incarnation. However, on the opposing side of the debate, there are those who argue that Jesus' assumption of a fallen nature makes him culpable and no longer worthy of being our savior.[2] It has even been argued that it

1. Irving, *CW* 5, 441.

2. This can be seen in the recently published books regarding this topic and this doesn't include the many journal articles that have been written on this topic as well.

is "not possible to make logical sense of the notion that Christ's humanity was fallen."[3] Those on the fallen side of the argument are clear to say that while Jesus had a fallen human nature he was always without sin himself and therefore not guilty of sinning himself. How, though, does Jesus assume the fallen nature and then sanctify that nature? Oliver Crisp offers a possible argument that "Christ had a fallen but not sinful human nature that was 'healed' of its fallenness at the moment of assumption by the Word."[4] However, this is not agreed upon by all those who wish to argue for Jesus' fallen human nature. For instance, Thomas F. Torrance, relying on Luke 2:52, argues that Jesus lived his entire human life leading up to the cross restoring our nature.[5] Irving rejects the idea that the human nature of Jesus was healed upon assumption on the grounds that it lacks teleological insight into redemption.

In this discussion of the fallen human nature of Christ there is a lack of discussion of the role of the Spirit in Jesus' life. If we are to move forward in this debate as I, and others, have argued elsewhere, we must begin to explore the relationship between Christ and the Spirit.[6] That is, we must begin to explore Spirit Christology. This chapter serves this end.

Plenty of ink has been spilled in discussion of Karl Barth and T.F. Torrance on the fallen nature view and significantly less has been spilled regarding Edward Irving on this point. However, the argument could be

---

See the following publications: Rafael N. Bello, *Sinless Flesh: A Critique of Karl Barth's Fallen Christ* (Bellingham, WA: Lexham, 2020); Daniel J. Cameron, *Flesh and Blood: A Dogmatic Sketch concerning the Fallen Nature View of Christ's Human Nature* (Eugene, OR: Wipf and Stock, 2016); Oliver D. Crisp, *Divinity and Humanity: The Incarnation Reconsidered* (Cambridge: Cambridge University Press, 2007); Jerome Van Kuiken, *Christ's Humanity in Current and Ancient Controversy: Fallen or Not?* (London: T.&T. Clark, 2017); Kevin Chiarot. *The Unassumed Is the Unhealed: The Humanity of Christ in the Christology of T. F. Torrance* (Eugene, OR: Pickwick, 2013).

3. Oliver Crisp, "Did Christ Have a Fallen Human Nature?" *International Journal of Systematic Theology* 6.3 (2004) 270. Granted, it appears as though Crisp has somewhat changed his thought regarding this topic in his 2019 article "On the Vicarious Humanity of Christ." *International Journal of Systematic Theology* 21.3 (2019) 235–50.

4. Crisp "On the Vicarious Humanity of Christ," 235.

5. Torrance scholars struggle to understand Torrance at this point and some even accuse him of inconsistency making the claim that Torrance argues that it was a once-and-for-all sanctification of our flesh upon assumption and yet he argues for the sanctification of our flesh throughout his life. A full answer to when exactly Torrance understands our flesh to be sanctified by Christ is yet to be seen.

6. Cameron, *Flesh and Blood*, chapter 5. See also, Myk Habets, "The Fallen Christ: A Pneumatological Clarification of the Theology of Thomas F. Torrance." *Participatio* 5 (2015) 18–44; Graham McFarlane, *Christ and the Spirit: Doctrine of the Incarnation according to Edward Irving* (Carlisle, UK: Paternoster, 1996); David Dorries, *Edward Irving's Incarnational Christology* (Xulon, 2002).

made that Irving is responsible for the modern flavor of this fallen-nature view. Donald Macleod has argued that this Irvingite Christology was passed down to those like H.R. Mackintosh, John Ballie, Karl Barth, T.F. Torrance, and J.B. Torrance.[7] And yet, Irving's unique contribution to this conversation regarding the role of the Spirit in Christ's assumption of the fallen nature seems to have been lost in translation. Thus, this chapter serves as a work of retrieval in order to rediscover and open Irving's views regarding the relationship of the Spirit and Jesus in order to contribute to this conversation. In order to accomplish this, I will show how this plays out in his argument for Christ's assumption of a fallen human nature. Then I will show how Irving understands the relationship between the Spirit and Jesus. This will include how Irving's Spirit Christology can answer some modern critiques of the fallen nature view.

OPENING IRVING'S FALLEN CHRIST

As the church has attempted to understand salvation they have focused on the importance and centrality of the cross of Jesus. However, this tendency has, at times, led to an emphasis on the *work* of Jesus and has failed to give proper place to the person and humanity of Jesus. In other words, Jesus has become the means to an end. Jesus' humanity in particular only has importance as it was required for him to die, to be mortal. For Irving, this is problematic for Christology and soteriology must not be separated. Thus, he develops his thinking regarding the fallen nature of Jesus giving soteriological importance to the incarnation. As he writes, "The question of the atonement [. . .] doth not so much flow out of, as it is involved in, and thorough implicated with, being of the very essence of, the incarnation; not a circumstance of its manifestation, but an original and substantial element in the idea itself."[8] What follows in this section is an attempt to open Irving's fallen Jesus for the purposes of our thesis. I will begin by exploring how Irving understands the composition of Jesus incarnate. I will conclude this section by opening Irving's definition of fallenness in order to gain a clear understanding of how Jesus can be fallen and sinless.

Important for understanding Irving's doctrine of Jesus, incarnation, and atonement and thus the fallen humanity of Jesus, is his understanding of the Trinity as "a first principle in all sound theology."[9] Out of his explora-

---

7. Donald Macleod, "The Doctrine of the Incarnation in Scottish Theology: Edward Irving." *Scottish Bulletin of Evangelical Theology* 9.1 (1991) 40–50.

8. Irving, *CW* 5, 29–30.

9. Irving, *CW* 4, 252.

tion of the Trinity he came to understand Jesus as the epistemological center for understanding God.

> He was not the Word merely, but He was the will of the Father, so that He could say, "He that hath seen me hath seen the Father;" and He was not only the fullness of the Father's will, and of the word of the Son, but He was also the fullness of the power of the Holy Ghost, who dwelleth in Him without measure; so that He could say of the Spirit, "He shall testify of me;" "whatsoever He shall hear that shall He speak. . . . He shall teach you all things, and bring all things to your remembrance whatsoever I have said unto you." Which mystery of the fullness of the Godhead— Father, Son, and Spirit—that was manifest in Christ is expressed by Himself in these words: "All things that the Father hath are mine: therefore said I that he (the Spirit of truth) shall take of mine, and shall shew it unto you."[10]

How then did he understand the human nature of Christ? Irving's concern when it came to Christology was first and foremost about Jesus' goal in saving humanity.[11] Thus, as he discusses the constitution of Jesus, he always has at the forefront the soteriological significance of the person of Christ.

In his sermon on the method of the incarnation, he begins with an exploration of the "composition of His Divine person, from His conception even unto His resurrection, observing the most notable changes he underwent during that period [. . .]."[12] At the beginning of Irving's argument is his understanding of the pre-existence of the divine person of Christ. In the incarnation, the second person of the Trinity, the Logos, took "up into His own *eternal* personality the human nature [. . .]."[13] The subject of the incarnation is the pre-existent second person of the Trinity. The Logos, in the incarnation, assumes an *anhypostatic* human nature.[14] That is, in the

---

10. Irving, *CW* 4, 223.

11. It is on this point that Irving actually gives us insight into his theological method. "This seemeth to me the logical way of handling any act of the Godhead: first, to shew wherein it originates; then, whereto it tendeth; then, by what method it proceedeth; then, in what way it transacted; and finally, with what fruit or effects it is followed." Irving, *CW* 5, 114.

12. *CW* 5, 114.

13. *CW* 5, 115. Emphasis mine.

14. Van Kuiken reflects on this idea in Irving arguing that "the Son's role in the Incarnation was to supply personhood for the human nature (the doctrine of anhypostasia) and to accommodate his divine will to direct his human will faithfully within the constraints of the latter's finitude." Kuiken. *Christ's Humanity in Current and Ancient Controversy*, 14. It is also important to note that this is a more modern analytic term than Irving himself would have used though the idea is present in his work.

incarnation, the Logos does not assume some pre-existent human nature. He does not indwell someone who already existed and somehow empowered them to live obediently, die, and rise again. Rather, the humanity of Jesus only ever was *his* humanity (the doctrine of *enhypostasia) contra* any form of Adoptionism. For Irving, as McFarlane argues, a faithful approach to understanding takes into account the "location and intention of salvation."[15] The location and intention of salvation for Irving is "manhood fallen, which He took up into His Divine Person, in order to prove the grace and might of the Godhead in redeeming it."[16]

Now we turn to examine how Irving understood the location of the Incarnation in Jesus' assumption of the *anhypostatic* humanity. As stated previously, the location of salvation is humanity and in particular fallen humanity. Irving indicates three types of humanity that exist/have existed: prelapsarian humanity, fallen humanity, and resurrected humanity.[17] Many have argued challenging the fallen nature view that Christ did not have to assume a fallen human nature for it is not required for him to be fully human as fallen humanity is not the only type of humanity that exists. Thus, some say, we can (and should!) argue that Christ assumed an unfallen prelapsarian humanity like Adam before the fall.[18] In order to maintain this unfallen nature of Christ, the Roman Catholic church has the doctrine of the immaculate conception in which Mary herself is preserved from the stain of sin in order to be a pure vessel from which Jesus came.[19] Seeing

15. Graham McFarlane, *Christ and the Spirit*, 141.

16. Irving, *CW* 5, 3.

17. Edward Irving, *Orthodox and Catholic Doctrine of our Lord's Human Nature* (London, 1830), 50–51.

18. See the arguments of those like Crisp, *Divinity and Humanity* or Crisp, "Did Christ Have a Fallen Human Nature?" *International Journal of Systematic Theology* 6.3 (2004) 270–88. See also Luke Stamps "Did Jesus Assume a Fallen Human Nature?" The Gospel Coalition Blog; accessed September 15, 2020, https://www.thegospelcoalition.org/article/you-asked-did-jesus-assume-a-fallen-human-nature/

19. While Protestant theology does not hold to the same Roman Catholic understanding of the immaculate conception, the common view seems to me to be that of the unfallen nature view of Christ. Without the immaculate conception they still wish to maintain the unstained nature of Christ's human nature. Rather than needing Mary to be pure in order to assume an unfallen nature, the argument that I most often hear in support of this is the doctrine of the virgin birth. Because Jesus was born of a virgin he was kept from the stain of sin. This argument assumes a very strong Augustinian understanding of the transmission of sin through the seed of the man. Thus, as Jesus is not the biological son of a man, his humanity is protected from the stain of sin. However, I am not sure that this is the best way to understand the transmission of sin. It seems more logical, in order to maintain the unfallen human nature of Christ, to hold to a doctrine of immaculate conception than to argue that the virgin birth protects Jesus from fallenness. While the virgin birth teaches us that the incarnation has nothing

a critical connection between incarnation and salvation, Irving challenged the Roman Catholic doctrine arguing that "unless God had created the Virgin in Adam's first estate, (which is a figment of Romish superstition,) it was impossible to find in existence any human nature but human nature fallen, whereof Christ might partake with the brethren."[20] In other words, "Christ took our fallen nature . . . because there was no other existence to take."[21] For Irving, Christ's assumption of a fallen human nature is not simply about being 'fully human' but, rather, about salvation. Prelapsarian humanity does not need to be saved. That humanity does not need resurrection as it has not yet been corrupted by the stain of sin.

It is now appropriate to discuss how Irving understood the means or the mode of the incarnation. There has been debate regarding this aspect of Irving's theology. Jerome Van Kuiken and Graham McFarlane argue that on this point Irving is kenotic.[22] However, Colin Gunton argues, "As a theory, kenotic Christology holds that in order to become incarnate the eternal Son divests himself of some aspects of his divinity in order to be, so to speak, made compatible with the human experience. Is Irving's Christology in that sense kenotic? The answer is, surely not."[23] Gunton makes the point that Irving's point here is to show the incarnation as the ultimate expression of the "Son's self-giving."[24] So how are we to understand Irving at this point? As stated before, Irving seeks to understand the acts of Jesus as an act of the Trinity with the goal of redemption in mind.[25] Thus, as McFarlane argues, it is fair to interpret Irving along the lines of more modern interpretations of

---

to do with the will of humans but is only an act of the will of God. See the argument of Thomas F. Torrance, *Incarnation: The Person and Life of Christ.* Edited by Robert T. Walker (Milton Keynes, UK: Paternoster, 2015), 88–104. I am not sure that it is fair to make the argument that Jesus does not assume his humanity from Mary. Protestant theology argues that Mary was fallen and thus, if Jesus takes his humanity from her, he takes into himself a fallen humanity. As Irving argues, "He was of the seed of David; that He was of the seed of Abraham, as well as the seed of the woman; yea, that He was of the seed of the woman after she fell, and not before she fell." Irving, *CW* 5, 116.

20. Irving, *CW* 5, 116.

21. Irving, *CW* 5, 115–116.

22. See Graham McFarlane's argument in his book *Christ and the Spirit* and Jerome E. Van Kuiken. "Edward Irving on Christ's Sinful Flesh and Sanctifying Spirit: A Wesleyan Appraisal." *Wesleyan Theological Journal* 49.1 (2014) 175–85.

23. Colin Gunton. "Two Dogmas Revisited: Edward Irving's Christology." *Scottish Journal of Theology* 41.3 (August 1988) 372.

24. Gunton. "Two Dogmas Revisited," 372.

25. "Before the infinite Godhead in the Son could act in the finite form, whether before taking that form or after, He must act not of Himself only, but with the consent and concurrence of the other persons of the Trinity. And this is not a small matter but is in fact that which determineth all the rest." Irving, *CW* 5, 405.

Philippians 2 in that the idea of 'emptying' has more to do with "Godlike-ness essentially as giving and spending oneself out."[26] Thus, Christ gives us himself in the incarnation without any change to his eternal divine being.

> He had been sacrificed from the foundation of the world; and for them He had now laid aside the mantle of His uncreated and incommunicable glory, and taken on the veils of flesh; clothed Himself in likeness of man; entered the charmed region, which the curse of God did over-canopy, and which Satan had filled with his damned influences—all for the love of man, all to re-deem the sons of men, and introduce them into the glorious liberty of the sons of God.[27]

McFarlane summarizes Irving's trinitarian understanding of kenosis well saying, "The Son's self-limitation is never separated from the Spirit's enabling: in his divine person the Son is at all times related to the Father through the Spirit. So, too, in his humanity, there is a pneumatic, Spirit dimension."[28]

In becoming incarnate, Jesus "took unto Himself a true body and a reasonable soul; and . . . the flesh of Christ, like my flesh, was in its proper nature mortal and corruptible."[29] For Irving, Christ takes upon himself this fallen nature for there is no other human nature that exists and because this is the human nature that needs to be saved. This again points us to Irving's stress on the soteriological nature of the incarnation. But how exactly does Irving understand this fallen nature?[30]

As Irving discusses the fallen nature of Jesus three things are important to understand. When Irving discusses the term 'flesh,' he is referring to two things, the body, and the totality of the fallen human nature both 'body' and 'soul.' Thus, Irving argues that the Holy Spirit, in the conception of Jesus, did not keep him from being under the 'law of sin', "For if in his conception the particles of his flesh were changed from unholy to holy, from mortal to

---

26. Charles Francis Digby Moule, "The Manhood of Jesus in the New Testament" in *Christ, Faith and History. Cambridge Studies in Christology*, edited by S.W. Sykes, J.P. Clayton (Cambridge: Cambridge University Press, 1972), 97.

27. Irving, *CW* 5, 280.

28. McFarlane, *Christ and the Spirit*, 155.

29. McFarlane, *Christ and the Spirit*, 116.

30. This is key, for there are many ways to think about the fallen nature. Some have critiqued Torrance for being inconsistent at this point for in one instance he seems to argue that we are to understand fallenness as being subject to the fallen human experi-ence and then in another instance arguing that fallenness is to be understood in terms of the corruption of the nature defined by original sin. See Cameron, *Flesh and Blood.* Crisp, "On the Vicarious Humanity of Christ," 235–50.

immortal, then what was left to be done at the resurrection?"[31] Despite the verdict at his trial that Irving should be removed from ministry for teaching that Jesus was fallen and thus a sinner, Irving adamantly maintained the sinlessness of Jesus due to his distinction between 'person' and 'nature.' In the incarnation Jesus never assumes to himself a human person but only a human nature. Thus, *enhypostasis* helps us to understand that Jesus assumes actual human nature while remaining the second *person* of the trinity and thus when Irving attributes fallenness to Jesus it is only in his human nature yet it is not characteristic of his divine person. As Irving argues,

> Christ had a body and soul of man's substance, without thereby having a human person; and, therefore, we can assert the sinfulness of the whole, the complete, the perfect human nature, which He took, without in the least implicating Him with sin: yea, verily, seeing He subdued those properties which it had in itself, and made it holy, we assert Him to be the only Redeemer of man from sin.[32]

When Irving attributes 'sinfulness' to the human nature of Christ, how does he understand sin? Irving understands sin in three ways: original sin, constitutional sin/original guilt, and actual sin.[33] For Irving, original sin is Adam's "willful forfeiting of his created state," a state in which all created beings participate in through their persons.[34] But, since Jesus is not created and thus does not have a human person he is shielded from participation in this original sin. Irving argues, "He hath taken part with the children, with the fallen children; but He came by that part, not through connexion with Adam, but by His own free will, and his Father's free will, and the free will of the Holy Ghost; and thus original sin is avoided, though yet the body He took is in the fallen state, and liable to all temptations."[35] Irving does not attribute original sin to Jesus due to the fact that, for Irving, original sin is an attribute of persons and Jesus does not have a human person. However, Irving does attribute original guilt to Jesus. That is, in the incarnation, Jesus takes upon himself a human nature that is, he shares in the "common mass of sinful human nature [. . .] sharing in the sins and carnal temptations

---

31. Irving, "On the Human Nature of Christ," 97.

32 Irving, *CW* 5, 565. In Irving, *Orthodox and Catholic Doctrine*, vii, Irving argues, "Whenever I attribute sinful properties and dispositions and inclinations to our Lord's human nature, I am speaking of it considered as apart from Him, in itself."

33. This is helpfully pointed out by Van Kuiken in *Christ's Humanity*, 16.

34. Van Kuiken, *Christ's Humanity*, 16.

35. Van Kuiken, *Christ's Humanity*, 159.

of the whole race."[36] There has been disagreement on Irving at this point. McFarlane argues that Irving understands Jesus to have assumed original guilt but not original sin for, original sin is an attribute of persons and thus inseparable from actual sin. Thus, Jesus assumes a human nature (not a human person) tainted by original guilt. Van Kuiken argues that it is more accurate to describe Irving's position in terms of constitutional guilt rather than original guilt. It seems to me that understanding Irving in terms of Jesus' assumption of original guilt makes more sense given Irving's argument that Jesus assumed a nature that participates in original guilt. Irving argues,

> When the Son of God took flesh, He entered upon the travail of salvation; when He carried that work triumphant to the right hand of God, He finished the work. By saving His own human nature, by preserving it from the taint of sin, by delivering it from the power of Satan, by carrying it into the region of glory, He did obtain eternal redemption for us.[37]

In making this argument it almost seems as though Irving is being inconsistent in arguing that Jesus assumed a fallen nature and he preserved it from the taint of sin. However, this is a misapprehension; he is speaking about actual sin. That is, Jesus preserved, though fallen, his human nature from participating in sin as an act of his person.

With Christ's humanity in this state, McFarlane notes an important question that Irving seeks to answer. That is, "how shall human nature, in the fallen state, be brought into harmony with the acting of the holy Godhead?"[38] The answer to this question of how lies in Irving's understanding of the soul of Jesus. For Irving, when Jesus became incarnate, he assumed a human soul. As Irving describes the incarnation as a

> threefold spiritual substance, the only begotten Son, the human soul, and the Holy Spirit [. . .] the Eternal Son, therefore, humbling Himself to the human soul, and the human soul taken possession of by the Holy Ghost, this spiritual substance (of two natures only, through of three parts) did animate and give life to the flesh of the Lord Jesus; which was flesh in the fallen state,

---

36. Van Kuiken, *Christ's Humanity*, 17.

37. Irving, *CW* 4, 341. Irving argues elsewhere "As Christ was man, and not *a* man, he cannot be spoken of as a human person, without being brought in guilty of original sin. As a divine person he is clear of it, and no one can impute it to him. His not having natural generation, clears him of it altogether." E. Irving, *Christ's Holiness in the Flesh, the Form, Fountain Head, and Assurance to Us of Holiness in the Flesh.* (Edinburgh: John Lindsay and Co, 1831), 5.

38. McFarlane, *Christ and the Spirit*, 156.

> and liable to all the temptations to which flesh is liable: but the
> soul of Christ, thus anointed with the Holy Ghost, did ever resist
> and reject the suggestions of evil.[39]

Thus, in the incarnation, Jesus assumes to himself a human nature and thus a human soul which was a product of fallenness. However, he sinlessly assumes this fallen nature and soul in lieu of the Holy Spirit's possession of the human soul of Jesus. Key for Irving's understanding of how Jesus can assume this fallen human nature and remain sinless lies in the role of the Holy Spirit in the incarnation and life of Jesus. It is at this point that we must now turn to open Irving's Spirit Christology.

OPENING IRVING'S SPIRIT CHRISTOLOGY

In Colin Gunton's article "Two Dogmas Revisited: Edward Irving's Christology," he argues that it is not accurate to describe Irving's theology in terms of Spirit Christology.[40] Gunton makes his argument based on the definition of Spirit Christology laid out by G.W.H. Lampe in his book *God as Spirit*.[41] Gunton argues that Lampe attempts to define Spirit Christology in unitary terms. That is, for Lampe, the Spirit is a reference to the immanence and action of God. Thus, the incarnation is the action of the God-Spirit in space and time. As Lampe argues, "By the 'Christ-Spirit' is meant the indwelling presence of God as Spirit in the freely responding spirit of man as this is concretely exhibited in Christ and reproduced in some measure in Christ's followers."[42] This understanding of the Trinity's action in the incarnation is problematic and does not capture the distinction between the persons of the Trinity nor their existence as individual persons and Gunton is correct to say that this is not what Irving is doing in his theology regarding the role of the Spirit in the life of Jesus. If Irving does not have a Spirit Christology in the same way that Lampe describes, how are we to understand Spirit Christology in a way that is faithful to the theology of Irving?

There are three formulated and somewhat distinct understandings of Spirit Christology that I want to look at briefly now. The first I have already mentioned and that is the understanding of Lampe. Lampe argues, "The use of this concept [Spirit Christology] enables us to say that God indwelt and motivated the human spirit of Jesus in such a way that in him, uniquely, the

39. Irving, *CW* 5, 126.

40. Gunton, "Two Dogmas Revisited," 373. "His Christology is sometimes referred to as a 'Spirit Christology,' but that is precisely what it is not"

41. G. W. H. Lampe, *God as Spirit* (London: SCM, 1977).

42. Lampe, *God as Spirit*, 114.

relationship for which man is intended by his Creator was fully realized."[43] In other words, Spirit Christology is a way of talking about the indwelling of the human spirit of Jesus in such a way that empowered him to live out the relationship with God that we were always meant to have. Roman Catholic theologian, Ralph Del Colle argues that the Spirit Christology has to do with the role of the Holy Spirit in sustaining the human nature of Jesus from the incarnation through his private and public ministry.[44] The third perspective I want to mention is that of John Owen. Owen argues that "the only singular immediate act of the person of the Son on the human nature was the assumption of it into subsistence with himself. [. . .] The Holy Ghost, as we have proved before, is the immediate, peculiar, efficient cause of all external divine operations: for God worketh by his Spirit, or in him immediately applies the power and efficacy of the divine excellencies unto their operation; when the same work is equally the work of each person."[45] In other words, for Owen, the work of the Holy Spirit is the power of God in action while the action of God remains "the work of each person."[46] Thus, Owen can argue that the Spirit is at the heart of the action of God and still maintain the responsibility for the action of each person of the Godhead.

In looking at these three interpretations of Spirit Christology, it seems that there is less of a hard and fast distinction between their interpretations but rather much more nuanced understandings of the more basic assertion of Spirit Christology. This most basic assertion being that the Holy Spirit had a role in the empowerment of Jesus' humanity during his life on earth from the incarnation on. Thus, we can argue that Irving has a Spirit Christology based on this understanding of Spirit Christology's basic assumption. So, the question we can ask now is how does Irving describe the role of the Spirit in empowering the humanity of Jesus?

In discussions regarding the fallen nature of Christ a question continues to arise from both supporters and opponents alike. If the assumption of the fallen nature is an act of redemption and healing of that fallen nature when and how is it healed? Is it healed upon assumption?[47] Irving, however,

43. Lampe, *God as Spirit*, 11.

44. See Ralph Del Colle, *Christ and the Spirit: Spirit Christology in Trinitarian Perspective* (Oxford: Oxford University Press, 1994).

45. John Owen, *The Works of John Owen*. Vol. 3, (Edinburgh: Banner of Truth, 1966), 160, 162.

46. Owen, *The Works of John Owen*, Vol. 3162. It is also important to note that Graham McFarlane notes the similarities and probable influence of John Owen on Edward Irving. See McFarlane, *Christ and the Spirit*, 160–61.

47. This has come up in conversations particularly concerning T.F. Torrance's theology regarding this conversation. As I have argued elsewhere, I do not think that

is adamant that the fallen nature was not healed upon assumption for this would destroy his oneness with us and Jesus would no longer be able to sympathize with us as Hebrews 4:15 states. He also argues that, "if in his conception the particles of his flesh were changed from unholy to holy, from mortal to immortal, then what was left to be done at the resurrection?"[48] Thus, crucial for Irving, is that throughout Jesus' life he sanctifies and heals the fallen nature through the power of the Holy Spirit. Irving sees the Spirit in three aspects of the life of Christ: first, in his conception in the womb of Mary; second, in the miracles and work of Christ throughout his life; and third, in maintaining the sinlessness of Christ in his sacrifice.[49] Thus, in the incarnation, Irving understands Jesus to be "of two natures only, though of three parts."[50] That is, the composition of Jesus was that of the divine nature, a human nature, and the Spirit as the third part. The human nature "was flesh in the fallen state, and liable to all the temptations to which flesh is liable."[51] However, this fallen flesh did not overcome the person of Jesus for it was assumed by the Holy Spirit empowering Jesus to overcome the liability to temptation.

It is on this point that Oliver Crisp raises an important concern. He argues that Spirit Christology "leaves no metaphysical room for the interposition of another divine person between the intentions of God the Son and the intentional actions brought about in his human nature."[52] In other words, Spirit Christology actually drives a wedge between the Logos and the human nature that he assumed in the incarnation. Myk Habets helpfully responds to Crisp's critique saying that "Crisp's central critique is that a Spirit Christology

Torrance was clear enough in his writings concerning this issue in order to give an answer. He seems to say in one place that it is healed upon assumption and in others, in reference to Luke 2:52, that Jesus heals it throughout his life by beating back the continued desires of the fallen nature. It seems to me that Irving is helpful here with his Spirit Christology.

48. Irving, "On the Human Nature of Christ," 97.

49. "This comes from the omission of the third part in the composition of Christ, which is, the substance of the Godhead in the person of the Holy Ghost: to whose divine presence and power it is that the creation of the body in the womb of the virgin is given, the might works which Christ did ascribed, and the spotlessness of His sacrifice attributed, in the Holy Scripture." Irving, *CW5*, 124. Van Kuiken points out that "Due to the Spirit coming on Christ at conception he never experienced the life of the unregenerate but instead "is the prototype for the holy, sinless life in sinful flesh that Christians ought to and can lead from the start of their regenerate lives." Van Kuiken, *Christ's Humanity in Current and Ancient Controversy*, 19.

50. Irving, *CW* 5, 126.

51. Irving, *CW* 5, 126.

52. Oliver Crisp, *Revisioning Christology: Theology in the Reformed Tradition* (Farnham, UK: Ashgate. 2011), 92.

is untenable on the grounds that once the Son has assumed human nature he steps back and lets the Holy Spirit act in all future works."[53] Irving would adamantly reject this critique on trinitarian grounds. He argues, "in the manhood of Christ was exhibited all of the Godhead that shall ever be exhibited, Father, Son, and Spirit; according as it is written, 'In Him dwelt all the fullness of the Godhead bodily, or in a body.'"[54] Irving carefully places emphasis on the idea of *perichoresis*. That is, that the Trinity is one undivided substance not just united in being but united in action. As I have argued elsewhere we can thus say that "while the Son is the main character in the incarnation it is never without the participation of the Father and the Son."[55] This is known as the doctrine of inseparable operations. Karl Barth argues "From creation by way of revelation and reconciliation to the coming redemption it is always true that He who acts here is the Father and the Son and the Spirit."[56] In other words, we must avoid the temptation to so distinguish each person of the Trinity that we divide the operations of the Trinity into three separate operations. Irving is clear to argue that the human soul of Christ was "thus anointed with the Holy Ghost [and] did ever resist and reject the suggestions of evil."[57] However, it was never the Spirit despite the divine Son but rather "Christ's [human] soul was so held in possession by the Holy Ghost, *and so supported by the Divine nature*, as that it never assented unto an evil suggestion, and never originated an evil suggestion."[58]

Van Kuiken also raises a critique here arguing that "If Christ saves us primarily as a Spirit-filled human being, then was the Incarnation truly necessary? Could we not have saved ourselves with but the assistance of the Holy Spirit?"[59] Irving argues the possibility of this in his discussion of the prophet Jeremiah and John the Baptist. He argues,

> For though Jeremiah and [John] the Baptist are declared to have
> been filled with the Holy Ghost from their mother's womb, yet
> their souls came not possessed with the Holy Ghost, for they
> were born by ordinary generation; and therefore they must have
> been capable of regeneration; which implies that they were in

53. Myk Habets, "The Fallen Humanity of Christ: A Pneumatological Clarification of the Theology of Thomas F. Torrance." *Participatio* 5 (2015) 41. Habets argues on similar grounds as Irving seeing Trinitarian perichoresis as key to understanding the action of the persons of the Godhead.

54. Irving, *CW* 5, 124.

55. Cameron. *Flesh and* Blood, 78.

56. Karl Barth. *Church Dogmatics. Volume 1* (London: T.&T. Clark, 2010), 374.

57. Irving, *CW* 5, 126.

58. Irving, *CW* 5, 126, *emphasis mine.*

59. Jerome Van Kuiken. "Edward Irving on Christ's Sinful Flesh," 183.

their creation-state sinful, seeing they needed the washing of regeneration and renewing of the Holy Ghost. It is not the time during which we are unregenerate, nor is it the number of sins which we have committed in our unregenerate state, but it is the fact that we need regeneration, which constitutes our original sinfulness in the sight of a holy God.[60]

Thus, for Irving, the reason that we cannot redeem ourselves with simply the help of the Holy Spirit has to do with the fact that we are born of the will of man and thus are in need of the regeneration of our original sinfulness. Remember that Irving makes the argument that Christ is free from original sin due to his not being a human person but rather the Logos, the second person of the Trinity. So, Jesus then assumes the fallen nature and original guilt and as the second person of the Trinity with his human soul in possession of his human soul he lives out his human life in perfect sinlessness as 2 Corinthians 5:21 makes clear ("For our sake he made him to be sin who knew no sin").[61]

CONCLUSION

"Rev. Edward Irving having previously been delated and convicted before this Presbytery on the ground of teaching heresy concerning the human nature of our Lord Jesus Christ, has been declared to be no longer a member thereof."[62] On May 3, 1832, James Reid Brown, the moderator of the Church of Scotland, passed down this sentence on Irving for his teaching that Jesus, in the incarnation, assumed a fallen human nature. Though Irving was no longer allowed to be a pastor in the Church of Scotland this condemnation of Irving's views did not stop his teaching that Christ assumed a fallen human nature from continuing. Those who came after him like H.R. Mackintosh, Karl Barth, T.F. Torrance, and J.B. Torrance taught this as well, though different in nuance. This topic has arisen again in Christological conversation

---

60. Irving, *CW* 5, 128–29.

61. ESV

62. Edward Irving. *The Trial of the Rev. Edward Irving, M.A., Before the London Presbytery: Containing the Whole of the Evidence, Exact Copies of the Documents, Verbatim Report of the Speeches and Opinions of the Presbyters, &. Being the Only Authentic and Complete Record of the Processing* (London: W. Harding, 1832), 87. I wonder if the reason for his condemnation as a heretic is due to the strength to which he argues in several places throughout his work that he considers this teaching regarding the fallen human nature of Christ as an article of faith and thus to deny the fallen nature of Christ brings your faith into question. This seems to be too strong an argument regarding this issue. It is not an issue of salvation but of clarity regarding the how of the incarnation and atonement.

and has lacked some of what Irving has to offer. Thus, this critical response has been an attempt at a work of retrieval in order to rediscover or open Irving's views regarding the relationship of the Spirit and Jesus in order to contribute to this conversation.

Irving started from a place of the importance of connecting Christology and soteriology, a connection which I believe too often be lost in systematic theology. This teleological way of looking at the Incarnation led Irving to believe that the human nature of Jesus was fallen. That is, in the Incarnation the eternal Son took up the anhypostatic fallen human nature as that was the only kind of human nature that existed and that was the human nature that needed healing. This means that he assumed original guilt and not original sin as he was not a human person. For Irving this means that Jesus participates in the sinful human nature that all humanity shares in thus sharing in our sin and 'carnal temptations.' This could be potentially problematic leaving Jesus himself in need of a savior. Irving overcomes this danger by arguing that Jesus, though assuming a fallen human nature, never himself is guilty of sinning. How does Irving get to this point?

Irving's understanding of the role of the Holy Spirit in the life of Christ is key for understanding how Jesus can assume this fallen nature and not himself be guilty of sinning. In the assumption of a fallen human nature, Jesus condescended to assume a human soul as well. It is this soul that the Holy Spirit joins itself too in order to begin the act of sanctification. Some have argued that this makes the Son useless in the act of redeeming the flesh since it was an act of the Spirit. Irving, however, is careful to say that the Spirit joined himself to the human soul of Jesus *while being fully supported by the divine person of the Son.* An act of one is an act of both.

This short chapter is not the 'closing' of this conversation, but I hope that it truly is the 'opening' of the box. It is time to take this information and go further. Future research needs to continue to press further into constructive theology building a robust Spirit Christology that can help to further clarify and expand our knowledge of the fallen human nature of Christ.[63]

---

63. Myk Habets is doing good work in this area with several books on this topic such as *The Anointed Son: A Trinitarian Spirit Christology* (Eugene, OR: Pickwick, 2010) and his new book *The Progressive Mystery: Tracing the Elusive Spirit in Scripture & Tradition* (Bellingham, WA: Lexham, 2019).

Recommended Resources

FURTHER READING ON EDWARD IRVING AND CONTEMPORANEOUS SCOTTISH THEOLOGY

Dorries, D. *Edward Irving's Incarnational Christology.* Fairfax: Xulon, 2002.

Fergusson, D., and M. Elliot. *The History of Scottish Theology, Volume II: From the Early Enlightenment to the Late Victorian Era.* Oxford: Oxford University Press, 2019.

Lee, B.S. *"Christ Sinful Flesh": Edward Irving's Christological Theology within the Context of His Life and Times.* Newcastle upon Tyne, UK: Cambridge Scholars Publishing, 2013.

MacLeod, D. "The Doctrine of the Incarnation in Scottish Theology: Edward Irving." *Scottish Bulletin of Evangelical Theology* 9.1 (1991) 40–50.

McFarlane, G.W.P. *Christ and the Spirit: Doctrine of the Incarnation according to Edward Irving.* Carlisle, UK: Paternoster, 1996.

Torrance, T.F. *Scottish Theology from John Knox to John McLeod Campbell.* Edinburgh: T.&T. Clark, 1996.

ARISING CHRISTOLOGICAL THEMES

Bello, R.N. *Sinless Flesh: A Critique of Karl Barth's Fallen Christ.* Bellingham, WA: Lexham, 2020.

Cameron, D.J. *Flesh and Blood: A Dogmatic Sketch concerning the Fallen Nature View of Christ's Human Nature.* Eugene, OR: Wipf and Stock, 2016.

Chiarot, K. *The Unassumed Is the Unhealed: The Humanity of Christ in the Christology of T. F. Torrance.* Eugene, OR: Pickwick, 2013.

Crisp, O. "Did Christ Have a Fallen Human Nature?" *International Journal of Systematic Theology* 6.3 (2004) 270–88.

———. *Divinity and Humanity: The Incarnation Reconsidered.* Cambridge: Cambridge University Press, 2007.

———. "On the Vicarious Humanity of Christ." *International Journal of Systematic Theology* 21.3 (2019) 235–50.

Del Colle, R. *Christ and the Spirit: Spirit Christology in Trinitarian Perspective.* Oxford: Oxford University Press, 1994.

Gunton, C. "Two Dogmas Revisited: Edward Irving's Christology." *Scottish Journal of Theology* 41.3 (1988) 359–76.

Habets, M. *The Anointed Son: A Trinitarian Spirit Christology.* Eugene, OR: Pickwick, 2010.

van Kuiken, E. J. *Christ's Humanity in Current and Ancient Controversy: Fallen or Not?* London: T.&T. Clark, 2017.

———. "Edward Irving on Christ's Sinful Flesh and Sanctifying Spirit: A Wesleyan Appraisal." *Wesleyan Theological Journal* 49.1 (2014) 175–85.